LANGUAGE!
The Comprehensive Literacy Curriculum

Jane Fell Greene, Ed.D.

Sopris West®
EDUCATIONAL SERVICES

A Cambium Learning Company

BOSTON, MA • LONGMONT, CO

Harvard Medical School is a registered trademark of the President and Fellow of Harvard College. Baylor College of Medicine is a registered trademark of Baylor University. Dacron is a registered trademark of E.I. du Pont de Nemours and Company. Guardian Unlimited is a registered trademark of Guardian Newspapers Limited. Weekly Reader is a registered trademark of Weekly Reader Corporation. New Scientist is a registered trademark of IPC Magazines Limited. New England Journal of Medicine is a registered trademark of the Massachusetts Medical Society. Miami Herald is a registered trademark of Knight-Ridder, Inc. U.S. Army Corps of Engineers is a registered trademark of the Office of the Judge Advocate General. Scientific American is a registered trademark of Scientific American, Inc. University of South Carolina is a registered trademark of the University of South Carolina. Harvard University is a registered trademark of the President and Fellows of Harvard College. University of San Francisco is a registered trademark of the University of San Francisco. Frisbee is a registered trademark of Wham-O, Inc. New York University is a registered trademark of New York University. Academy Award is a registered trademark of the Academy of Motion Picture Arts and Sciences. Shrek is a registered trademark of DreamWorks Animation, LLC. MIT is a registered trademark of the Massachusetts Institute of Technology. ExxonMobil is a registered trademark of Exxon Corporation. Lexus is a registered trademark of the Toyota Motor Corporation. BMW is a registered trademark of Beyerische Motoren Werke Aktiengesellschaft. PowerPoint is a registered trademark of Microsoft Corporation.

ISBN 13 digit: 978-1-60218-701-6
ISBN 10 digit: 1-60218-701-0

Printed in the United States of America

Published and distributed by

Sopris West®
EDUCATIONAL SERVICES

A Cambium Learning Company

4093 Specialty Place • Longmont, CO 80504 • (303) 651-2829
www.sopriswest.com

170077/3-08

Table of Contents

Check off the activities you complete with each lesson. Evaluate your accomplishments at the end of each lesson. Pay attention to teacher evaluations and comments.

Unit Objectives	Lesson 1 (Date:_____)	Lesson 2 (Date:_____)
STEP 1 • Say the vowel sounds for the letter combinations: **ear/air/ar** for / âr / as in *bear, air, care*; **ar/arr** for / ăr / as in *parody, arrow*; **ear** for / är / as in *heart*; **ar/er/err** for / ĕr / as in *primary, very, berry*; **oar** for / ôr /, **ear** for / ûr / as in *earth*; **ear/eir/ier/er/eer** for / îr / as in *ear, weird, pier, series, deer*. • Say the variant sounds for the consonants **s** (/ s /, / z /, / sh /, and / zh /) and **g** (/ g /, / j /, and / zh /). • Write the various letter combinations representing **r**-controlled vowel sounds and the consonants **g** and **s**.	❏ Exercise 1: Listening for Sounds in Words: Sound-Spelling Patterns	❏ Exercise 1: Listening for Sounds in Words: Sound-Spelling Patterns
STEP 2 • Read and spell words based on unit sound-spelling combinations. • Read and spell the **Essential Words:** *bury, buy, cough, penguin, soldier, toward*. • Read and spell words with Latin and Greek number prefixes. • Spell confusing words correctly.	❏ Exercise 2: Spelling Pretest 1	❏ Exercise 2: Write It: Essential Words ❏ Word Fluency 1
STEP 3 • Identify and define Latin and Greek number prefixes. • Use knowledge of word relationships to build word meanings.	❏ Review: Synonyms ❏ Word Wheel	❏ Introduce: Latin Number Prefixes ❏ Exercise 3: Match It: Number Prefixes ❏ Exercise 4: Choose It: Affixed Words
STEP 4 • Identify correct adjective order. • Identify dangling participles. • Identify basic sentence patterns: simple, compound, and complex. • Use capital letters correctly in titles and letters.	❏ Review: Participles ❏ Exercise 3: Find It: Functions of Participles ❏ Introduce: Dangling Participial Phrases ❏ Exercise 4: Identify It: Dangling Participial Phrases	❏ Review: Dangling Participial Phrases ❏ Exercise 5: Rewrite It: Dangling Participial Phrases
STEP 5 • Use text features to understand informational text. • Use context-based strategies to define words. • Identify elements of plot. • Identify, understand, and answer questions that use different types of signal words. • Identify the strategies in SQ3R.	❏ Independent Text: **"The Heart of Our Land"** ❏ SQ3R: Working with Text	❏ Passage Fluency ❏ Exercise 6: How To: Write an E-mail Message
STEP 6 • Use text features to develop study questions. • Write responses to questions using the signal words. • Organize information in a plot analysis graphic organizer. • Write a literary analysis essay. • Use a genre-specific Writer's Checklist to revise and edit a literary analysis essay.	❏ Write It: Summary Paragraph	❏ Exercise 7: Write It: E-mail Message
Self-Evaluation (5 is the highest) **Effort** = I produced my best work. **Participation** = I was actively involved in tasks. **Independence** = I worked on my own.	**Effort:** 1 2 3 4 5 **Participation:** 1 2 3 4 5 **Independence:** 1 2 3 4 5	**Effort:** 1 2 3 4 5 **Participation:** 1 2 3 4 5 **Independence:** 1 2 3 4 5
Teacher Evaluation	**Effort:** 1 2 3 4 5 **Participation:** 1 2 3 4 5 **Independence:** 1 2 3 4 5	**Effort:** 1 2 3 4 5 **Participation:** 1 2 3 4 5 **Independence:** 1 2 3 4 5

Lesson 3 (Date:_____)	**Lesson 4** (Date:_____)	**Lesson 5** (Date:_____)
❑ Exercise 1: Listening for Sounds in Words: Sound-Spelling Patterns	❑ Exercise 1: Listening for Sounds in Words: Sound Spelling Patterns ❑ Exercise 2: Variant Sound-Spelling Patterns	❑ Content Mastery: Variant Sound-Spelling Patterns
❑ Word Fluency 2 ❑ Divide It: Preview Vocabulary Text Connection 1	❑ Make a Mnemonic ❑ Present It: Mnemonics for Confusing Word Pairs and Triplets	❑ Content Mastery: Spelling Posttest 1 ❑ Present It: Mnemonics for Confusing Word Pairs
❑ Use the Clues: Preview Vocabulary Text Connection 1 ❑ Write It: Journal Entry	❑ Introduce: Greek Number Prefixes ❑ Exercise 3: Match It: Number Prefixes ❑ Exercise 4: Choose It: Affixed Words	❑ Exercise 1: Sort It: Latin and Greek Number Prefixes ❑ Exercise 2: Choose It: Affixed Words
❑ Review: Capitalization in Titles and Letters ❑ Find It: Use of Capital Letters Text Connection 1	❑ Review: Sentence Structure ❑ Exercise 5: Diagram It: Different Sentence Types	❑ Introduce: Adjective Order ❑ Exercise 3: Choose It: Order of Adjectives
❑ Instructional Text: **"Dear Rosita"**	❑ Comprehend It: **"Dear Rosita"** Text Connection 1	❑ Introduce: A Quick Outline ❑ Answer It: Using Signal Words
❑ Comprehend It Text Connection 1	❑ Exercise 6: Write It: E-mail Message	❑ Review: How to Write an E-mail Message ❑ Exercise 4: Speaking and Writing Using the Challenge Text: Pre-Write It: Brainstorming Ideas for a Story
Effort: 1 2 3 4 5 **Participation:** 1 2 3 4 5 **Independence:** 1 2 3 4 5	**Effort:** 1 2 3 4 5 **Participation:** 1 2 3 4 5 **Independence:** 1 2 3 4 5	**Effort:** 1 2 3 4 5 **Participation:** 1 2 3 4 5 **Independence:** 1 2 3 4 5
Effort: 1 2 3 4 5 **Participation:** 1 2 3 4 5 **Independence:** 1 2 3 4 5	**Effort:** 1 2 3 4 5 **Participation:** 1 2 3 4 5 **Independence:** 1 2 3 4 5	**Effort:** 1 2 3 4 5 **Participation:** 1 2 3 4 5 **Independence:** 1 2 3 4 5

Check off the activities you complete with each lesson. Evaluate your accomplishments at the end of each lesson. Pay attention to teacher evaluations and comments.

	Unit Objectives	Lesson 6 (Date:_____)	Lesson 7 (Date:_____)
STEP 1	• Say the vowel sounds for the letter combinations: **ear/air/ar** for / âr / as in *bear, air, care*; **ar/arr** for / ăr / as in *parody, arrow*; **ear** for / är / as in *heart*; **ar/er/err** for / ĕr / as in *primary, very, berry*; **oar** for / ôr /; **ear** for / ûr / as in *earth*; **ear/eir/ier/er/eer** for / îr / as in *ear, weird, pier, series, deer*. • Say the variant sounds for the consonants **s** (/ s /, / z /, / sh /, and / zh /) and **g** (/ g /, / j /, and / zh /). • Write the various letter combinations representing **r**-controlled vowel sounds and the consonants **g** and **s**.	❏ Content Mastery: Using Student Performance	❏ Exercise 1: Using a Dictionary
STEP 2	• Read and spell words based on unit sound-spelling combinations. • Read and spell the **Essential Words:** *bury, buy, cough, penguin, soldier, toward*. • Read and spell words with Latin and Greek number prefixes. • Spell confusing words correctly.	❏ Exercise 1: Spelling Pretest 2 ❏ Word Fluency 3	❏ Build It: Words with Number Prefixes ❏ Word Fluency 4
STEP 3	• Identify and define Latin and Greek number prefixes. • Use knowledge of word relationships to build word meanings.	❏ Vocabulary Focus Text Connection 2 ❏ Use the Clues: Vocabulary Review ❏ Expression of the Day	❏ Review: Antonyms ❏ Exercise 2: Fill In: Words with Number Prefixes ❏ Expression of the Day
STEP 4	• Identify correct adjective order. • Identify dangling participles. • Identify basic sentence patterns: simple, compound, and complex. • Use capital letters correctly in titles and letters.	❏ Adjective Use ❏ Exercise 2: Rewrite It: Sentences	❏ Review: Role of Articles ❏ Find It: Nouns with Articles and Adjectives Text Connection 2
STEP 5	• Use text features to understand informational text. • Use context-based strategies to define words. • Identify elements of plot. • Identify, understand, and answer questions that use different types of signal words. • Identify the strategies in SQ3R.	❏ Instructional Text: **"The Tell-Tale Heart"**	❏ Comprehend It: **"The Tell-Tale Heart"** ❏ Map It: Plot Analysis Text Connection 2
STEP 6	• Use text features to develop study questions. • Write responses to questions using the signal words. • Organize information in a plot analysis graphic organizer. • Write a literary analysis essay. • Use a genre-specific Writer's Checklist to revise and edit a literary analysis essay.	❏ Exercise 3: Analyze It: Literary Analysis Essay	❏ Review Plot Development: Cause and Effect Text Connection 2
	Self-Evaluation (5 is the highest) **Effort** = I produced my best work. **Participation** = I was actively involved in tasks. **Independence** = I worked on my own.	**Effort:** 1 2 3 4 5 **Participation:** 1 2 3 4 5 **Independence:** 1 2 3 4 5	**Effort:** 1 2 3 4 5 **Participation:** 1 2 3 4 5 **Independence:** 1 2 3 4 5
	Teacher Evaluation	**Effort:** 1 2 3 4 5 **Participation:** 1 2 3 4 5 **Independence:** 1 2 3 4 5	**Effort:** 1 2 3 4 5 **Participation:** 1 2 3 4 5 **Independence:** 1 2 3 4 5

Lesson 8 (Date:_____)	Lesson 9 (Date:_____)	Lesson 10 (Date:_____)
❑ Exercise 1: Listening for Word Parts: Number Prefixes		
❑ Build It: Words with Number Prefixes	❑ Chain It	❑ Content Mastery: Spelling Posttest 2
❑ Exercise 2: Identify It: Unit Words ❑ Exercise 3: Choose It: Unit Words	❑ Content Mastery: Vocabulary; Morphology	❑ Content Mastery: Using Student Performance ❑ Find It: Words with Number Prefixes ❑ Write a Mini-Dialog: Idioms
❑ Exercise 4: Rewrite It: Adjective Order ❑ Review: Uses of Capital Letters	❑ Content Mastery: Dangling Participial Phrases; Adjective Usage; Capitalization	❑ Content Mastery: Using Student Performance
❑ Comprehend It: **"The Tell-Tale Heart"** ❑ Map It: Plot Analysis Text Connection 2 ❑ How Authors Build Suspense	❑ Answer It: Using Signal Words	❑ Review: Literary Analysis Essay
❑ Prepare to Write: Literary Analysis Essay	❑ Write It: Literary Analysis Essay	❑ Revising and Editing: Literary Analysis Essay
Effort: 1 2 3 4 5 **Participation:** 1 2 3 4 5 **Independence:** 1 2 3 4 5	**Effort:** 1 2 3 4 5 **Participation:** 1 2 3 4 5 **Independence:** 1 2 3 4 5	**Effort:** 1 2 3 4 5 **Participation:** 1 2 3 4 5 **Independence:** 1 2 3 4 5
Effort: 1 2 3 4 5 **Participation:** 1 2 3 4 5 **Independence:** 1 2 3 4 5	**Effort:** 1 2 3 4 5 **Participation:** 1 2 3 4 5 **Independence:** 1 2 3 4 5	**Effort:** 1 2 3 4 5 **Participation:** 1 2 3 4 5 **Independence:** 1 2 3 4 5

Exercise 1 · Listening for Sounds in Words: Sound-Spelling Patterns

▶ Say each sound in the Sound Bank with your teacher.

Sound Bank

/ âr /	/ är /

▶ Listen to your teacher read each word in the first column. Repeat each word.

▶ Identify the sound in the **Sound Bank** that is heard in each of the words.

▶ Underline the letters in each word that represent the sound.

▶ Label the column with the correct sound-spelling pattern and sound from the **Sound Bank**.

▶ Repeat this process for the remaining columns.

_____ = _____	_____ = _____	_____ = _____	_____ = _____
bear	heart	area	chair
wear	hearth	compare	pair
pear	heartbeat	rare	fair

▶ Practice reading the words in each column with a partner.

Which sound has three different spelling patterns? _____

Which spelling pattern represents two different sounds? _____

Exercise 2 · Spelling Pretest 1

▸ Write the word your teacher repeats.

1. _____
2. _____
3. _____
4. _____
5. _____

6. _____
7. _____
8. _____
9. _____
10. _____

11. _____
12. _____
13. _____
14. _____
15. _____

Exercise 3 · Find It: Functions of Participles

▸ Read each sentence.

▸ Identify the participle and underline it.

▸ Determine the function of the participle.

▸ Read the answer choices and circle the correct answer.

1. The immigrants, who had struggled to survive overseas, made homes in the Heartland.

   a. part of a verb phrase   b. adjective   c. start of participial phrase

2. The prairies stretching across the midwestern states contain rich soil.

   a. part of a verb phrase   b. adjective   c. start of participial phrase

3. Drenching rains provide water for crops.

   a. part of a verb phrase   b. adjective   c. start of participial phrase

4. Flowing through the Heartland, three major rivers provide essential water for the crops.

   a. part of a verb phrase   b. adjective   c. start of participial phrase

5. Today, machines are replacing human labor on farms.

   a. part of a verb phrase   b. adjective   c. start of participial phrase

Exercise 4 · Identify It: Dangling Participial Phrases

▸ Read each pair of sentences.

▸ Underline the participial phrase in each sentence.

▸ Determine which sentence is written correctly.

▸ In the correct sentence, draw an arrow from the participial phrase to the word it modifies.

1. Growing in the fields, the farmer picked the corn.

   The farmer picked the corn growing in the fields.

2. Playing with enthusiasm, the spectators watched the team.

   The spectators watched the team playing with enthusiasm.

3. The fisherman had a worm dangling at the end of the line.

   Dangling at the end of the line, the fisherman had a worm.

4. Barking loudly at the raccoon, I tried to silence the dog.

   I tried to silence the dog barking loudly at the raccoon.

5. Tom watched the traffic lights turning red.

   Turning red, Tom watched the traffic lights.

Exercise 1 · Listening for Sounds in Words: Sound-Spelling Patterns

▸ Say each sound in the **Sound Bank** with your teacher.

Sound Bank

/ âr /	/ ĕr /

▸ Listen to your teacher read each word in the first column. Repeat each word.

▸ Identify the sound in the **Sound Bank** that is heard in each of the words.

▸ Underline the letters in each word that represent the sound.

▸ Label the column with the correct sound-spelling pattern and sound from the **Sound Bank**.

▸ Repeat this process for the remaining columns.

_____ = _____	_____ = _____	_____ = _____	_____ = _____	_____ = _____
comparison	berry	dictionary	barrel	very
paragraph	territory	library	carry	inherit
parody	terrible	necessary	narrow	heritage

▸ Practice reading the words in each column with a partner.

Which spelling pattern represents two different sounds shown in the chart? _____

Unit 31 · Lesson 2

Exercise 2 · Write It: Essential Words

▸ Review the **Essential Words** in the **Word Bank**.

Word Bank

bury	toward	buy	cough	soldier	penguin

▸ Put the words in alphabetical order and write them on the lines.

▸ Write one sentence for each **Essential Word**.

▸ Check that each sentence uses correct capitalization, commas, and end punctuation.

▸ Read each sentence to a partner.

1. _____

_____

2. _____

_____

3. _____

_____

4. _____

_____

5. _____

_____

6. _____

_____

Exercise 3 · Match It: Number Prefixes

▸ Sort the **Morphemes for Meaning Cards** to find the Latin number prefixes.

▸ Complete each line in the chart by writing the correct prefix in the Latin Prefix column beside its numeral.

Number	Latin Prefix	Greek Prefix
1		
2		
3		
4		
5		
6		
7		
8		
9		
10		
100		
1000		
10,000		
million		
billion		
trillion		
quadrillion		
quintillion		

Unit 31 · Lesson 2

Exercise 4 · Choose It: Affixed Words

▸ Read each sentence.

▸ Choose the correct word to complete the sentence, and write it in the blank.

▸ Circle the number prefix.

▸ Use the chart in Unit 31, Lesson 2, Exercise 3 and a dictionary as references.

1. Each of the farmer's fields had four sides and was in the shape of a_____.

   a. quintuplet   b. quadruped   c. quadrangle

2. In 1976 there were great celebrations to mark the two hundredth year, or

   _____, of the Declaration of Independence.

   a. bicentennial   b. biennial   c. centennial

3. My grandmother lived ninety years, so she was a _____.

   a. nonagon   b. nonagenarian   c. septuagenarian

4. A _____ is one thousandth of a meter.

   a. millimeter   b. millipede   c. decimeter

5. A one-celled organism is called _____.

   a. unicellular   b. unilateral   c. bilateral

Exercise 5 · Rewrite It: Dangling Participial Phrases

▶ Read each sentence.

▶ Underline the dangling participial phrase.

▶ Rewrite the sentence on the lines provided to make the sentence clearer.

▶ Underline the strategy you used.

1. Migrating to the Heartland, new homes were built across the prairie.

   _____

   _____

   _____

   Which strategy did you use?   A. Moved the participial phrase in the sentence

   B. Added words to the sentence

   C. Revised the sentence to create a dependent clause

2. Building new farms, the number of cattle herds increased rapidly.

   _____

   _____

   _____

   Which strategy did you use?   A. Moved the participial phrase in the sentence

   B. Added words to the sentence

   C. Revised the sentence to create a dependent clause

3. The summer days passed quickly growing crops and raising cattle.

   _____

   _____

   _____

   Which strategy did you use?   A. Moved the participial phrase in the sentence

   B. Added words to the sentence

   C. Revised the sentence to create a dependent clause

(continued)

Unit 31 · Lesson 2

4. Repairing the tractor, the coyotes attacked the chickens in the hen house.

_____

_____

_____

Which strategy did you use? A. Moved the participial phrase in the sentence

B. Added words to the sentence

C. Revised the sentence to create a dependent clause

5. Driving across the prairie, cornfields stretched for miles and miles.

_____

_____

_____

Which strategy did you use? A. Moved the participial phrase in the sentence

B. Added words to the sentence

C. Revised the sentence to create a dependent clause

Exercise 6 · How To: Write an E-mail Message

▶ Read the sample e-mail message below.

▶ Label each of the features of the e-mail message.

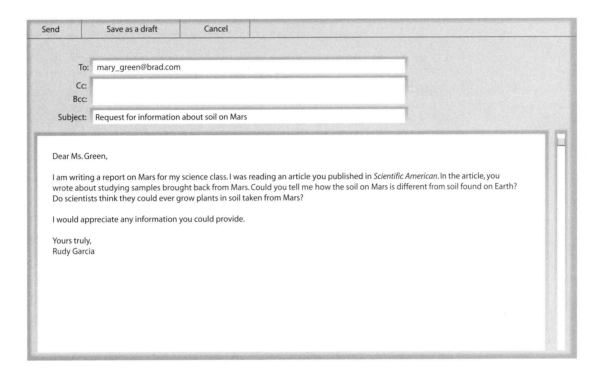

Send	Save as a draft	Cancel

To: mary_green@brad.com

Cc:
Bcc:

Subject: Request for information about soil on Mars

Dear Ms. Green,

I am writing a report on Mars for my science class. I was reading an article you published in *Scientific American*. In the article, you wrote about studying samples brought back from Mars. Could you tell me how the soil on Mars is different from soil found on Earth? Do scientists think they could ever grow plants in soil taken from Mars?

I would appreciate any information you could provide.

Yours truly,
Rudy Garcia

Unit 31 · Lesson 2

Exercise 7 · Write It: E-mail Message

▸ Refer to the sample e-mail message on the previous page.

▸ Think of one or more questions to ask a geography expert about the Heartland.

▸ Write an e-mail to the address your teacher provides.

Send	Save as a draft	Cancel	

To:

Cc:
Bcc:

Subject:

Exercise 1 · Listening for Sounds in Words: Sound-Spelling Patterns

▶ Say each sound in the **Sound Bank** with your teacher.

Sound Bank

/ ôr /	/ ûr /	/ îr /

▶ Listen to your teacher read each word in the first column. Repeat each word.

▶ Identify the sound in the **Sound Bank** that is heard in each of the words.

▶ Underline the letters in each word that represent the sound.

▶ Label the column with the correct sound-spelling pattern and sound from the **Sound Bank**.

▶ Repeat this process for the remaining columns.

___ = ___	___ = ___	___ = ___	___ = ___	___ = ___	___ = ___	___ = ___
board	experience	learn	appear	fierce	weir	cheer
coarse	material	early	clear	pier	weird	deer
roar	severe	research	year	pierce		steer

▶ Practice reading each column with a partner.

Which spelling pattern represents two different sounds shown in the chart? _____

Exercise 1 · Listening for Sounds in Words: Sound-Spelling Patterns

▶ Say each sound in the **Sound Bank** with your teacher.

Sound Bank

/ sh /	/ zh /

▶ Listen to your teacher read each word in the first column. Repeat each word.

▶ Identify the sound in the **Sound Bank** that is heard in each of the words.

▶ Underline the letters in each word that represent the sound.

▶ Label the column with the correct sound-spelling pattern and sound from the **Sound Bank**.

▶ Repeat this process for the remaining columns.

_____ = _____	_____ = _____	_____ = _____	_____ = _____
measure	issue	mirage	sugar
usually	tissue	regime	sure
visual		camouflage	

▶ Practice reading each column with a partner.

Which spelling pattern represents two different sounds shown in the chart?_____

Exercise 2 · Variant Sound-Spelling Patterns

▶ Read each list of words with a partner. Underline the letters in each word that represent the same sound in the list.

▶ Review these words from Unit 31, Lesson 1:

bear	heart	area	chair
wear	hearth	compare	pair
pear	heartbeat	rare	fair

▶ Review these words from Unit 31, Lesson 2:

comparison	berry	dictionary	barrel	very
paragraph	territory	library	carry	inherit
parody	terrible	necessary	narrow	heritage

▶ Review these words from Unit 31, Lesson 3:

board	experience	learn	appear	fierce	weir	cheer
coarse	material	early	clear	pier	weird	deer
roar	severe	research	year	pierce		steer

Unit 31 · Lesson 4

Exercise 3 · Match It: Number Prefixes

▶ Sort the **Morphemes for Meaning Cards** to find the Greek number prefixes.

▶ Complete each line in the chart by writing the correct prefix in the **Greek Prefix** column beside its numeral.

Number	Latin Prefix	Greek Prefix
1	uni-	
2	bi-	
3	ter-	
4	quadr-/quar-	
5	quint-	
6	sex-	
7	sept-	
8	oct-	
9	nona-/nove-	
10	dec-	
100	cent-	
1000	mille-/milli-	
10,000		
million		
billion		
trillion		
quadrillion		
quintillion		

Exercise 4 · Choose It: Affixed Words

▶ Read each sentence.

▶ Choose the correct word to complete the sentence, and write it in the blank.

▶ Circle the number prefix.

▶ Use the chart in Unit 31, Exercise 3, **Match It: Number Prefixes**, and a dictionary as references.

1. Standing on his own, the talk show host started the evening by giving a funny

   _____.

   a. tetrapod   b. monolith   c. monologue

2. Bonnie's new computer has a memory capacity of more than six _____ and mine only has half that capacity, about three billion bytes.

   a. gigameter   b. gigabytes   c. megahertz

3. The five-sided building in which the Defense Department works is called the

   _____.

   a. Pentagon   b. Octagon   c. Pentameter

4. Our school year is divided into three sections, or _____.

   a. tricycles   b. kilometers   c. trimesters

5. A six-sided cube is an example of a _____ shape.

   a. hexadecimal   b. hexagonal   c. diagonal

Unit 31 · Lesson 4

Exercise 5 · Diagram It: Different Sentence Types

▸ Work in the previously assigned groups.

▸ Find the sentence assigned to your group.

▸ Diagram the sentence.

▸ Share your diagramming with the rest of the class.

▸ Complete all the sentence diagrams as other groups present them.

1. Rosita wrote letters to her father.

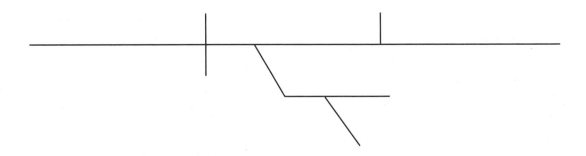

2. Rosita attended classes, and she also worked in an office.

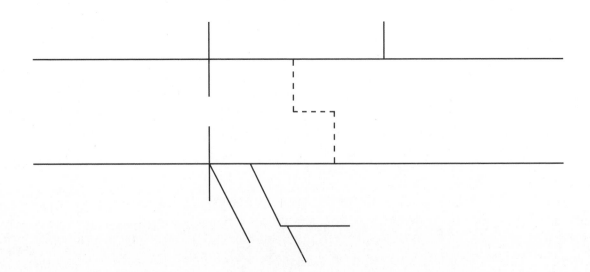

(continued)

Exercise 5 (continued) · Diagram It: Different Sentence Types

3. Since Rosita left for college, her father has written many letters to her.

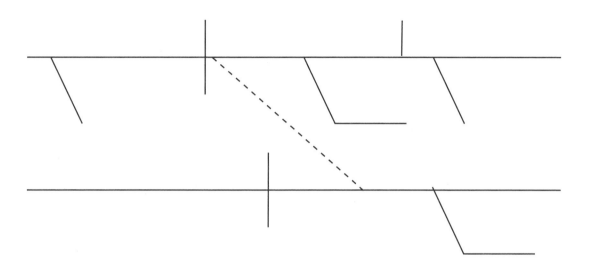

4. Rosita's father missed his daughter, who was attending college.

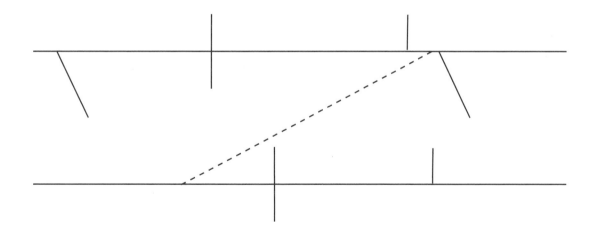

(continued)

5. Mama worried about her daughter, and she waited for her return.

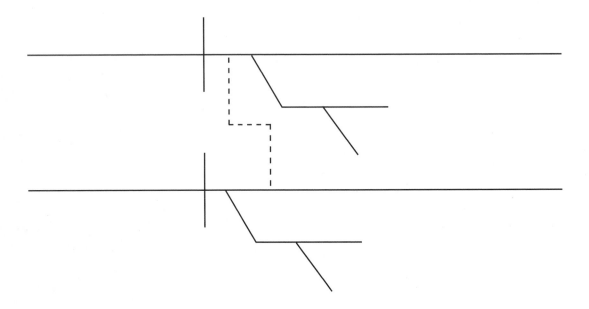

Exercise 6 · Write It: E-mail Message

▸ Open the *Student Text* to the letter in **"Dear Rosita"** that you discussed with your partner.

▸ Draft an e-mail note that Rosita might have written to her father before he wrote either letter three or letter four in reply.

Send	Save as a draft	Cancel

To:

Cc:
Bcc:

Subject:

Exercise 1 · Sort It: Latin and Greek Number Prefixes

▶ Read the list of words with your teacher.

▶ Circle the prefix in each word. Decide if it is a Latin prefix, a Greek prefix, or both.

▶ Copy the prefix into the correct column in the chart. Add the meaning.

▶ Refer to Exercise 3 in Unit 31, Lesson 4, Step 3, **Match It: Number Prefixes**, and a dictionary as needed.

	Latin Number Prefixes	Greek Number Prefixes
1. triathlon		
2. kilometer		
3. bicycle		
4. megatons		
5. millibar		
6. unicorn		
7. quarter		
8. octopus		
9. decimal		
10. digraph		

Exercise 2 · Choose It: Affixed Words

▸ Read each sentence.

▸ Fill in the blank with one of the words from the list in Unit 31, Exercise 1, **Sort It: Latin and Greek Number Prefixes**.

▸ Use a dictionary if you need help.

▸ Reread the sentence to make sure it makes sense.

1. The money was to be divided equally among the four of us so we would each get one _____.

2. The mythical animal with one horn is called a _____.

3. The _____ has three events: swimming, biking, and running.

4. In many countries, distances are measured in _____, not miles.

5. A two-letter grapheme that represents one sound is called a _____.

Unit 31 · Lesson 5

Exercise 3 · Choose It: Order of Adjectives

▶ Read the group of adjectives in each category in the **Word Bank**, then read the list of nouns in the **Order of Adjectives** chart.

▶ Choose adjectives to describe each noun and write them in the correct columns.

Word Bank

Number	Opinion	Size	Shape	Age	Color	Origin	Material	Qualification
billion	beautiful	large	narrow	old	blue	Mexican	golden	fishing
several	comfortable	small	octagonal	mature	green	American	woolen	prepared
six	delicious	huge	square	young		Italian	silken	
a/an	talented					Spanish		
the	lively							

Order of Adjectives

Number	Opinion	Size	Shape	Age	Color	Origin	Material	Qualification	Noun
									car
									soup
									painter
									scarf
									music

Exercise 4 · Pre-Write It: Brainstorming Ideas for a Story

▶ Work on this activity with a group of classmates to get ideas for a short story. For this activity, each person in the group will need four index cards and one sheet of lined paper.

1. Take two index cards. Write a problem or situation on the back of each card. Make these general rather than specific ideas. Here are two examples:

   Someone loses something important.

   Someone learns surprising news.

2. Put the cards face down in a pile with the cards of the other students in the group.

3. Shuffle the cards. Take turns drawing two cards each. (It is okay if you draw one of your own cards.)

4. Using the remaining two index cards, write a specific situation for each general situation you drew. For example, if you drew the general situation **Someone loses something important**, then you might write this specific situation.

   A 15-year-old boy loses an autographed baseball that his father gave him.

5. Once you have written a specific problem or situation for each general problem on a card, put the two cards in a pile with the cards of everyone else in the group.

6. Shuffle the cards. Lay them all face up on a desk or table so that everyone can see them. Walk around and read each card.

7. Choose one problem or situation that you might like to write about.

8. Write this one problem or situation on the top of a sheet of paper. Imagine that it is the initiating event in a short story. Then write for ten minutes on what might happen as a result of this situation.

Exercise 1 · Spelling Pretest 2

▸ Write the word your teacher repeats.

1. _____   6. _____   11. _____

2. _____   7. _____   12. _____

3. _____   8. _____   13. _____

4. _____   9. _____   14. _____

5. _____   10. _____   15. _____

Exercise 2 · Rewrite It: Sentences

▶ Read the composition in the box.

▶ Identify and correct errors in the first sentence with your teacher.

▶ Identify and use editing marks to correct errors in the remaining sentences in the composition. Write your revised sentences on the lines that are provided.

▶ Fill in the problem and an explanation of the revision in the chart.

▶ Pay special attention to capitalization, choice of adjectives, order of adjectives, dangling participles, and sentence variety.

---

1. Edgar allan Poe wrote "the tell-tale heart." 2. It is a good story about a crazy madman. 3. He plans to kill the old defenseless man he looks after. 4. Giving the reader a look inside a deranged mind, the plot unfolds as the madman explains what he is thinking. 5. He carries out his bad plan perfectly. 6. His guilty conscience makes him confess. 7. I thought this story was nice. 8. Describing the madman's thoughts, the author was fascinating.

_____

_____

_____

_____

_____

_____

_____

_____

_____

(continued)

Exercise 2 (continued) · Rewrite It: Sentences

_____

_____

_____

_____

Sentence #	Trait(s)	Problem(s)	Revision

Exercise 3 · Analyze It: Literary Analysis Essay

▸ Read the example student essay on **"Dear Rosita"** with your teacher.

▸ Number the paragraphs 1–5.

▸ Label the paragraphs in the margins **Introduction**, **Body**, and **Conclusion**.

▸ Locate the thesis statement and underline it. Then locate and underline the topic sentence in each of the body paragraphs.

▸ Use your **Literary Analysis Essay Checklist** to analyze the essay.

What Characters Teach Us in "Dear Rosita"

What kind of story characters do you most enjoy reading about? The characters I most enjoy are ordinary people who face challenges and learn from life. Strong, believable characters are one of the things that makes "Dear Rosita," by Nash Candelaria, so enjoyable to read. "Dear Rosita" is a story told through letters. Rosita is the first member of her family to go to college. Her father writes her many letters because he is very proud of her and it is her first time away from the family. We only see Papá's letters, not Rosita's, but we can tell what Rosita has written by reading Papá's responses. We learn a lot about both characters and their relationship. We learn that Papá is a very strong character who has had a great influence on Rosita because he works hard, he honestly communicates his feelings, and he feels it is important for people to stand up for what they believe in.

One of Papá's main character traits is that he is a hard worker. Papá and his family work on a farm in New Mexico. In each letter Papá tells Rosita something about his work on the farm. He writes, "I got to go to the corral and feed the animals." He also writes that he filled a ditch with water from the Rio Grande because the land is dry. When Rosita writes to Papá about doctors who say that healthy people should exercise and not eat meat, Papá thinks that is ridiculous. He writes that he has worked hard his whole life, and now he finally has enough money to enjoy steak. He writes, "Who needs to go out and run on purpose? Or sweat and breathe hard on purpose? Man, that's the way we live—sweating and breathing hard." By setting an

(continued)

example of hard work, Papá has prepared Rosita to succeed at college. Rosita goes to school, studies six hours a day, and works a part-time job.

Another character trait we learn about Papá is that he is honest. He writes to Rosita that her mother is worried that Rosita is going to change at college. Her mother worries that she's not going to be smart enough for her daughter. Papá tells her not to worry. But he also confesses to Rosita that he has the same concern. He writes, "But the truth is, I worry a little too. We are so proud of you. And want you not to be ashamed of us poor country folks." It takes a very honest person to share that fear with his daughter. You can tell that Rosita has learned to be honest, too. She tells her father when she is put in jail for protesting at the university.

Papá has taught his family to work hard and be honest. He has also taught them to stand up for what they believe. When Rosita tells Papá that she was arrested for protesting at her college, at first he is upset and concerned. He thinks taking over the university president's office was a bad idea. He suggests that the students go on strike instead, like he did when he was a farm worker. But in his next letter, Papá tells Rosita that he's been thinking more about the different reasons why people get arrested. He writes, "Lots of good people been put in jail. Jesus. That Indian man Gandhi." He shows Rosita that he is proud of her for standing up for what she believes.

I really enjoyed reading "Dear Rosita" because Papá and Rosita are such strong characters, yet they continue to learn from life, and from each other. Papá is an especially interesting character. Although he lives a traditional life and is not as educated as his daughter, he has much wisdom to teach her, and he has much to teach readers, as well.

Exercise 1 · Using a Dictionary

▸ Turn to the **Vocabulary** section (dictionary) in the back of the *Student Text*.

▸ Find the word **sluice** and its pronunciation.

▸ Write the diacritical markings for that word on the line in item 1 below.

▸ Use the markings to read the word aloud.

▸ Complete numbers 2–5 using the same process.

Word	Pronunciation
1. sluice	_____
2. scholarship	_____
3. sagacity	_____
4. shrieked	_____
5. meticulous	_____

▸ Use a classroom dictionary or an online reference source to complete numbers 6–10.

6. camouflage	_____
7. regime	_____
8. bacteria	_____
9. caribou	_____
10. inherited	_____

Unit 31 · Lesson 7

Exercise 2 · Fill In: Words with Number Prefixes

▸ Read each sentence and the underlined word.

▸ Use strategies from **Use the Clues**, including the meanings of prefixes, to determine meaning of the underlined word in each sentence.

▸ Circle the correct answer and write it in the blank.

▸ Use a dictionary as a resource.

1. If a quintet is a group of five, then a <u>septet</u> must be a group of _____.

   a. three   b. six   c. seven   d. none of the above

2. A <u>tercet</u> is a group of _____ lines of verse, often rhyming together or with another triplet.

   a. three   b. six   c. seven   d. none of the above

3. A <u>unilateral</u> decision is made by only _____ of two groups, nations, or persons.

   a. one   b. two   c. four   d. none of the above

4. If triceps are muscles with three points of attachment, then <u>biceps</u> are muscles with

   _____ points of attachment.

   a. several   b. one   c. two   d. four

5. If a decigram is a metric unit equal to one-tenth of a gram, then a <u>centigram</u> is equal

   to _____ of a gram.

   a. 1/100   b. 1/1000   c. 1/10   d. none of the above

Exercise 1 · Listening for Word Parts: Number Prefixes

▶ Listen to each word your teacher says.

▶ Repeat the word.

▶ Mark **Yes** or **No** to tell if you hear a number prefix.

▶ If **yes**, write the number prefix you hear under the heading **Number Prefix**.

Number Prefixes		
Do you hear a **number prefix** in the word?		If **Yes**, write the **number prefix**.
Yes	No	Number Prefix
1.		
2.		
3.		
4.		
5.		
6.		
7.		
8.		
9.		
10.		
11.		
12.		
13.		
14.		
15.		

Unit 31 · Lesson 8

Exercise 2 · Identify It: Unit Words

▸ Read each sentence, paying special attention to the underlined word.

▸ Circle the correct meaning for the underlined word.

▸ Reread each sentence, substituting the word or phrase you circled for the underlined word.

▸ Use a dictionary for help if necessary.

1. Meet us <u>here</u> after school.

   a. ear   b. at this location   c. near   d. nearby

2. <u>Usually</u> he walks his dog in the early morning.

   a. rarely   b. sometimes   c. as a rule   d. once in a while

3. I am <u>very</u> excited that you are in my class!

   a. merry   b. vary   c. terrible   d. extremely

4. She nearly tripped over the loose <u>board</u>.

   a. not interested   b. piece of lumber   c. saw   d. nails

5. My good friend sent me a <u>sincere</u> letter of apology.

   a. dishonest   b. poetic   c. heartfelt   d. lengthy

Exercise 3 · Choose It: Unit Words

▶ Read each sentence and the word choices below the sentence.

▶ Select the correct word for the context of the sentence.

▶ Circle the correct word and write the word in the blank.

▶ Reread the sentence to check your work.

1. It is important to _____ the food you eat to have a healthy heart.
   a. vary   b. very

2. The attorney asked for the _____ facts in the case.
   a. bear   b. bare

3. The young _____ leapt through the open meadow.
   a. deer   b. dear

4. The cardiologist will be _____ in just a moment.
   a. hear   b. here

5. Many people like to _____ fruit before eating it.
   a. pear   b. pare

Exercise 4 · Rewrite It: Adjective Order

▶ Read the set of words in each item.

▶ Arrange the words in the correct order.

▶ Rewrite the group of words in correct order as a noun phrase.

▶ Refer to the **Order of Adjectives Chart** in the *Student Text* if needed.

1. lonely   young   girl   a   _____

2. newsy   letters   many   long   _____

3. large   cotton   eight   T-shirts   _____

4. corn   yellow   mature   juicy   _____

5. silver   shiny   badge   a   _____

Check off the activities you complete with each lesson. Evaluate your accomplishments at the end of each lesson. Pay attention to teacher evaluations and comments.

Unit Objectives	Lesson 1 (Date:_____)	Lesson 2 (Date:_____)
STEP 1 • Say the vowel sounds for phonograms **-old**, **-oll**, **-ost** for / ō / as in *cold, toll, most*; **-ind**, **-ild** for / ī / as in *find, wild*. • Write the letter combinations for the phonograms representing / ō / and / ī /.	❏ Exercise 1: Listening for Sounds in Words: Sound-Spelling Patterns	❏ Exercise 1: Listening for Sounds in Words: Sound-Spelling Patterns
STEP 2 • Read and spell words based on unit sound-spelling combinations. • Read and spell the **Essential Words:** *blood, both, door, flood, floor, pint*. • Read and spell words composed of Greek combining forms. • Spell confusing words correctly.	❏ Exercise 2: Spelling Pretest 1	❏ Exercise 2: Write It: Essential Words ❏ Word Fluency 1
STEP 3 • Identify and define Greek combining forms. • Use knowledge of word relationships to build word meanings.	❏ Unit Words ❏ Review: Synonyms ❏ Word Wheel	❏ Introduce: Greek Combining Forms ❏ Introduce: Euphony ❏ Define It
STEP 4 • Identify linking verbs. • Identify correct subject-verb agreement. • Identify correctly formed negative statements.	❏ Exercise 3: Check What You Know: The Verb **be** ❏ Introduce: Linking Verbs Other Than **be** ❏ Exercise 4: Identify It: Linking Verbs	❏ Review: Subject-Verb Agreement ❏ Introduce: Subject-Verb Agreement—Special Conditions ❏ Exercise 3: Identify It: Subject-Verb Agreement
STEP 5 • Use text features to understand informational text. • Apply SQ3R to read informational text. • Use context-based strategies to define words. • Identify mood, meter, and melody in poetry. • Identify features of a screenplay. • Identify, understand, and answer questions that use different types of signal words.	❏ Review: SQ3R: Study Skills ❏ SQ3R: Study Skills: Working With Text	❏ Passage Fluency ❏ Exercise 4: How To: Read a Web Page ❏ Exercise 5: How To: Search for Information on the Internet
STEP 6 • Use text features to develop study questions. • Write responses to questions using the signal words. • Develop an informal outline to prepare to write. • Write literary analysis compositions • Present a literary analysis orally. • Apply a genre-specific Writer's Checklist to revise and edit literary analysis compositions.	❏ Write It: Study Guide ❏ Using a Study Guide	❏ Exercise 6: Apply It: Do an Internet Search
Self-Evaluation (5 is the highest) **Effort** = I produced my best work. **Participation** = I was actively involved in tasks. **Independence** = I worked on my own.	**Effort:** 1 2 3 4 5 **Participation:** 1 2 3 4 5 **Independence:** 1 2 3 4 5	**Effort:** 1 2 3 4 5 **Participation:** 1 2 3 4 5 **Independence:** 1 2 3 4 5
Teacher Evaluation	**Effort:** 1 2 3 4 5 **Participation:** 1 2 3 4 5 **Independence:** 1 2 3 4 5	**Effort:** 1 2 3 4 5 **Participation:** 1 2 3 4 5 **Independence:** 1 2 3 4 5

Lesson 3 (Date:_____)	**Lesson 4** (Date:_____)	**Lesson 5** (Date:_____)
❏ Exercise 1: Listening for Sounds in Words: Sound-Spelling Patterns	❏ Exercise 1: Listening for Sounds in Words: Sound Spelling Patterns	❏ Content Mastery: Sound-Spelling Patterns
❏ Word Fluency 2 ❏ Instructional Text: **"Nothing Gold Can Stay"** Text Connection 3	❏ Review: Contractions ❏ Exercise 2: Contract It ❏ Make a Mnemonic ❏ Present It: Mnemonics for Confusing Word Pairs	❏ Content Mastery: Spelling Posttest 1 ❏ Present It: Mnemonics for Confusing Word Pairs
❏ Instructional Text: **"Nothing Gold Can Stay"** Text Connection 3 ❏ Write It: Journal Entry	❏ Review: Latin and Greek Number Prefixes ❏ Review: Greek Combining Forms ❏ Exercise 3: Match It: Greek Combining Forms	❏ Exercise 1: Choose It: Words with Greek Combining Forms
❏ Review: Subject-Verb Agreement ❏ Find It: Subject-Verb Agreement	❏ Introduce: Negative Sentences ❏ Exercise 4: Rewrite It: Negative Sentences	❏ Review: Verb Choice ❏ Exercise 2: Rewrite It: Strong Verbs ❏ Exercise 3: Rewrite It: Sentences
❏ Instructional Text: **"Nothing Gold Can Stay"**	❏ Instructional Text: **"Nothing Gold Can Stay"** Text Connection 3	❏ Answer It: Using Signal Words
❏ Analyze It: Elements of Poetry	❏ Prepare to Write: Literary Analysis Paragraph	❏ Write It: Literary Analysis Paragraph
Effort: 1 2 3 4 5 **Participation:** 1 2 3 4 5 **Independence:** 1 2 3 4 5	**Effort:** 1 2 3 4 5 **Participation:** 1 2 3 4 5 **Independence:** 1 2 3 4 5	**Effort:** 1 2 3 4 5 **Participation:** 1 2 3 4 5 **Independence:** 1 2 3 4 5
Effort: 1 2 3 4 5 **Participation:** 1 2 3 4 5 **Independence:** 1 2 3 4 5	**Effort:** 1 2 3 4 5 **Participation:** 1 2 3 4 5 **Independence:** 1 2 3 4 5	**Effort:** 1 2 3 4 5 **Participation:** 1 2 3 4 5 **Independence:** 1 2 3 4 5

Check off the activities you complete with each lesson. Evaluate your accomplishments at the end of each lesson. Pay attention to teacher evaluations and comments.

	Unit Objectives	Lesson 6 (Date:_____)	Lesson 7 (Date:_____)
STEP 1	• Say the vowel sounds for phonograms **-old**, **-oll**, **-ost** for / ō / as in *cold*, *toll*, *most*; **-ind**, **-ild** for / ī / as in *find*, *wild*. • Write the letter combinations for the phonograms representing / ō / and / ī /.	❑ Content Mastery: Using Student Performance	❑ Exercise 1: Using a Dictionary
STEP 2	• Read and spell words based on unit sound-spelling combinations. • Read and spell the **Essential Words:** *blood, both, door, flood, floor, pint.* • Read and spell words composed of Greek combining forms. • Spell confusing words correctly.	❑ Exercise 1: Spelling Pretest 2 ❑ Word Fluency 3	❑ Build It: Words with Greek Combining Forms ❑ Word Fluency 4
STEP 3	• Identify and define Greek combining forms. • Use knowledge of word relationships to build word meanings.	❑ Review: Negative Words ❑ Instructional Text: **"The Treasure of the Sierra Madre"** Text Connection 4 ❑ Use the Clues: Vocabulary Strategies ❑ Expression of the Day	❑ Review: Synonyms ❑ Introduce: Asian Loan Words ❑ Expression of the Day
STEP 4	• Identify linking verbs. • Identify correct subject-verb agreement. • Identify correctly formed negative statements.	❑ Introduce: Avoidance of Double Negatives ❑ Exercise 2: Rewrite It: Negative Statements ❑ Exercise 3: Rewrite It: Sentences	❑ Exercise 2: Identify It: Linking Verbs ❑ Instructional Text: **"The Treasure of the Sierra Madre"** Text Connection 4
STEP 5	• Use text features to understand informational text. • Apply SQ3R to read informational text. • Use context-based strategies to define words. • Identify mood, meter, and melody in poetry. • Identify features of a screenplay. • Identify, understand, and answer questions that use different types of signal words.	❑ Instructional Text: **"The Treasure of the Sierra Madre"**	❑ Review: Theme ❑ Instructional Text: **"The Treasure of the Sierra Madre"** Text Connection 4
STEP 6	• Use text features to develop study questions. • Write responses to questions using the signal words. • Develop an informal outline to prepare to write. • Write literary analysis compositions • Present a literary analysis orally. • Apply a genre-specific Writer's Checklist to revise and edit literary analysis compositions.	❑ Prepare to Write: Literary Analysis Essay	❑ Prepare to Write: Literary Analysis Essay
	Self-Evaluation (5 is the highest) **Effort** = I produced my best work. **Participation** = I was actively involved in tasks. **Independence** = I worked on my own.	**Effort:** 1 2 3 4 5 **Participation:** 1 2 3 4 5 **Independence:** 1 2 3 4 5	**Effort:** 1 2 3 4 5 **Participation:** 1 2 3 4 5 **Independence:** 1 2 3 4 5
	Teacher Evaluation	**Effort:** 1 2 3 4 5 **Participation:** 1 2 3 4 5 **Independence:** 1 2 3 4 5	**Effort:** 1 2 3 4 5 **Participation:** 1 2 3 4 5 **Independence:** 1 2 3 4 5

Lesson 8 (Date:_____)	Lesson 9 (Date:_____)	Lesson 10 (Date:_____)
❑ Exercise 1: Listening for Word Parts: Greek Combining Forms		
❑ Chain It	❑ Review: Compound Words ❑ Exercise 1: Find It: Compound Words	❑ Content Mastery: Spelling Posttest 2
❑ Write It: Sentences ❑ Present It: Loan Words from Asian Languages	❑ Content Mastery: Vocabulary; Morphology	❑ Content Mastery: Using Student Performance ❑ Find It: Words with Greek Combining Forms ❑ Write a Mini-Dialog: Idioms
❑ Review: Negative Statements ❑ Review: Double Negative ❑ Exercise 2: Rewrite It: Negative Statements	❑ Content Mastery: Subject-Verb Agreement; Negative Sentences	❑ Content Mastery: Using Student Performance
❑ Instructional Text: **"The Treasure of the Sierra Madre"** Text Connection 4 ❑ Comprehend It ❑ Answer It: Using Signal Words	❑ Speaking Application: Reading a Screenplay Text Connection 4 ❑ Present It	❑ Review: Literary Analysis Text Connection 4
❑ Prepare to Write: Literary Analysis Essay ❑ Write It: Literary Analysis Essay	❑ Revise It: Literary Analysis Essay	❑ Speaking Application: Literary Analysis
Effort: 1 2 3 4 5 **Participation:** 1 2 3 4 5 **Independence:** 1 2 3 4 5	**Effort:** 1 2 3 4 5 **Participation:** 1 2 3 4 5 **Independence:** 1 2 3 4 5	**Effort:** 1 2 3 4 5 **Participation:** 1 2 3 4 5 **Independence:** 1 2 3 4 5
Effort: 1 2 3 4 5 **Participation:** 1 2 3 4 5 **Independence:** 1 2 3 4 5	**Effort:** 1 2 3 4 5 **Participation:** 1 2 3 4 5 **Independence:** 1 2 3 4 5	**Effort:** 1 2 3 4 5 **Participation:** 1 2 3 4 5 **Independence:** 1 2 3 4 5

Exercise 1 · Listening for Sounds in Words: Sound-Spelling Patterns

▶ Say each sound in the **Sound Bank** with your teacher.

Sound Bank

/ ōl /	/ ōld /	/ ōlt /	/ ōst /

▶ Listen to your teacher read each word in the first column. Repeat each word.

▶ Identify the sound in the **Sound Bank** that is heard in each of the words.

▶ Underline the letters in each word that represent the sound.

▶ Label the column with the correct sound-spelling pattern and sound from the **Sound Bank**.

▶ Repeat this process for the remaining columns.

____ = ____	____ = ____	____ = ____	____ = ____	____ = ____
poll	bold	control	almost	bolt
roll	household	patrol	host	revolt
swollen	untold	bolster	postpone	jolt

▶ Practice reading each column with a partner.

These sound-spelling patterns contain the same vowel sound. What is it? _____

Which sound has two different spelling patterns? _____

Exercise 2 · Spelling Pretest 1

▸ Write the words your teacher repeats.

1. _____

2. _____

3. _____

4. _____

5. _____

6. _____

7. _____

8. _____

9. _____

10. _____

11. _____

12. _____

13. _____

14. _____

15. _____

Unit 32 · Lesson 1

Exercise 3 · Check What You Know: The Verb *be*

▸ Read each question.

▸ Write the answer.

▸ Refer to the Handbook section of the *Student Text* for reference as needed.

1. Write the correct present tense form of the verb **be** after each pronoun or group of pronouns.

Singular	Plural
I	We
You	You
He/she/it	They

2. What are the present and past participles of the verb **be**?

_____

_____

3. What are **two** functions of the verb **be**?

_____

_____

4. How is the verb **be** used in this verb phrase: **is holding**?

_____

_____

5. What is a linking verb?

_____

_____

Exercise 4 · Identify It: Linking Verbs

▸ Read each sentence and underline the linking verb.

▸ Identify the function of the word following the linking verb.

▸ Circle the correct answer.

1. The family became ill after drinking polluted water.
   a. predicate nominative   b. predicate adjective

2. Robert Frost is a famous American poet.
   a. predicate nominative   b. predicate adjective

3. Frost's poems appear simple, but they have a deeper meaning.
   a. predicate nominative   b. predicate adjective

4. At first, the task looked overwhelming.
   a. predicate nominative   b. predicate adjective

5. The surface of the gold felt smooth.
   a. predicate nominative   b. predicate adjective

Exercise 1 • Listening for Sounds in Words: Sound-Spelling Patterns

▶ Say each sound in the **Sound Bank** with your teacher.

Sound Bank

/ īld /	/ īnd /

▶ Listen to your teacher read each word in the first column below. Repeat each word.

▶ Identify the sound in the **Sound Bank** that you hear in each of the words.

▶ Underline the letters in each word that represent the sound.

▶ Label the column with the correct sound-spelling pattern and sound from the **Sound Bank**.

▶ Repeat this process for the remaining column.

_____ = _____	_____ = _____
behind	child
bind	mild
grindstone	wild
unkind	wildfire
blind	wildlife
remind	grandchild

▶ Practice reading each column with a partner.

These sound-spelling patterns contain the same vowel sound. What is it? _____

Exercise 2 · Write It: Essential Words

▶ Review the **Essential Words** in the **Word Bank**.

Word Bank

flood	door	both	floor	blood	pint

▶ Put the words in alphabetical order and write them on the lines.

▶ Write one sentence for each **Essential Word**.

▶ Check that each sentence uses correct capitalization, commas, and end punctuation.

▶ Read each sentence to a partner.

1. _____

   _____

2. _____

   _____

3. _____

   _____

4. _____

   _____

5. _____

   _____

6. _____

   _____

Unit 32 · Lesson 2

Exercise 3 · Identify It: Subject-Verb Agreement

▸ Read each sentence and underline the simple subject once and the simple predicate twice.

▸ Circle the correct answer.

▸ Rewrite the corrected sentence on the lines.

1. The students, given the task of learning a Frost poem, was helping one another.

    a. correct subject-verb agreement   b. incorrect subject-verb agreement

    _____

    _____

2. The author of those articles about Robert Frost is visiting our school tomorrow.

    a. correct subject-verb agreement   b. incorrect subject-verb agreement

    _____

    _____

3. Robert Frost, one of America's great poets, were honored at President John F. Kennedy's inauguration.

    a. correct subject-verb agreement   b. incorrect subject-verb agreement

    _____

    _____

4. Simple descriptions of everyday life is found in Frost's poems.

    a. correct subject-verb agreement   b. incorrect subject-verb agreement

    _____

    _____

5. One of Frost's most famous poems is the poem "Nothing Gold Can Stay."

    a. correct subject-verb agreement   b. incorrect subject-verb agreement

    _____

    _____

Exercise 4 · How To: Read a Web Page

The Internet provides access to millions of Web pages. Each Web page may look different, but most have common elements you can look for to make it easier for you to find and read the information you need. Most Web pages include these elements:

1. **A URL:** This is the address of the Web page. It is found at the top of the page under the navigation bar.

2. **Links:** The links are usually underlined. Clicking on a link will take you to another page or another Web site.

3. **A Title:** Usually this is at the top of the page. (Many Web pages also have headings, just like a textbook chapter.)

4. **Graphics:** Some graphics present important information. Others are just decorative.

5. **A Copyright date:** This date tells when the page was first displayed. Often this is found at the very bottom of the page.

6. **Menu bars:** These provide buttons you can click on to go to other pages at the same Web site. The menu bars may be found on the sides, the top, or the bottom of the page.

Refer to the information above and the images on the next page to complete the following activity.

1. What is the URL of the California Historical Society Web page?

   _____

2. What is the title of the Web page?

   _____

3. What is the copyright date of the Web page?

   _____

4. Circle the button you would click on if you wanted to read about what life was like for the miners who were digging for gold.

5. Circle the link that takes you to the California Historical Society Web page.

(continued)

Unit 32 · Lesson 2

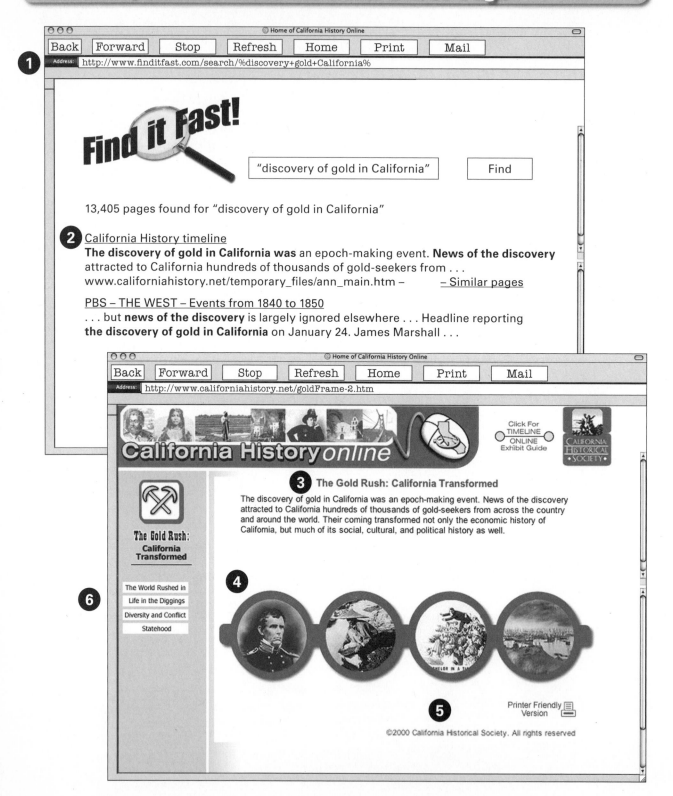

Home of California History Online

1 Address: http://www.finditfast.com/search/%discovery+gold+California%

Back | Forward | Stop | Refresh | Home | Print | Mail

Find it Fast!

"discovery of gold in California"   Find

13,405 pages found for "discovery of gold in California"

2 California History timeline
The discovery of gold in California was an epoch-making event. **News of the discovery** attracted to California hundreds of thousands of gold-seekers from . . .
www.californiahistory.net/temporary_files/ann_main.htm –   – Similar pages

PBS – THE WEST – Events from 1840 to 1850
. . . but **news of the discovery** is largely ignored elsewhere . . . Headline reporting
the discovery of gold in California on January 24. James Marshall . . .

Home of California History Online

Back | Forward | Stop | Refresh | Home | Print | Mail

Address: http://www.californiahistory.net/goldFrame-2.htm

California History online

Click For
TIMELINE
ONLINE
Exhibit Guide

CALIFORNIA
HISTORICAL
SOCIETY

The Gold Rush:
California
Transformed

3 **The Gold Rush: California Transformed**

The discovery of gold in California was an epoch-making event. News of the discovery attracted to California hundreds of thousands of gold-seekers from across the country and around the world. Their coming transformed not only the economic history of California, but much of its social, cultural, and political history as well.

6
The World Rushed in
Life in the Diggings
Diversity and Conflict
Statehood

4

5 Printer Friendly
Version

©2000 California Historical Society. All rights reserved

Exercise 5 · How To: Search for Information on the Internet

Use this activity to learn the steps involved in searching for information on the Internet. First read the steps for using a search engine. Then complete the activity below.

▸ Locate a search engine by typing its URL into the Web browser.

▸ Type a keyword or phrase into the search box. Use combinations of words with or without quotation marks as necessary.

▸ Click the **Search** or **Find** button.

▸ The results page will provide links to all the pages that contain those keywords. The total number of pages found is usually towards the top of the results page.

Read each question below. Imagine you wanted to find the answer to that question. Write the keyword or phrase you would use to search for your answer. Include quotes if you think they would be helpful.

1. Who was the leader of the Aztecs when Cortez conquered Tenochtitlan?

   _____

2. Can people visit King Tut's tomb today?

   _____

3. What is the value of one ounce of gold in U.S. dollars?

   _____

4. What role did Sam Brannan play in the California gold rush?

   _____

5. What are other uses for gold not mentioned in **"Good as Gold"**?

   _____

Unit 32 · Lesson 2

Exercise 6 · Apply It: Do an Internet Search

Use this activity to practice searching for information on the Internet and evaluating your results.

1. Think of a question you would like to find the answer to. You may use one of the questions from Exercise 5, **How To: Search for Information on the Internet**, or one of your own. Write your question here:

   _____

2. Locate a search engine by typing its URL into the Web browser.

   Name of the search engine you used: _____

3. Type a keyword or phrase into the search engine. Use quotation marks as appropriate.

   Keyword or phrase you typed into the search engine: _____

4. Click the Search or Find button.

5. Click on three of the links that the search locates. Fill in the following information for each Web site that the link takes you to.

URL: _____

Title of the Web site or article: _____

Copyright date (if there is one): _____

URL: _____

Title of the Web site or article: _____

Copyright date (if there is one): _____

URL: _____

Title of the Web site or article: _____

Copyright date (if there is one): _____

Exercise 1 • Listening for Sounds in Words: Sound-Spelling Patterns

▶ Say each sound in the **Sound Bank** with your teacher.

Sound Bank

/ ōld /	/ ōl /	/ īld /	/ ōlt /	/ ōst /	/ īnd /

▶ Listen to your teacher read each word in the first column. Repeat each word.

▶ Identify the sound in the **Sound Bank** that you hear in each of the words.

▶ Underline the letters in each word that represent the sound.

▶ Label the column with the correct sound-spelling pattern and sound from the **Sound Bank**.

▶ Repeat this process for the remaining columns.

____ = ____	____ = ____	____ = ____
payroll	threshold	unwind
enroll	scold	humankind
swollen	goldenrod	grind
troll	scaffold	mind

____ = ____	____ = ____	____ = ____	____ = ____
control	childcare	foremost	colt
patrol	wildcat	hostess	bolt
holster	mild	postwar	revolt
patrolman	wild	innermost	jolt

▶ Practice reading each column with a partner.

Exercise 1 • Listening for Sounds in Words:
Sound-Spelling Patterns

▶ Say each sound in the **Sound Bank** with your teacher.

Sound Bank

/ ōld /	/ ōl /	/ īld /	/ ōlt /	/ ōst /	/ īnd /

▶ Listen to each word your teacher says. Repeat each word.

▶ Listen for the sound pattern.

▶ Select and write the sound pattern from the **Sound Bank** in the space provided.

1. _____

2. _____

3. _____

4. _____

5. _____

6. _____

7. _____

8. _____

9. _____

10. _____

Exercise 2 · Contract It

▸ Read each phrase.

▸ Write the contraction for each one.

▸ Check the answers with your teacher.

1. are not   _____

2. cannot   _____

3. did not   _____

4. does not   _____

5. do not   _____

6. is not   _____

7. was not   _____

8. were not   _____

9. should not   _____

10. could not   _____

Unit 32 · Lesson 4

Exercise 3 · Match It: Greek Combining Forms

▶ Read each word and circle each combining form.

▶ Read the definitions.

▶ Use what you know about the meanings of the combining forms to match each word to its definition.

▶ Write the letter for the correct definition in the blank next to each word.

▶ Use **Morphemes for Meaning Cards** and a dictionary as references.

Word		Definitions
1. telescope	_____	**a.** a symbol that represents a sound in speech
2. autobiography	_____	**b.** an instrument used to observe or detect distant objects
3. telegraph	_____	**c.** an instrument that magnifies images of small objects
4. phonogram	_____	**d.** a communications system that transmits and receives electric impulses
5. microscope	_____	**e.** an account of your life that you write

Exercise 4 · Rewrite It: Negative Sentences

▸ Read each sentence and underline the verb or verb phrase.

▸ Rewrite the sentence using the adverb **not** so the sentence becomes a negative statement.

Note: Items 6–10 contain contractions. When you rewrite these sentences, remember to shift the contraction from the subject to the helping verb.

1. The Frost poems were collected into an anthology.

   _____

   _____

2. Our class has had many lessons on poetry.

   _____

   _____

3. The group stayed to hear the poetry reading.

   _____

   _____

4. In winter, the trees can sprout their first leaves.

   _____

   _____

5. The library has a collection of Frost's poems.

   _____

   _____

(continued)

Exercise 4 *(continued)* · Rewrite It: Negative Sentences

6. You've read these Frost poems.

_____

_____

7. We've written poems in class.

_____

_____

8. We'll meet him after the presentation.

_____

_____

9. He's coming with us to the festival.

_____

_____

10. They've lost their festival tickets.

_____

_____

Exercise 1 · Choose It: Words with Greek Combining Forms

▸ Read each sentence and the word choices below the sentence.

▸ Choose the correct word to complete the sentence, and write it in the blank.

▸ Circle each Greek combining form in the word you selected.

▸ Reread each completed sentence to make sure it makes sense.

1. The _____ about Robert Frost provided many details about his life.

   a. autobiography   b. biography   c. telegraphy

2. Our biology class will look at organisms under the _____.

   a. microscope   b. telescope   c. bioscope

3. The _____ enabled us to see the rings of the planet Saturn.

   a. telegram   b. telegraph   c. telescope

4. The students waited to get the athlete's _____.

   a. autobiography   b. telegraph   c. autograph

5. Our class has studied most of the _____ that make up English words.

   a. telephones   b. phonograms   c. phonographs

Unit 32 · Lesson 5

Exercise 2 · Rewrite It: Strong Verbs

▶ Read each sentence and underline the verb.

▶ Rewrite the sentence using a more descriptive verb that fits the context of the sentence.

▶ Use a thesaurus as a reference as needed.

1. Kelvin told his secret plan to us.

_____

_____

_____

2. The athlete runs down the track toward the finish line.

_____

_____

_____

3. The postal carrier takes letters to more than 500 homes each day!

_____

_____

_____

4. My younger brother likes it when I help him with his homework.

_____

_____

_____

5. Juan said the poem perfectly.

_____

_____

_____

Exercise 3 · Rewrite It: Sentences

▶ Read each sentence.

▶ Decide if the sentence is written incorrectly.

▶ Circle the type of error.

▶ Rewrite the sentence correctly on the lines.

1. The brothers who live down the street was not going to the play.

a. incorrect subject-verb agreement   b. incorrect negative use   c. sentence is correct.

_____

_____

2. The band not is going to march in the parade.

a. incorrect subject-verb agreement   b. incorrect negative use   c. sentence is correct.

_____

_____

3. The musicians, who have a large fan club, often arrive late for concerts.

a. incorrect subject-verb agreement   b. incorrect negative use   c. sentence is correct.

_____

_____

4. These books on my desk was a graduation present.

a. incorrect subject-verb agreement   b. incorrect negative use   c. sentence is correct.

_____

_____

5. The men wearing yellow isn't allowing anyone through the barricade.

a. incorrect subject-verb agreement   b. incorrect negative use   c. sentence is correct.

_____

_____

Exercise 1 · Spelling Pretest 2

▶ Write the word your teacher repeats.

1. _____

2. _____

3. _____

4. _____

5. _____

6. _____

7. _____

8. _____

9. _____

10. _____

11. _____

12. _____

13. _____

14. _____

15. _____

Exercise 2 · Rewrite It: Negative Statements

▸ Read each sentence and underline the negative words.

▸ Rewrite the sentence correctly.

▸ Reread the sentence to make sure it makes sense.

Note: There are two ways to correct each of the sentences.

1. There wasn't no place to hide the gold inside the tent.

   _____

   _____

2. At first the men didn't find no gold.

   _____

   _____

3. Dobbs had no trust for nobody.

   _____

   _____

4. Curtin hadn't said nothing about the hiding place for his gold.

   _____

   _____

5. Howard thought his two companions were not going nowhere.

   _____

   _____

Exercise 3 · Rewrite It: Sentences

▸ Read the composition in the box.

▸ Identify and correct errors in the first sentence with your teacher.

▸ Identify and use editing marks to correct errors in the remaining sentences in the composition. Write your revised sentences on the lines that are provided.

▸ Fill in the problem and an explanation of the revision in the chart.

▸ Pay special attention to improve weak verbs and errors in subject-verb agreement and double negatives.

---

1. Two men, Dobbs and Curtin, meets an old prospector by the name of Howard, who tells them that there is gold to be found in the Sierra Madre. 2. Dobbs and Curtin do not have no money, so they joins forces with Howard and follows him into the mountains to try to find gold. 3. Howard tell Dobbs and Curtin how to get gold. 4. The two men find that prospecting ain't no easy job. 5. At first they don't find no gold. 6. Then they get a lot. 7. After they get more gold, they don't trust no one.

_____

_____

_____

_____

_____

_____

_____

_____

_____

Exercise 3 (continued) · Rewrite It: Sentences

Sentence #	Trait(s)	Problem(s)	Revision

Exercise 1 · Using a Dictionary

▶ Turn to the **Vocabulary** section (dictionary) in the Handbook section of the *Student Text*.

▶ Find the word **inauguration** and its pronunciation.

▶ Write the diacritical markings for that word on the line in item 1 below.

▶ Use the markings to read the word aloud.

▶ Complete numbers 2–5 using the same process.

Word	Pronunciation
1. inauguration	_____
2. grief	_____
3. irony	_____
4. prophetic	_____
5. consecutive	_____

▶ Use a classroom dictionary or online reference source to complete numbers 6–10.

6. scaffold	_____
7. orangutan	_____
8. typhoon	_____
9. kimono	_____
10. samurai	_____

Exercise 2 · Identify It: Linking Verbs

▸ Read each sentence and underline the linking verb.

▸ Determine whether that verb relates to the senses or reflects a state of being, and then circle the correct answer.

▸ Refer to the Handbook section of the *Student Text* for a list of linking verbs as needed.

1. The real name of the author of the book *The Treasure of the Sierra Madre* remains unknown.

   senses   state of being

2. The clouds above the mountains looked majestic.

   senses   state of being

3. The old prospector named Howard seemed confident that gold could be found in the mountains.

   senses   state of being

4. Howard's warning about greed apparently sounded silly to Dobbs and Curtin.

   senses   state of being

5. The sand in which the gold rested appeared ordinary.

   senses   state of being

6. After a long day's work in the goldfields, the prospectors felt exhausted.

   senses   state of being

7. As more gold piled up, the prospectors became greedy.

   senses   state of being

8. Dobbs grew suspicious of his partners.

   senses   state of being

9. Howard, the old prospector, remained calm.

   senses   state of being

10. To prospectors searching for gold in the desert, water tastes sweet.

    senses   state of being

Exercise 1 · Listening for Word Parts: Greek Combining Forms

▸ Listen as your teacher reads a word pair.

▸ Repeat the word pair.

▸ Listen for a Greek combining form contained in both words.

▸ Write the Greek combining form in the space provided.

▸ Repeat this process with the remaining word pairs.

1. _____   6. _____

2. _____   7. _____

3. _____   8. _____

4. _____   9. _____

5. _____   10. _____

Exercise 2 · Rewrite It: Negative Statements

▶ Read each sentence and underline the negative words.

▶ Rewrite the sentence correctly.

▶ Reread the sentence to make sure it makes sense.

▶ Refer to the Handbook section of the *Student Text* for the list of negative words as necessary.

Note: There may be more than one way to correct each sentence with a double negative error.

1. Dobbs and Curtin hadn't nothing to lose by going with Howard.

_____

_____

_____

_____

2. Howard didn't express his opinion of the two men to nobody.

_____

_____

_____

_____

3. In their desire to get the gold, the men were not going to take no rest days.

_____

_____

_____

_____

(continued)

4. Curtin didn't show meanness towards no one.

_____

_____

_____

_____

5. At first Dobbs hadn't no idea how gold was extracted.

_____

_____

_____

_____

Exercise 1 · Find It: Compound Words

▶ Turn to **"The Treasure of the Sierra Madre"** in the *Student Text*.

▶ Find 10 compound words.

▶ Decide whether the word you find is an open compound, a closed compound, or a hyphenated compound.

▶ Record each word under the proper heading.

Closed Compound	Open Compound	Hyphenated Compound

Check off the activities you complete with each lesson. Evaluate your accomplishments at the end of each lesson. Pay attention to teacher evaluations and comments.

	Unit Objectives	Lesson 1 (Date:_____)	Lesson 2 (Date:_____)
STEP 1	• Say the vowel sounds for the phonograms: **-eigh** for / ā / as in *eight*; **-igh** for / ī / as in *light*; **-ough** for / ō / as in *although*. • Write the letter combinations for the phonograms representing / ā /, / ī /, and / ō /.	❑ Exercise 1: Listening for Sounds in Words: Sound-Spelling Patterns	❑ Exercise 1: Listening for Sounds in Words: Sound-Spelling Patterns
STEP 2	• Read and spell words based on unit sound-spelling combinations. • Read and spell the **Essential Words:** *auxiliary, daughter, dinosaur, mortgage, ocean, tongue.* • Read and spell words composed of Greek combining forms. • Spell confusing words correctly.	❑ Exercise 2: Spelling Pretest 1	❑ Exercise 2: Write It: Essential Words ❑ Word Fluency 1
STEP 3	• Identify and define Greek combining forms. • Identify multiple meanings for words.	❑ Unit Words ❑ Review: Synonyms ❑ Multiple Meaning Map ❑ Write It: Journal Entry	❑ Introduce: Additional Greek Combining Forms ❑ Exercise 3: Build It: Words with Greek Combining Forms
STEP 4	• Identify gerunds and gerund phrases. • Identify the function of gerunds and gerund phrases. • Identify passive voice verbs. • Review sentences to change passive to active voice verbs.	❑ Review: Present Participle ❑ Introduce: Gerunds and Gerund Phrases ❑ Exercise 3: Identify It: Gerunds and Gerund Phrases ❑ Exercise 4: Identify It: Functions of Gerunds and Gerund Phrases	❑ Introduce: Active and Passive Voice ❑ Exercise 4: Rewrite It: Active Voice and Passive Voice
STEP 5	• Use text features to understand informational text. • Apply SQ3R to read informational text. • Use context-based strategies to define words. • Identify features of a report. • Identify features of a journal. • Use a notetaking system to research content for a report. • Identify, understand, and answer questions that use different types of signal words.	❑ Independent Text: **"Playing with the Logic of Space"** ❑ Review: SQ3R Study Skills ❑ SQ3R: Study Skills: Working with Text	❑ Passage Fluency ❑ Exercise 5: How To: Choose the Right Reference Source ❑ Exercise 6: How To: Evaluate Sources
STEP 6	• Use text features to develop study questions. • Write responses to questions using the signal words. • Answer open-ended questions under timed conditions. • Prepare to write a research report including selecting and shaping a topic. • Organize information into an outline to write a research report. • Use the Guide to Writing a Research Report as a reference tool for writing a research report.	❑ Write It: Study Guide	❑ Exercise 7: Apply It: Evaluate Internet Sources
	Self-Evaluation (5 is the highest) **Effort** = I produced my best work. **Participation** = I was actively involved in tasks. **Independence** = I worked on my own.	**Effort:** 1 2 3 4 5 **Participation:** 1 2 3 4 5 **Independence:** 1 2 3 4 5	**Effort:** 1 2 3 4 5 **Participation:** 1 2 3 4 5 **Independence:** 1 2 3 4 5
	Teacher Evaluation	**Effort:** 1 2 3 4 5 **Participation:** 1 2 3 4 5 **Independence:** 1 2 3 4 5	**Effort:** 1 2 3 4 5 **Participation:** 1 2 3 4 5 **Independence:** 1 2 3 4 5

Lesson 3 (Date:_____)	Lesson 4 (Date:_____)	Lesson 5 (Date:_____)
❏ Exercise 1: Listening for Sounds in Words: Sound-Spelling Patterns	❏ Vowel Chart ❏ Exercise 1: Listening for Sounds in Words: Sound-Spelling Patterns	❏ Content Mastery: Variant Sound-Spelling Patterns
❏ Word Fluency 2 ❏ Instructional Text: **"The First Amendment"** Text Connection 5	❏ Make a Mnemonic ❏ Present It: Mnemonics for Confusing Word Pairs and Triplets	❏ Content Mastery: Spelling Posttest 1 ❏ Present It: Mnemonics for Confusing Word Pairs
❏ Instructional Text: **"The First Amendment"** Text Connection 5 ❏ Use the Clues: Vocabulary Strategies	❏ Review: Greek Combining Forms ❏ Exercise 2: Choose It: Words with Greek Combining Forms	❏ Exercise 1: Choose It: Words with Greek Combining Forms
❏ Review: Gerunds and Gerund Phrases ❏ Review: Active and Passive Voice ❏ Identify It: Gerunds, Gerund Phrases, and Active and Passive Voice Text Connection 5	❏ Exercise 3: Rewrite It: Gerunds ❏ Review: Passive Voice ❏ Introduce: When to Use Passive Voice ❏ Exercise 4: Rewrite It: Passive-Voice Sentences	❏ Review: Strong Verbs and Active Voice ❏ Exercise 2: Rewrite It: Strong Verbs and Active Voice
❏ Introduce: Reports ❏ Instructional Text: **"The First Amendment"** Text Connection 5 ❏ Comprehend It	❏ Instructional Text: **"The First Amendment"** Text Connection 5 ❏ Answer It: Using Signal Words	❏ Prepare to Write: Research Report Exercise 3: Write It: Taking Notes on Index Cards
❏ Prepare to Write: Research Report	❏ Prepare to Write: Research Report Exercise 5: Shape It: Choose a Research Topic Text Connection 5	❏ Prepare to Write: Research Report
Effort: 1 2 3 4 5 **Participation:** 1 2 3 4 5 **Independence:** 1 2 3 4 5	**Effort:** 1 2 3 4 5 **Participation:** 1 2 3 4 5 **Independence:** 1 2 3 4 5	**Effort:** 1 2 3 4 5 **Participation:** 1 2 3 4 5 **Independence:** 1 2 3 4 5
Effort: 1 2 3 4 5 **Participation:** 1 2 3 4 5 **Independence:** 1 2 3 4 5	**Effort:** 1 2 3 4 5 **Participation:** 1 2 3 4 5 **Independence:** 1 2 3 4 5	**Effort:** 1 2 3 4 5 **Participation:** 1 2 3 4 5 **Independence:** 1 2 3 4 5

Check off the activities you complete with each lesson. Evaluate your accomplishments at the end of each lesson. Pay attention to teacher evaluations and comments.

	Unit Objectives	Lesson 6 (Date:_____)	Lesson 7 (Date:_____)
STEP 1	• Say the vowel sounds for the phonograms: **-eigh** for / ā / as in *eight*; **-igh** for / ī / as in *light*; **-ough** for / ō / as in *although*. • Write the letter combinations for the phonograms representing / ā /, / ī /, and / ō /.	❏ Content Mastery: Using Student Performance	❏ Exercise 1: Using a Dictionary
STEP 2	• Read and spell words based on unit sound-spelling combinations. • Read and spell the **Essential Words:** *auxiliary, daughter, dinosaur, mortgage, ocean, tongue.* • Read and spell words composed of Greek combining forms. • Spell confusing words correctly.	❏ Exercise 1: Spelling Pretest 2 ❏ Word Fluency 3	❏ Exercise 2: Build It: Words with Greek Combining Forms ❏ Word Fluency 4
STEP 3	• Identify and define Greek combining forms. • Identify multiple meanings for words.	❏ Instructional Text: **"A Printer's Journal in Revolutionary America"** Text Connection 6 ❏ Expression of the Day	❏ Review: Antonyms ❏ Multiple Meaning Map ❏ Expression of the Day
STEP 4	• Identify gerunds and gerund phrases. • Identify the function of gerunds and gerund phrases. • Identify passive voice verbs. • Review sentences to change passive to active voice verbs.	❏ Exercise 2: Rewrite It: Sentences	❏ Identify It: Functions of Gerunds Text Connection 6
STEP 5	• Use text features to understand informational text. • Apply SQ3R to read informational text. • Use context-based strategies to define words. • Identify features of a report. • Identify features of a journal. • Use a notetaking system to research content for a report. • Identify, understand, and answer questions that use different types of signal words.	❏ Instructional Text: **"A Printer's Journal in Revolutionary America"**	❏ Instructional Text: **"A Printer's Journal in Revolutionary America"** Text Connection 6 ❏ Comprehend It
STEP 6	• Use text features to develop study questions. • Write responses to questions using the signal words. • Answer open-ended questions under timed conditions. • Prepare to write a research report including selecting and shaping a topic. • Organize information into an outline to write a research report. • Use the Guide to Writing a Research Report as a reference tool for writing a research report.	❏ Prepare to Write: Research Report	❏ Prepare to Write: Research Report
	Self-Evaluation (5 is the highest) **Effort** = I produced my best work. **Participation** = I was actively involved in tasks. **Independence** = I worked on my own.	**Effort:** 1 2 3 4 5 **Participation:** 1 2 3 4 5 **Independence:** 1 2 3 4 5	**Effort:** 1 2 3 4 5 **Participation:** 1 2 3 4 5 **Independence:** 1 2 3 4 5
	Teacher Evaluation	**Effort:** 1 2 3 4 5 **Participation:** 1 2 3 4 5 **Independence:** 1 2 3 4 5	**Effort:** 1 2 3 4 5 **Participation:** 1 2 3 4 5 **Independence:** 1 2 3 4 5

Lesson 8 (Date:_____)	**Lesson 9** (Date:_____)	**Lesson 10** (Date:_____)
❏ Exercise 1: Listening for Word Parts: Greek Combining Forms		
❏ Chain It	❏ Review: Compound Words ❏ Review: Greek Combining Forms ❏ Exercise 1: Sort It: Compound Words and Greek Combining Forms	❏ Content Mastery: Spelling Posttest 2
❏ Review: Greek Combining Forms ❏ Write It: Sentences	❏ Content Mastery: Vocabulary; Morphology	❏ Content Mastery: Using Student Performance ❏ Find It: Words with Greek Combining Forms ❏ Write a Mini-Dialog: Idioms
❏ Review: Gerunds and Passive and Active Voice	❏ Content Mastery: Gerunds and Gerund Phrases; Active and Passive Voice	❏ Content Mastery: Using Student Performance
❏ Instructional Text: **"A Printer's Journal in Revolutionary America"** Text Connection 6 ❏ Answer It: Using Signal Words	❏ Organize Information: A Formal Outline ❏ Exercise 2: Analyze It: Outline for **"The First Amendment"** Text Connection 5	❏ Exercise 1: Answering Open-Ended Questions
❏ Prepare to Write: Research Report	❏ Organize Information: Reading and Sorting Research Notes	❏ Organize Information: Research Report ❏ Discuss It: Research Report Outline
Effort: 1 2 3 4 5 **Participation:** 1 2 3 4 5 **Independence:** 1 2 3 4 5	**Effort:** 1 2 3 4 5 **Participation:** 1 2 3 4 5 **Independence:** 1 2 3 4 5	**Effort:** 1 2 3 4 5 **Participation:** 1 2 3 4 5 **Independence:** 1 2 3 4 5
Effort: 1 2 3 4 5 **Participation:** 1 2 3 4 5 **Independence:** 1 2 3 4 5	**Effort:** 1 2 3 4 5 **Participation:** 1 2 3 4 5 **Independence:** 1 2 3 4 5	**Effort:** 1 2 3 4 5 **Participation:** 1 2 3 4 5 **Independence:** 1 2 3 4 5

Exercise 1 · Listening for Sounds in Words: Sound-Spelling Patterns

▶ Say each sound in the **Sound Bank** with your teacher.

Sound Bank

/ ā /	/ ē /	/ ī /	/ ō /	/ o͞o /

▶ Listen to your teacher read each word in the first column. Repeat each word.

▶ Identify the vowel sound that is heard in all the words in the column.

▶ Label the column with that sound from the **Sound Bank**.

▶ Underline the letters in each word that represent the common vowel sound.

▶ Repeat this process for the second column.

though	eight
dough	freight
thorough	weigh
although	weight

▶ Practice reading the words in each column with a partner.

Exercise 2 · Spelling Pretest 1

▶ Write the word your teacher repeats.

1. _____   6. _____   11. _____

2. _____   7. _____   12. _____

3. _____   8. _____   13. _____

4. _____   9. _____   14. _____

5. _____   10. _____   15. _____

Exercise 3 · Identify It: Gerunds and Gerund Phrases

▶ Read each sentence with your teacher.

▶ With your teacher, find the gerund or gerund phrase and then underline it.

1. Creating optical illusions requires a lot of skill.

2. Careful planning is a key to success.

3. Playing with cut shapes helped Escher produce unusual artwork.

4. You can learn more about optical illusions by studying Escher's work.

5. Painting is a wonderful form of self-expression.

Exercise 4 · Identify It: Functions of Gerunds and Gerund Phrases

▸ Read each sentence and the underlined gerund or gerund phrase.

▸ Determine how the gerund or gerund phrase is functioning in the sentence.

▸ Circle the correct function.

1. <u>Painting</u> is an appealing art form.

   a. subject   b. direct object   c. object of the preposition   d. predicate nominative

2. Escher became skillful at <u>drawing</u>.

   a. subject   b. direct object   c. object of the preposition   d. predicate nominative

3. He loved <u>challenging the viewer</u>.

   a. subject   b. direct object   c. object of the preposition   d. predicate nominative

4. My friend's hobby is <u>illustrating</u>.

   a. subject   b. direct object   c. object of the preposition   d. predicate nominative

5. Once I tried <u>sketching</u>, but I did not like the colorless results.

   a. subject   b. direct object   c. object of the preposition   d. predicate nominative

Exercise 1 · Listening for Sounds in Words: Sound-Spelling Patterns

▶ Say each sound in the **Sound Bank**.

Sound Bank

/ ā /	/ ē /	/ ī /	/ ō /	/ o͞o /

▶ Listen to your teacher read each word. Repeat each word.

▶ Identify the vowel sound that is heard in all the words and label the column with that sound from the **Sound Bank**.

▶ Underline the letters in each word that represent the vowel sound.

high
sigh
bright
slight
fright

▶ Practice reading the words in the column with a partner.

Unit 33 · Lesson 2

Exercise 2 · Write It: Essential Words

▶ Review the **Essential Words** in the **Word Bank**.

Word Bank

| dinosaur | mortgage | tongue | ocean | auxiliary | daughter |

▶ Put the words in alphabetical order and write them on the lines.

▶ Write one sentence for each **Essential Word**.

▶ Check that each sentence uses sentence signals—correct capitalization, commas, and end punctuation.

▶ Read each sentence to a partner.

1. _____

_____

2. _____

_____

3. _____

_____

4. _____

_____

5. _____

_____

6. _____

_____

Exercise 3 · Build It: Words with Greek Combining Forms

▸ Read each sentence.

▸ Fill in the blanks with Greek combining forms to create a word to fit the provided definition.

▸ Use the Unit 33 **Morphemes for Meaning Cards** as a reference as needed.

1. _____ _____ literally means "time measure."

2. _____ _____ literally means "many angles."

3. _____ _____ literally means "earth specialist."

4. _____ _____ literally means "around measure."

5. _____ _____ literally means "time study."

6. _____ _____ literally means "earth measure."

7. _____ _____ literally means "light specialist."

8. _____ _____ literally means "heat measure."

9. _____ _____ literally means "together measure."

10. _____ _____ literally means "life science."

Unit 33 · Lesson 2

Exercise 4 · Rewrite It: Active Voice and Passive Voice

▸ Read each sentence in the chart and then circle the passive-voice verb in it.

▸ Rewrite the sentence so its verb is in active voice.

▸ Underline the doer in the sentence and draw an arrow from the action to the receiver of the action.

▸ Refer to the Handbook section of the *Student Text* as a reference as needed.

Passive-Voice Verb	Active-Voice Verb
1. Surprising images were made by Escher.	
2. Cubes are shown in the pictures.	
3. The cut sandwich was eaten by the child.	
4. The human eye was tricked by the shapes.	
5. The drawings are interpreted by the viewer.	

Exercise 5 · How To: Choose the Right Reference Source

You will find a variety of information in the classroom, at the local library, or on the Internet. Here are some different kinds of sources and the kind of information you will find in each:

almanac: short articles and lists of facts and statistics on topics such as sports, weather, politics, and geography

atlas: collections of maps; may include historical maps, world maps, road maps, or maps of Earth's oceans

encyclopedia: short articles on general topics (listed alphabetically)

magazine: articles on a variety of topics

newspaper: short news articles and feature articles on a variety of topics

nonfiction books: books written on various topics; histories and biographies

audiovisual materials: CDs, cassette tapes, video tapes, and DVDs

Internet Web sites: articles and information on almost any topic; includes online reference sources such as dictionaries, encyclopedias, magazines, and newspapers

(continued)

Exercise 5 (continued) · How To: Choose the Right Reference Source

▶ Use the information above to answer these questions.

1. Which sources would you use if you wanted to find general information about M.C. Escher?

_____

2. Which sources would you use if you wanted to find out about recent discoveries in science?

_____

3. Which sources would you use if you wanted to find out how many colleges there are in the United States?

_____

4. Which sources would you use if you wanted to find out what rivers run through central China?

_____

5. Where would you look if you wanted to find out what bills were being discussed in Congress?

_____

Unit 33 · Lesson 2

Exercise 6 · How To: Evaluate Sources

Once you locate information, you must judge whether it is reliable. Here are some questions to ask of any reference source that you consult:

1. Who wrote it? Be wary of information that does not name an author or an editor. Read any information about the author provided on the back or inside cover of the book jacket.

2. When was it written? Look for the copyright date. The copyright date in a book is usually found on the back of the title page. On a Web site, the copyright is often found at the bottom of the page. If possible, try to avoid using sources that are more than ten or twenty years old.

3. Is the information well researched? Most reference books (such as encyclopedias and atlases) are thoroughly researched and are therefore reliable. To find out if other nonfiction books are well researched, look at the back of the book for the bibliography, or a list of reference sources that the author used to write the book.

4. Is the information biased? When information is biased, it shows a preference for or against an idea, thing, or group of people. Its conclusions are not based on impartial judgment. In biased writing, statements that are presented as facts may not be true and factual. Check any questionable information by looking it up in another source.

▸ Use the information above to answer these questions.

1. Why do you think it is wise to choose a source that names an author or an editor?

   _____

   _____

2. In most books, where is the copyright date located?

   _____

   _____

3. How can you determine if a book is well researched?

   _____

   _____

(continued)

4. Which of the following would you expect to provide a **less** biased discussion of air pollution? Why?

   • A report by environmental scientists at a university

   • A report by a car manufacturer

   _____

   _____

   _____

   _____

   _____

   _____

5. Which of the following would you expect to provide **less** biased information on the nutritional value of a fast food meal? Why?

   • The owner of a fast food restaurant

   • A dietician

   _____

   _____

   _____

   _____

   _____

   _____

Unit 33 · Lesson 2

Exercise 7 · Apply It: Evaluate Internet Sources

Internet Web sites are created not only by a number of governmental and educational institutions, but also by many individuals and groups. It is therefore very important to consider who is providing the information on a Web site and whether that information is reliable or accurate. Here are some tips for evaluating Internet sources:

1. Look at the **top-level domain** of the Web site. The top-level domain is indicated by the abbreviation or word at the end of the main Web address. These are some of the most common top-level domains:

    .gov—Governmental institutions such as state and federal agencies, museums, and parks.

    .edu—Educational institutions such as schools and universities.

    .com—Commercial institutions, such as private companies; often these sites sell a product or have paid advertising.

    .org—Organizations such as historical associations, museums, nonprofit institutions, and political groups.

    .net—Networks such as Internet service providers and anyone else who chooses to use this top-level domain.

2. Try to draw most of your facts from educational, governmental, and museum Web sites.

3. Confirm each fact you find with one or two other sources. (Try to include one print source.)

▸ Do an Internet search for information on M.C. Escher. Use **"M.C. Escher"** and **exhibition** as your search words. Choose sites from two different domains. Then complete this activity.

First site

URL: _____

Circle the domain: gov   edu   com   org   other _____

Title of the Web site or article: _____

Author or editor: _____ Copyright date (if there is one): _____

Does the information seem well researched? (Circle one.)   yes   no

Does the information seem biased? (Circle one.)   yes   no

Based on all of the above, does the information seem reliable? (Explain your answer.)

_____

(continued)

Exercise 7 (continued) · Apply It: Evaluate Internet Sources

Second site

URL: _____

Circle the domain: gov   edu   com   org   other _____

Title of the Web site or article: _____

Author or editor: _____   Copyright date (if there is one): _____

Does the information seem well researched? (Circle one.)   yes   no

Does the information seem biased? (Circle one.)   yes   no

Based on all of the above, does the information seem reliable? (Explain your answer.)

_____

Exercise 1 · Listening for Sounds in Words: Sound-Spelling Patterns

▶ Read each word in the first column.

▶ Underline the letters that represent / ā /, / ī /, or / ō /.

▶ Place a √ under the vowel sound that matches the sound-spelling pattern in each word.

	/ ā /	/ ī /	/ ō /
1. eighteen			
2. although			
3. delight			
4. weight			
5. might			
6. furlough			
7. copyright			
8. neighbor			
9. lightning			
10. tonight			

▶ Practice reading the words with a partner.

▶ Answer the following questions:

Which letters are common to all three sound-spelling patterns? _____

What sound do these letters produce? _____

Exercise 1 · Listening for Sounds in Words: Sound-Spelling Patterns

▸ Say each sound in the **Sound Bank**.

Sound Bank

| / ā / | / ī / | / ō / |

▸ Listen to each word your teacher says. Repeat each word.

▸ Listen for the vowel sound.

▸ Select and write the vowel sound from the **Sound Bank** in the space provided.

1. right _____
2. eight _____
3. though _____
4. straight _____
5. time _____

6. my _____
7. boat _____
8. play _____
9. show _____
10. guide _____

▸ List the words from this exercise with spelling variations for / ā / according to their order of frequency as shown on the **Vowel Chart**.

▸ Underline the letters representing / ā /.

1st: _____   2nd: _____   3rd: _____

▸ List the words from this exercise with spelling variations for / ī / according to their order of frequency as shown on the **Vowel Chart**.

▸ Underline the letters representing / ī /.

1st: _____   2nd: _____   3rd: _____

(continued)

Exercise 1 (continued) · Listening for Sounds in Words: Sound-Spelling Patterns

▶ List the words from this exercise with spelling variations for / ō / according to their order of frequency as shown on the **Vowel Chart**.

▶ Underline the letters representing / ō /.

1st: _____   2nd: _____   3rd: _____

Exercise 2 · Choose It: Words with Greek Combining Forms

▶ Read each sentence and the answer choices below.

▶ Select the correct answer and write it in the blank.

▶ Circle the Greek combining forms in the word.

▶ Use the **Morphemes for Meaning Cards** and a dictionary as a reference as needed.

▶ Identify and underline clues in the sentence that helped you select the word.

1. The length of each side of a square must be added together to get the

   _____.

   a. chronometer   b. thermometer   c. perimeter

2. As both sides of the building had the same measurements, the building had

   _____.

   a. telemetry   b. symmetry   c. thermometry

3. The student decided to become a _____ and study the structure of the earth.

   a. geologist   b. chronologist   c. biologist

4. The figure had many sides and many angles so it was an example of a

   _____.

   a. polychrome   b. polygon   c. polygraph

5. A _____ was used to measure the heat in the room.

   a. photometer   b. perimeter   c. thermometer

Exercise 3 · Rewrite It: Gerunds

▸ Read each sentence.

▸ Form a gerund from the verb under the blank and write that gerund in the blank.

▸ Determine how the gerund or gerund phrase is functioning in the sentence.

▸ Circle the correct function.

1. _____ a constitution is a daunting task.
   write

   a. subject   b. direct object   c. object of the preposition   d. predicate nominative

2. The lawyer was given the task of _____ her client's rights.
   defend

   a. subject   b. direct object   c. object of the preposition   d. predicate nominative

3. Politicians sometimes suggest _____ more amendments to the
   United States Constitution.   add

   a. subject   b. direct object   c. object of the preposition   d. predicate nominative

4. _____ the Bill of Rights was the lawyer's goal.
   protect

   a. subject   b. direct object   c. object of the preposition   d. predicate nominative

5. One aim of the Bill of Rights is _____ individuals' rights.
   protect

   a. subject   b. direct object   c. object of the preposition   d. predicate nominative

Unit 33 · Lesson 4

Exercise 4 · Rewrite It: Passive-Voice Sentences

▸ Read each sentence and underline the verb.

▸ Rewrite the sentence in active voice if that can be done.

1. Thomas Jefferson was made unhappy by the omission of a bill of rights.

   _____

   _____

2. Citizens' rights will be protected.

   _____

   _____

3. Criticism of the king was not permitted by the laws of some colonies.

   _____

   _____

4. The original United States Constitution was drafted by a committee of leaders from 12 states.

   _____

   _____

5. Amendments to the Constitution were added later.

   _____

   _____

Exercise 5 · Shape It: Choose a Research Topic

Here are four of the twenty-seven amendments to the United States Constitution.

   1. Read the text of each amendment as well as the summary below it.

   2. Discuss the amendment with a partner. Talk about why you think the amendment was added and whether you think it is an important right.

The Tenth Amendment

"The powers not delegated to the United States by the Constitution, nor prohibited by it to the states, are served to the states respectively, or to the people."

In Brief: This amendment grants states or the people power that is not given specifically to the federal government.

The Nineteenth Amendment

"The right of citizens of the United States to vote shall not be denied or abridged by the United States or by any State on account of sex. Congress shall have power to enforce this article by appropriate legislation."

In Brief: This amendment gives women the right to vote.

The Twenty-Second Amendment

"No person shall be elected to the office of the President more than twice, and no person who has held the office of President, or acted as President, for more than two years of a term to which some other person was elected President shall be elected to the office of the President more than once..."

In Brief: This amendment limits the number of times a President of the United States can be elected to office.

The Twenty-Sixth Amendment

"The right of citizens of the United States, who are eighteen years of age or older, to vote shall not be denied or abridged by the United States or by any State on account of age."

In Brief: This amendment gives any citizen over the age of 18 the right to vote.

Exercise 1 · Choose It: Words with Greek Combining Forms

▶ Read the words in the **Word Bank**.

Word Bank

thermometer	photography	telephoto	pentagon
biology	chronology	microbiologist	phonology
kilometer	microphone	octagon	monopoly

▶ Read each sentence and choose a word from the **Word Bank** to complete the sentence.

▶ Use the **Morphemes for Meaning Cards** and a dictionary as needed.

▶ Identify and underline clues in the sentence that helped you select the word.

1. The camera has a special _____ lens so it can see distant light.

2. We study the life cycle of a frog in _____ class.

3. The instrument that picks up small sounds and enlarges them is called a

   _____.

4. The patient's temperature was taken regularly using a _____.

5. An _____ has eight angles and sides.

6. Ansel Adams used his _____ to record the light and shade of images.

7. The historian presented the time sequence, or _____, of events leading up to the disaster.

8. The specialist who studies small living organisms is called a _____.

9. There are a thousand meters in a _____.

10. The five-sided building that houses the Defense Department is called the

    _____.

Exercise 2 · Rewrite It: Strong Verbs and Active Voice

▸ Read each sentence and underline the verb.

▸ Decide if the verb can be replaced by a more precise and descriptive synonym.

▸ Rewrite the sentence using active voice and a more descriptive verb.

▸ Use a thesaurus when needed.

1. The liberties outlined in the Constitution are liked by Americans.

_____

_____

2. James Madison was told by Thomas Jefferson that there should be a bill of rights.

_____

_____

3. The Constitution was made by a select committee in 1787.

_____

_____

4. Zenger was put in jail by New York's colonial governor.

_____

_____

5. In a time of war, some Constitutional rights may be taken away by government officials.

_____

_____

Unit 33 · Lesson 5

Exercise 3 · Write It: Taking Notes on Index Cards

Once you have selected sources that are useful and reliable, you are ready to begin taking notes. Here are some tips for how to take notes effectively:

1. Use different colored index cards, one color for each subtopic in your report. This will help you organize your notes.

2. Refer to the information you recorded on the **Keeping Track of Sources** template. At the top of each index card, write the number of the reference source and the exact page number of the information you use so that you can find it again if necessary.

3. List notes in your own words.

4. Only write down main ideas and supporting details. Do not write in complete sentences and do not write down every word.

5. Write only on one side of each card and include only one main point per card. List related points on other cards as needed. (Remember to write the number of the source from your source list and use cards of the same color for the same subtopic.)

Imagine you were to use Lucy Bledsoe's report **"The First Amendment"** as a reference source. Turn to the section titled **Historical Purpose for the First Amendment** in the *Student Text*. Read lines 39–46. Take the notes that you might take if you were doing research on the history of the First Amendment.

Source Number _____
Question: What is the history of the First Amendment?
- colonists from Europe
- countries ruled by kings and queens
- dangerous to express ideas or practice religion different from ruler
(could be fined, killed, or put in prison)
e.g., Queen Mary I (ruled 1553–1558): had many non-Catholics burned at stake

Exercise 1 · Spelling Pretest 2

▶ Write the word your teacher repeats.

1. _____

2. _____

3. _____

4. _____

5. _____

6. _____

7. _____

8. _____

9. _____

10. _____

11. _____

12. _____

13. _____

14. _____

15. _____

Unit 33 · Lesson 6

Exercise 2 · Rewrite It: Sentences

▸ Read the composition in the box.

▸ Identify and correct errors in the first sentence with your teacher.

▸ Identify and use editing marks to correct errors in the remaining sentences in the composition. Write your revised sentences on the lines that are provided.

▸ Fill in the problem and an explanation of the revision in the chart.

▸ Pay special attention to improve passive voice and sentence fragments.

---

1. A constitution that does not guarantee individual liberties is bad. 2. The Bill of Rights was made by James Madison, Thomas Jefferson, and other leaders to give important individual rights. 3. Guaranteeing freedom of religion, speech, press, assembly, and petition. 4. Power is divided between the national and state governments by the United States Constitution. 5. The Constitution must be studied carefully by lawyers, judges, and legislators.

_____

_____

_____

_____

_____

_____

_____

_____

_____

Exercise 1 · Using a Dictionary

▶ Turn to the **Vocabulary** section (dictionary) in your *Student Text*.

▶ Find the word **persecution** and its pronunciation.

▶ Write the diacritical markings for that word on the line next to the word.

▶ Use the markings to read the word aloud.

▶ Complete numbers 2–5 using the same process.

Word	Pronunciation
1. persecution	_____
2. subsequent	_____
3. ratify	_____
4. recrimination	_____
5. vengeance	_____

▶ Use a classroom dictionary or an online reference source to complete numbers 6–10.

6. furlough	_____
7. righteous	_____
8. thoroughbred	_____
9. blight	_____
10. plight	_____

Unit 33 · Lesson 7

Exercise 2 · Build It: Words with Greek Combining Forms

▸ Read the word parts in each table.

▸ Combine two or three word parts to build words. Build as many words as you can.

▸ Record the words on the lines below the table.

▸ Check the dictionary to verify that you are building real words.

1.

bio	logy	logist	phono	chrono

_____ _____ _____

_____ _____ _____

2.

geo	metry	graphy	photo	logy

_____ _____ _____

_____ _____ _____

3.

penta	octa	poly	meter	gon

_____ _____ _____

_____ _____ _____

4.

thermo	meter	graph	poly	stat

_____ _____ _____

_____ _____ _____

5.

sym	metry	photo	hydro	tele

_____ _____ _____

_____ _____ _____

Exercise 1 · Listening for Word Parts: Greek Combining Forms

▶ Listen as your teacher reads a word pair.

▶ Repeat the word pair.

▶ Listen for a Greek combining form contained in both words.

▶ Write the Greek combining form in the space provided.

▶ Repeat this process with the remaining words.

1. _____

2. _____

3. _____

4. _____

5. _____

6. _____

7. _____

8. _____

9. _____

10. _____

Exercise 1 · Sort It: Compound Words and Greek Combining Forms

▸ Read each word in the **Word Bank**.

Word Bank

lightweight	symmetry	polygon	daylight	monopoly	chronograph
birthright	right-hand	graphologist	self-righteous	thermograph	sourdough

▸ Decide whether the word is a compound word or a word made of Greek combining forms.

▸ Write the word under the correct heading.

Compound Words	Greek Combining Forms

Exercise 2 · Analyze It: Outline for "The First Amendment"

Here is an outline that the writer used to write her report entitled **"The First Amendment."**
Read the outline and compare it to the final report. Then discuss the questions on the next page
with a partner.

"The First Amendment"

Introduction

▶ Text of 1st Amendment quoted

▶ 5 freedoms: religion, speech, press, assembly, petition

 I. Definition of the First Amendment

   A. First part: religious freedom + Jefferson quotation (separation of church & state)

   B. Second part: free expression

   C. Third part: right to assemble and petition

 II. Historical Purpose for the First Amendment

   A. religious persecution in Europe

   B. religious persecution in American colonies

   C. diversity of religions among colonists

   D. Zenger: colonial fight for freedom of press

   E. Original Constitution did not have Bill of Rights

   F. James Madison champions the Bill of Rights

III. Relevance in Today's World

   A. What religious freedom & freedom of expression mean today

   B. Supreme Court examples—supporting the 1st Amendment

Conclusion

▶ Sum up rights in 1st Amendment

▶ Why important for American citizens

(continued)

Unit 33 · Lesson 9

Exercise 2 (continued) · Analyze It: Outline for "The First Amendment"

1. Read the topics numbered I, II, and III. Where do you see these on the final report?

   _____

   _____

   _____

2. Find the two paragraphs in the report that correspond to the notes labeled I.A. in the outline. Could the writer have combined both paragraphs? Why do you think she chose not to?

   _____

   _____

   _____

3. Find the paragraph in the report that corresponds to the idea labeled I.C. in the outline. Why do you think the writer chose to group right to assemble and right to petition together in the same paragraph?

   _____

   _____

   _____

106 Unit 33 · Lesson 9

Lesson 10

Exercise 1 · Answering Open-Ended Questions

▶ In this assessment, you will have 30 minutes to read an article and answer a question about it. Your answer must be in the form of a paragraph.

▶ Carefully read the passage and the question that follows. Think about your answer and make a quick map or outline of points to include in your paragraph. Then write your paragraph. Be sure to proofread your answer.

The World's Largest Treasure
by Beth Turin Weston

Imagine! You have managed to obtain almost all the gold available throughout the world. But you haven't been able to get your hands on the last fifty billion dollars' worth of gold bars that you need to completely control the world's gold supply.

If you could get your hands on that gold, you might become the richest person in the world! But you're out of luck, because this gold belongs to the United States government, and over half of it is housed in a depository in Fort Knox, Kentucky.

The gold is protected by the United States Treasury Department's best security systems. The only people who are allowed near the gold are security guards who have passed the toughest of security tests and Treasury Department employees on official business. And that is just the beginning of the security measures that protect America's gold.

The gold bars, which are slightly smaller than bricks, are stored in steel and concrete vaults that are inside granite-block buildings with barred windows. The core of the depository is a two-level, steel and concrete vault. The vault doors weigh nearly thirty tons. The walls and roof are made of steel plates, I-beams, and cylinders, all surrounded by concrete. Guard boxes stand at each outside corner of the building. Steel fences surround them.

(continued)

Exercise 1 (continued) · Answering Open-Ended Questions

The depository is located on the corner of Gold Vault Drive and Bullion Boulevard. It is located on the Fort Knox military base, which was constructed in 1937. The military base also protects the gold, along with the latest security and alarm devices.

Silver is stored in a similar way at the U.S. Bullion Depository at West Point, New York. West Point is also a military reservation. Security is tight at West Point, too. This one-story windowless building was built in 1936, and it looks like a border fort. There are closed-circuit cameras and a complicated alarm system.

West Point does more than store silver. In 1973 West Point began minting coins. Each year, about two billion pennies are made at West Point. If your pennies don't show a mint mark, they were made at the West Point or the Philadelphia mint. The ten-dollar gold coin for the 1984 Olympics was also made at West Point.

Because of the high security at West Point and Fort Knox, visitors are forbidden. At Fort Knox, exceptions to that rule have been made. For example, President Franklin D. Roosevelt inspected the facility in 1943. Thirty-one years later, a special group of seven congressmen and one hundred reporters from around the world were given a tour of the gold vault. It was the first time photos were allowed to be taken.

A model of Fort Knox is on display at the George S. Patton Museum at the Fort Knox Military Reservation. Visiting that model and viewing the depository from the road are about the closest most people will ever get to America's vast gold reserves.

Question: Some people may think that it is not safe for the United States to store so much of the nation's wealth in Fort Knox. Do you agree or disagree with this idea? Support your answer with evidence from the selection.

Plan your answer here:

(continued)

Exercise 1 (continued) · Answering Open-Ended Questions

Write your paragraph here:

_____

_____

_____

_____

_____

_____

_____

_____

_____

_____

_____

Trait	Point
Ideas/Content	
Organization	
Word Choice	
Sentence Fluency	
Conventions	

Total Number
Correct _____ /5

Check off the activities you complete with each lesson. Evaluate your accomplishments at the end of each lesson. Pay attention to teacher evaluations and comments.

Unit Objectives	Lesson 1 (Date:_____)	Lesson 2 (Date:_____)
STEP 1 • Say the sounds for graphemes: **mb**, **mn**, and **lm** for / m / as in *comb*, *hymn*, *calm*; **kn** and **gn** for / n / as in *knock*, *sign*; **wr** and **rh** for / r / as in *wrong*, *rhyme*; **ps** for / s / as in *psychology*. • Write the letter combinations containing silent letters representing / m /, / n /, / r /, and / s /.	❏ Introduce: Silent Consonant Letters ❏ Exercise 1: Listening for Sounds in Words: Sound-Spelling Patterns	❏ Exercise 1: Listening for Sounds in Words: Sound-Spelling Patterns
STEP 2 • Read and spell words based on unit sound-spelling combinations. • Read and spell the **Essential Words:** *bargain, clothes, island, ninth, often, sword*. • Read and spell words composed of Greek combining forms. • Spell confusing words correctly.	❏ Exercise 2: Spelling Pretest 1	❏ Exercise 2: Write It: Essential Words ❏ Word Fluency 1
STEP 3 • Identify and define Greek combining forms. • Identify multiple meanings for words.	❏ Unit Words ❏ Review: Synonyms ❏ Word Wheel ❏ Expression of the Day	❏ Introduce: Additional Greek Combining Forms ❏ Exercise 3: Build It: Words with Greek Combining Forms
STEP 4 • Identify appositives and appositive phrases. • Identify the function of noun clauses. • Identify sentence fragments. • Rewrite sentences to change sentence fragments to complete sentences.	❏ Review: Noun Classifications ❏ Review: Noun Functions ❏ Review: Appositives ❏ Exercise 3: Identify It: Appositives	❏ Introduce: Noun Clauses ❏ Exercise 4: Identify It: Noun Clauses
STEP 5 • Use text features, such as tables and graphs, to understand informational text. • Use context-based strategies to define words. • Identify, understand, and answer questions that use different types of signal words.	❏ Independent Text: **"The Value of Knowledge"** ❏ Comprehend It: Reading Tables and Graphs	❏ Passage Fluency ❏ Exercise 5: How To: Write Footnotes
STEP 6 • Use text features to develop study questions. • Write responses to questions using signal words • Write a research report including a thesis, footnotes, and bibliography. • Present an oral summary of a research report. • Apply genre-specific Writer's Checklist to revise and edit a draft for a research report. • Use the Guide to Writing a Research Report as a reference tool for writing a research report.	❏ Exercise 4: Answer It: Using Tables and Graphs	❏ Exercise 6: Write It: Footnotes
Self-Evaluation (5 is the highest) **Effort** = I produced my best work. **Participation** = I was actively involved in tasks. **Independence** = I worked on my own.	**Effort:** 1 2 3 4 5 **Participation:** 1 2 3 4 5 **Independence:** 1 2 3 4 5	**Effort:** 1 2 3 4 5 **Participation:** 1 2 3 4 5 **Independence:** 1 2 3 4 5
Teacher Evaluation	**Effort:** 1 2 3 4 5 **Participation:** 1 2 3 4 5 **Independence:** 1 2 3 4 5	**Effort:** 1 2 3 4 5 **Participation:** 1 2 3 4 5 **Independence:** 1 2 3 4 5

Lesson 3 (Date:_____)	**Lesson 4** (Date:_____)	**Lesson 5** (Date:_____)
❏ Exercise 1: Listening for Sounds in Words: Sound-Spelling Patterns	❏ Exercise 1: Listening for Sounds in Words: Phonograms with Silent Letters	❏ Content Mastery: Sound-Spelling Patterns
❏ Word Fluency 2 ❏ Instructional Text: **"Maya Angelou: A Love of Knowledge"** Text Connection 7	❏ Make a Mnemonic ❏ Present It: Mnemonics for Confusing Word Pairs	❏ Content Mastery: Spelling Posttest 1 ❏ Present It: Mnemonics for Confusing Word Pairs
❏ Instructional Text: **"Maya Angelou: A Love of Knowledge"** Text Connection 7 ❏ Write It: Journal Entry	❏ Review: Greek Combining Forms ❏ Exercise 2: Choose It: Words with Greek Combining Forms	❏ Exercise 1: Choose It: Words with Greek Combining Forms
❏ Review: Noun Clauses ❏ Identify It: Noun Clauses Text Connection 7	❏ Review: Adjectival Clauses and Noun Clauses ❏ Exercise 3: Identify It: Adjectival Clauses and Noun Clauses ❏ Introduce: Essential and Nonessential Dependent Clauses ❏ Exercise 4: Punctuate It: Essential and Nonessential Clauses	❏ Review: Sentence Fragments ❏ Exercise 2: Rewrite It: Sentence Fragments
❏ Instructional Text: **"Maya Angelou: A Love of Knowledge"** Text Connection 7 ❏ Take Note	❏ Comprehend It: **"Maya Angelou: A Love of Knowledge"** ❏ Take Note Text Connection 7	❏ Answer It: Using Signal Words
❏ Review: Steps for Writing a Report ❏ Introduce: Research Report Writer's Checklist ❏ Report Structure: Ways to Introduce a Topic	❏ Introduce: When and How to Incorporate Quotations Exercise 5: When to Quote a Source ❏ Write It: Research Report Draft	❏ Write It: Research Report Draft ❏ Speaking and Writing Using the Challenge Text: Exercise 3: Poetry Interpretation Worksheet
Effort: 1 2 3 4 5 **Participation:** 1 2 3 4 5 **Independence:** 1 2 3 4 5	**Effort:** 1 2 3 4 5 **Participation:** 1 2 3 4 5 **Independence:** 1 2 3 4 5	**Effort:** 1 2 3 4 5 **Participation:** 1 2 3 4 5 **Independence:** 1 2 3 4 5
Effort: 1 2 3 4 5 **Participation:** 1 2 3 4 5 **Independence:** 1 2 3 4 5	**Effort:** 1 2 3 4 5 **Participation:** 1 2 3 4 5 **Independence:** 1 2 3 4 5	**Effort:** 1 2 3 4 5 **Participation:** 1 2 3 4 5 **Independence:** 1 2 3 4 5

Check off the activities you complete with each lesson. Evaluate your accomplishments at the end of each lesson. Pay attention to teacher evaluations and comments.

Unit Objectives	Lesson 6 (Date:_____)	Lesson 7 (Date:_____)
STEP 1 • Say the sounds for graphemes: **mb**, **mn**, and **lm** for / m / as in *comb*, *hymn*, *calm*; **kn** and **gn** for / n / as in *knock*, *sign*; **wr** and **rh** for / r / as in *wrong*, *rhyme*; **ps** for / s / as in *psychology*. • Write the letter combinations containing silent letters representing / m /, / n /, / r /, and / s /.	❑ Content Mastery: Using Student Performance	❑ Exercise 1: Listening for Word Parts: Greek Combining Forms
STEP 2 • Read and spell words based on unit sound-spelling combinations. • Read and spell the **Essential Words:** *bargain, clothes, island, ninth, often, sword.* • Read and spell words composed of Greek combining forms. • Spell confusing words correctly.	❑ Exercise 1: Spelling Pretest 2 ❑ Word Fluency 3	❑ Exercise 2: Build It: Words with Greek Combining Forms ❑ Word Fluency 4
STEP 3 • Identify and define Greek combining forms. • Identify multiple meanings for words.	❑ Instructional Text: **"Apollo 13: Ingenuity Saves the Mission"** Text Connection 8 ❑ Use the Clues: Vocabulary Strategies ❑ Expression of the Day	❑ Review: Synonyms ❑ Introduce: Native American Loan Words ❑ Write It: Journal Entry
STEP 4 • Identify appositives and appositive phrases. • Identify the function of noun clauses. • Identify sentence fragments. • Rewrite sentences to change sentence fragments to complete sentences.	❑ Review: Sentence Fragments ❑ Review: Appositives ❑ Exercise 2: Rewrite It: Sentences	❑ Identify It: Adjective Clauses and Noun Clauses Text Connection 8
STEP 5 • Use text features, such as tables and graphs, to understand informational text. • Use context-based strategies to define words. • Identify, understand, and answer questions that use different types of signal words.	❑ Instructional Text: **"Apollo 13: Ingenuity Saves the Mission"**	❑ Instructional Text: **"Apollo 13: Ingenuity Saves the Mission"** Text Connection 8 ❑ Comprehend It
STEP 6 • Use text features to develop study questions. • Write responses to questions using signal words • Write a research report including a thesis, footnotes, and bibliography. • Present an oral summary of a research report. • Apply genre-specific Writer's Checklist to revise and edit a draft for a research report. • Use the Guide to Writing a Research Report as a reference tool for writing a research report.	❑ Review: Steps to Write a Research Report ❑ Write It: Research Report Draft	❑ Review: Research Report Writer's Checklist ❑ Revise It: Research Report
Self-Evaluation (5 is the highest) **Effort** = I produced my best work. **Participation** = I was actively involved in tasks. **Independence** = I worked on my own.	**Effort:** 1 2 3 4 5 **Participation:** 1 2 3 4 5 **Independence:** 1 2 3 4 5	**Effort:** 1 2 3 4 5 **Participation:** 1 2 3 4 5 **Independence:** 1 2 3 4 5
Teacher Evaluation	**Effort:** 1 2 3 4 5 **Participation:** 1 2 3 4 5 **Independence:** 1 2 3 4 5	**Effort:** 1 2 3 4 5 **Participation:** 1 2 3 4 5 **Independence:** 1 2 3 4 5

Lesson 8 (Date:_____)	Lesson 9 (Date:_____)	Lesson 10 (Date:_____)
❏ Exercise 1: Using a Dictionary		
❏ Review: Silent Letter Spellings ❏ Exercise 2: Identify It: Base Words	❏ Review: Compound Words and Words with Greek Combining Forms ❏ Exercise 1: Sort It: Compound Words and Words with Greek Combining Forms	❏ Content Mastery: Spelling Posttest 2
❏ Present It: Loan Words from Native American Languages ❏ Sort It: Loan Words from Native American Languages	❏ Content Mastery: Vocabulary; Morphology	❏ Content Mastery: Using Student Performance ❏ Find It: Words with Greek Combining Forms ❏ Write a Mini-Dialog: Idioms
❏ Review: Gerunds and Passive and Active Voice	❏ Content Mastery: Noun Clauses; Fragments and Complete Sentences	❏ Content Mastery: Using Student Performance
❏ Instructional Text: **"Apollo 13: Ingenuity Saves the Mission"** Text Connection 8	❏ Answer It: Using Signal Words	❏ Discuss It: Research Report
❏ Revise It: Research Report ❏ Write It: Bibliography Text Connection 5	❏ Write It: Publish a Research Report	❏ Speaking Application: Oral Summary of Research Report
Effort: 1 2 3 4 5 **Participation:** 1 2 3 4 5 **Independence:** 1 2 3 4 5	**Effort:** 1 2 3 4 5 **Participation:** 1 2 3 4 5 **Independence:** 1 2 3 4 5	**Effort:** 1 2 3 4 5 **Participation:** 1 2 3 4 5 **Independence:** 1 2 3 4 5
Effort: 1 2 3 4 5 **Participation:** 1 2 3 4 5 **Independence:** 1 2 3 4 5	**Effort:** 1 2 3 4 5 **Participation:** 1 2 3 4 5 **Independence:** 1 2 3 4 5	**Effort:** 1 2 3 4 5 **Participation:** 1 2 3 4 5 **Independence:** 1 2 3 4 5

Exercise 1 · Listening for Sounds in Words: Sound-Spelling Patterns

▶ Read each sound in the **Sound Bank**.

Sound Bank

/ m /	/ h /	/ k /	/ n /
/ p /	/ r /	/ s /	/ w /

▶ Listen to your teacher read each word in the first column. Repeat each word.

▶ Identify the consonant sound that is heard in all of the words in the column.

▶ Label the column with that sound from the **Sound Bank**.

▶ Underline the letters in each word that represent the common consonant sound.

▶ Circle the letter that is silent.

▶ Repeat this process with the remaining columns.

___	___	___	___
wrap	rhyme	knew	psyche
wrote	rhythm	knee	pseudonym
wreck	rhinestone	knock	psychologist

▶ Practice reading the words in each column with a partner.

▶ Which consonant is pronounced in the **wr** and **rh** sound-spelling patterns? _____

▶ Which consonant is pronounced in the **kn** sound-spelling pattern? _____

▶ Which consonant is pronounced in the **ps** sound-spelling pattern? _____

Exercise 2 · Spelling Pretest 1

▶ Write the word your teacher repeats.

1. _____   6. _____   11. _____

2. _____   7. _____   12. _____

3. _____   8. _____   13. _____

4. _____   9. _____   14. _____

5. _____   10. _____   15. _____

Exercise 3 · Identify It: Appositives

▶ Read each sentence and underline the appositive.

▶ Place commas as needed.

1. Education a key to success should be available to everyone.

2. Mr. Seles the Minister of Education addressed the graduates.

3. I will study my favorite subject English.

4. Workers' income the money they make is affected by education and career choice.

5. My brother's job computer engineering requires a college education.

Unit 34 · Lesson 1

Exercise 4 · Answer It: Using Tables and Graphs

Use information from the text and the tables in **"The Value of Knowledge"** to answer each of these questions. Write complete sentences.

1. Generalize the relationship between education and income presented in the article.

   _____

   _____

   _____

   _____

   _____

   _____

2. According to the article, how does more education help us transition to new jobs?

   _____

   _____

   _____

   _____

3. Look at Table 1. What were the unemployment rate and the median weekly earnings of people with bachelor's degrees in 2006?

   _____

   _____

   _____

   _____

(continued)

4. Look at Table 2 and find the average annual income of $46,435. A person of what education level earned that level of income in 2006?

_____

_____

_____

_____

5. Compare the average lifetime incomes of a person who does not complete high school with that of a person who gets an associate's degree.

_____

_____

_____

_____

_____

Exercise 1 • Listening for Sounds in Words: Sound-Spelling Patterns

▸ Read each sound in the **Sound Bank**.

Sound Bank

/ b /	/ g /	/ l /	/ m /	/ n /

▸ Listen to your teacher read each word in the first column. Repeat each word.

▸ Identify the consonant sound that is heard in all of the words in the column.

▸ Label the column with that sound from the **Sound Bank**.

Hint: Sounds in the **Sound Bank** may be used more than once.

▸ Underline the letters in each word that represent the common consonant sound.

▸ Circle the letter that is silent.

▸ Repeat this process with the remaining columns.

design	climb	hymn	calm
sign	comb	column	salmon
reign	thumb	autumn	palm

▸ Practice reading the words in each column with a partner.

▸ Which consonant is pronounced in the **gn** sound-spelling patterns? _____

▸ Which sound has three different sound-spelling patterns shown in the columns above? _____

▸ Which consonant is pronounced in the **mb**, **mn**, and **lm** sound-spelling pattern? _____

Exercise 2 · Write It: Essential Words

▸ Review the **Essential Words** in the **Word Bank**.

Word Bank

often	island	ninth	clothes	bargain	sword

▸ Put the words in alphabetical order and write them on the lines.

▸ Write one sentence for each **Essential Word**.

▸ Check that each sentence uses sentence signals—correct capitalization, commas, and end punctuation.

▸ Read each sentence to a partner.

1. _____

   _____

2. _____

   _____

3. _____

   _____

4. _____

   _____

5. _____

   _____

6. _____

   _____

Unit 34 · Lesson 2

Exercise 3 · Build It: Words with Greek Combining Forms

▸ Read each sentence.

▸ Fill in the blanks with Greek combining forms to create a word to fit the provided definition.

▸ Use the Morphemes for Meaning Cards as a reference as needed.

1. _____ _____ literally means "people rule."

2. _____ _____ literally means "three feet."

3. _____ _____ literally means "god rule."

4. _____ _____ literally means "one rule."

5. _____ _____ literally means "mind specialist."

Exercise 4 · Identify It: Noun Clauses

▶ Read each sentence.

▶ Identify and underline the noun clause.

▶ Circle the word that introduces the clause.

▶ Determine the function of the noun clause and circle the answer.

Key	S= Subject	DO=Direct Object	OP= Object of Preposition
	PN= Predicate Nominative		A= Appositive

1. We learned that Mr. Pereira has a degree in accounting.

   a. S   b. DO   c. OP   d. PN   e. A

2. Whoever applies for the job has a chance of getting it.

   a. S   b. DO   c. OP   d. PN   e. A

3. All teachers, whoever they are, strive to help students succeed.

   a. S   b. DO   c. OP   d. PN   e. A

4. Financial stability should not be the only way by which we judge success.

   a. S   b. DO   c. OP   d. PN   e. A

5. Studying hard is what produces results.

   a. S   b. DO   c. OP   d. PN   e. A

Unit 34 · Lesson 2

Exercise 5 · How To: Write Footnotes

Read the information and look at the example footnotes below. Then answer the questions.

Steps for Writing a Footnote:

1. Put a small number 1 at the end of the sentence that contains the first source you need to reference.

2. At the bottom of the page, begin your footnote by writing the number 1 to match the reference you made in the text of your report.

3. Then write the author's last name, the title of the work, and the page number of the source you are referencing (unless you are citing an Internet source).

4. Number each footnote consecutively throughout your report; that is, 1, 2, 3, 4, and so on.

Body of the Report:

Thomas Jefferson convinced James Madison that this was a grave error.[3] In the first United States Congress, Madison proposed that a bill of rights be added to the Constitution. He drafted the amendments. Madison drew inspiration from the English Bill of Rights and the Virginia Declaration of Rights.[4]

Footnotes:

[3] Dueland, "A Voice From Paris," 36.

[4] Carey, "Declaration Hits the Road."

1. What is the last name of the author who wrote about Thomas Jefferson convincing Madison that it was an error to leave out a bill of rights?

   _____

2. What page can that information about Thomas Jefferson be found on?

   _____

3. What is the title of the article that presents information on where Madison got inspiration for our Bill of Rights?

   _____

4. What is the last name of the author of "Declaration Hits the Road"?

   _____

Exercise 6 · Write It: Footnotes

The two passages below are from a report. They are in the order in which they appear in the report. Read the reference information under each passage. Then use that information to write a footnote for that passage. Remember to include the number of the footnote at the end of each passage, as well as next to the footnote reference.

1. John Adams was among those who were disappointed that the passage Jefferson wrote condemning the slave trade had been removed from the Declaration of Independence. Later in his life, Adams stated that slavery was "an evil of colossal magnitude."[1]

Source information:
Title of book: *John Adams*
Author: David McCullough
Published in 2001 by Simon & Schuster in New York, NY
Page used: 134

Footnote: _____

_____

2. During the War for Independence, Abigail Adams wrote a letter to her husband, John Adams, requesting that Congress discuss not only the matter of the United States's independence from Britain, but the independence of women as well.[2]

Source information:
Title of book: *A New Age Now Begins: A People's History of the American Revolution*
Author: Page Smith
Published in 1976 by Penguin Books in New York, NY.
Page used: 1808

Footnote: _____

_____

Unit 34 Lesson 3

Exercise 1 · Listening for Sounds in Words: Sound-Spelling Patterns

▶ Read each word in the first column.

▶ Underline the letters that represent / m /, / n /, / r /, or / s /.

▶ Place a ✔ under the consonant sound that is represented by the sound-spelling pattern in each word.

	/ m /	/ n /	/ r /	/ s /
1. knife				
2. balm				
3. knot				
4. psychiatry				
5. wrist				
6. foreign				
7. wreck				
8. limb				
9. unknown				
10. rhinoceros				

▶ Practice reading the words in the first column with a partner.

Exercise 1 · Listening for Sounds in Words: Phonograms with Silent Letters

▶ Read each sound in the **Sound Bank**.

Sound Bank

/m/	/n/	/r/	/s/

▶ Listen to each word your teacher says. Repeat each word.

▶ Listen for the consonant sound.

▶ Write the consonant sound from the **Sound Bank** in the space provided.

▶ Underline the letters representing the sound.

▶ Circle the consonant letter that is silent.

1. wreath   _____

2. align   _____

3. wrong   _____

4. rhetoric   _____

5. knowledge   _____

6. autumn   _____

7. kneel   _____

8. column   _____

9. balm   _____

10. knight   _____

Exercise 2 · Choose It: Words with Greek Combining Forms

▸ Read each sentence and the answer choices below.

▸ Select the correct answer and write it in the blank.

▸ Circle the Greek combining forms in the word.

▸ Use the **Morphemes for Meaning Cards** and a dictionary as needed as a reference.

▸ Identify and underline clues in the sentence that helped you select the word.

1. England is ruled by one person, a queen or king, and is therefore a

   _____.

   a. democracy   b. biography   c. monarchy   d. patriarchy

2. A _____ is the name given to a large animal with thick skin, such as an elephant, rhinoceros, or hippopotamus.

   a. dermatologist   b. zoologist   c. hypodermic   d. pachyderm

3. A specialist who helps a patient understand behavior and emotions is called a

   _____.

   a. dermatologist   b. psychologist   c. geologist   d. aristocrat

4. In a(n) _____, citizens are encouraged to take part in government by voting.

   a. democracy   b. psychologist   c. aristocracy   d. autocracy

5. A _____, a large urban area where many people live, must have an evacuation plan that can be used in case of disaster.

   a. village   b. metropolis   c. city   d. suburb

Exercise 3 · Identify It: Adjectival Clauses and Noun Clauses

▸ Read each sentence.

▸ Identify the dependent clause and underline it.

▸ Decide whether the clause is an adjectival clause or a noun clause.

▸ Circle the correct answer.

1. Maya Angelou, who has been called a Renaissance woman, was born in Missouri in 1928.

   a. noun clause   b. adjectival clause

2. We learned that Maya Angelou speaks five languages.

   a. noun clause   b. adjectival clause

3. Whoever reads her autobiography will learn extraordinary facts about Maya Angelou.

   a. noun clause   b. adjectival clause

4. To this day, Maya Angelou remembers the books that Mrs. Flowers lent her.

   a. noun clause   b. adjectival clause

5. As a child, Maya Angelou would read whatever she was given.

   a. noun clause   b. adjectival clause

Unit 34 · Lesson 4

Exercise 4 · Punctuate It: Essential and Nonessential Clauses

▶ Read each sentence.

▶ Identify the dependent clause and underline it.

▶ Decide whether the clause is essential or nonessential to the meaning of the sentence, and circle the correct answer.

▶ Place commas where needed.

1. The American poet who spoke at President Bill Clinton's inauguration is world-renowned.

   a. essential   b. nonessential

2. Momma spoke to Mrs. Flowers who passed by on her way to the store.

   a. essential   b. nonessential

3. Mrs. Flowers purchased the things that she needed at the local store.

   a. essential   b. nonessential

4. Marguerite chose a school dress which she wore to Mrs. Flowers' house.

   a. essential   b. nonessential

5. The conversation, which centered around the poems we were writing was interrupted by giggles from my younger sister.

   a. essential   b. nonessential

Exercise 5 · When to Quote a Source

Most of the information in your report should be written in your own words. But adding quotations in moderation can strengthen your writing. Quotations show that you have done careful research: you have found words of others that support your points. Here are some guidelines that will help you decide when it is better to quote an author than to paraphrase the author's ideas.

Quote a source when:
- you need to state information directly from a historical document, such as the U.S. Constitution or the Bill of Rights.
- it is necessary for you to show exactly how a writer wrote or said something in his or her own words.
- an author or speaker expresses something in a way that is especially beautiful or interesting (for example, through the use of images or metaphors).

When you quote from a source:
- be sure to put the phrase, sentence, or passage in quotation marks.
- write down the name of the person who said or wrote the words you are quoting.

▶ Read each of these examples. Then write why you think the writer chose to quote this information rather than paraphrase it.

1. The Declaration of Independence states, "We hold these truths to be self-evident, that all men are created equal, that they are endowed by their Creator with certain unalienable Rights, that among these are Life, Liberty, and the pursuit of Happiness."

   _____

   _____

   _____

   _____

   _____

(continued)

Exercise 5 (continued) · When to Quote a Source

2. Thomas Jefferson wrote in a letter to the Danbury Baptists that "religion is a matter which lies solely between Man & his God, that he owes account to none other for his faith or his worship, that the legitimate powers of government reach actions only, & not opinions."

_____

_____

_____

_____

3. In fact, one of the authors of the American Constitution, Gouverneur Morris, praised the outcome of Zenger's trial. He said it was "the germ of American freedom—the morning star of that liberty which subsequently revolutionized America."

_____

_____

_____

_____

Exercise 1 · Choose It: Words with Greek Combining Forms

▶ Read the words in the **Word Bank**.

Word Bank

dermatologist	chronological	cosmopolitan	thermal
democracy	hypodermic	psychologist	kilogram
symphony	microphone	podium	monotone

▶ Read each sentence and choose a word from the **Word Bank** to complete the sentence.

▶ Use the **Morphemes for Meaning Cards** and a dictionary as needed.

▶ Identify and underline clues in the sentence that helped you select your answer.

1. The orchestra played a _____ in which all the instruments frequently sounded together in harmony.

2. The doctor used a _____ needle to inject antibiotics under the skin.

3. The speaker placed his feet on a wooden box behind the _____ so he could be seen more easily.

4. The _____ read a new scientific study about how people's minds work.

5. The _____ studied the rash that covered the child's skin.

6. The biographies of the presidents were placed in _____ order to show the time when each was in office.

7. My parents, who have lived in many different cities throughout the world, are very _____.

8. Many winter sports enthusiasts wear _____ undergarments to retain their body heat.

9. There are a thousand grams in a _____.

10. Because the United States is a _____, the people have the power to choose the nation's leaders.

Unit 34 · Lesson 5

Exercise 2 · Rewrite It: Sentence Fragments

▶ Read each sentence fragment.

▶ Rewrite the fragment as a complete sentence.

▶ Use correct punctuation.

▶ Reread your sentence to make sure it makes sense.

1. Who read her poetry and fiction.

_____

_____

2. Who taught young Marguerite the value of words.

_____

_____

3. Whomever we meet in life.

_____

_____

4. That there is beauty and strength in diversity.

_____

_____

5. Whatever words a poet uses.

_____

_____

Exercise 3 · Poetry Interpretation Worksheet

▶ Complete all of the activities and questions in regard to the poem you have selected.

1. Look at the punctuation at the end of each line. What is it? If there is a comma, you pause slightly. If there is a period, come to a full stop. If there is no punctuation, keep going to the next line. Now read your poem aloud several times, paying attention to the line breaks.

   _____

   _____

   _____

2. Underline any word in the poem that you do not know, find its definition in the dictionary, and write the definition below.

   _____

   _____

   _____

3. Who is the speaker in the poem? (Caution: it is not always the poet.) What can you tell about the speaker from reading the poem?

   _____

   _____

   _____

4. Look at the poem's title. What information does it give you? How does it connect to the rest of the poem?

   _____

   _____

   _____

(continued)

5. Underline the images in the poem. Then write the images below and note which of the five senses each image appeals to.

_____

_____

_____

6. Underline any instance of personification, metaphor, and/or simile in the poem. Write them below. What do these comparisons make you think about?

_____

_____

_____

7. What mood do the images, similes and metaphors create?

_____

_____

_____

8. What does this poem as a whole make you think about?

_____

_____

_____

Exercise 1 · Spelling Pretest 2

▸ Write the word your teacher repeats.

1. _____

2. _____

3. _____

4. _____

5. _____

6. _____

7. _____

8. _____

9. _____

10. _____

11. _____

12. _____

13. _____

14. _____

15. _____

Exercise 2 · Rewrite It: Sentences

▸ Read the composition in the box.

▸ Identify and correct errors in the first sentence with your teacher.

▸ Identify and use editing marks to correct errors in the remaining sentences in the composition. Write your revised sentences on the lines that are provided.

▸ Fill in the problem and an explanation of the revision in the chart.

▸ Pay special attention to improve sentence fragments and word choice.

1. When the system of power and oxygen got low. 2. The 3 astronauts got a problem in space. 3. Mission control worked hard. 4. To find a solution. 5. Using only things available on the spacecraft. 6. The men made an air scrubber. 7. Then they had to tell them how to make an identical air scrubber. 8. With tape, cardboard, and plastic. 9. It was O.K. 10. The spacecraft got them back to Earth.

_____

_____

_____

_____

_____

_____

_____

_____

_____

_____

(continued)

Exercise 2 (continued) · Rewrite It: Sentences

Sentence #	Trait(s)	Problem(s)	Revision

(continued)

Exercise 2 (continued) · Rewrite It: Sentences

Sentence #	Trait(s)	Problem(s)	Revision

Exercise 1 · Listening for Word Parts: Greek Combining Forms

▶ Listen as your teacher reads a word pair.

▶ Repeat the word pair.

▶ Listen for a Greek combining form contained in both words.

▶ Write the Greek combining form in the space provided.

▶ Repeat this process with the remaining words.

1. _____

2. _____

3. _____

4. _____

5. _____

6. _____

7. _____

8. _____

9. _____

10. _____

Unit 34 · Lesson 7

Exercise 2 · Build It: Words with Greek Combining Forms

▶ Read the word parts in each table.

▶ Combine word parts to build as many words as possible. (You can build words by combining two or three word parts.)

▶ Record the words on the lines below the table.

▶ Check a dictionary to verify that the words you have written are real words.

1.

aristo	demo	crat	cracy	ic

_____   _____   _____

_____   _____   _____

2.

an	y	arch	ive	hier

_____   _____   _____

_____   _____   _____

3.

psych	ologist	ology	ic	

_____   _____   _____

_____   _____   _____

4.

theo	crat	logy	logist	

_____   _____   _____

_____   _____   _____

5.

polit	polis	metro	ics	ical

_____   _____   _____

_____   _____   _____

Exercise 1 · Using a Dictionary

▸ Turn to the **Vocabulary** section (dictionary) in the back of your *Student Text*.

▸ Find the word **benign** and its pronunciation.

▸ Write the diacritical markings for that word on the line in item 1 below.

▸ Use the markings to read the word aloud.

▸ Complete numbers 2–5 using the same process.

Word	Pronunciation
1. benign	_____
2. pretensions	_____
3. essence	_____
4. expertise	_____
5. ochre	_____

▸ Use a classroom dictionary or an online reference source to complete numbers 6–10.

Word	Pronunciation
6. acknowledge	_____
7. rheumatism	_____
8. psychosis	_____
9. sovereign	_____
10. almond	_____

Exercise 2 · Identify It: Base Words

▶ Read each word.

▶ Underline the base word in each word.

▶ Write the base word on the line next to the word.

▶ Circle the silent letter in the base word.

1. signature _____

2. crumble _____

3. autumnal _____

4. resignation _____

5. hymnal _____

6. solemnity _____

7. malignant _____

8. condemnation _____

9. columnist _____

10. designation _____

Exercise 1 · Sort It: Compound Words and Words with Greek Combining Forms

▶ Read each word in the **Word Bank**.

Word Bank

demographics	handwriting	typewriter	doorknob	metropolitan
know-how	matriarch	aristocrat	honeycomb	podiatrist

▶ Identify the type of word.

▶ Write the word under the correct heading.

▶ Underline the Greek combing forms.

Compound Words	Words With Greek Combining Forms

Check off the activities you complete with each lesson. Evaluate your accomplishments at the end of each lesson. Pay attention to teacher evaluations and comments.

	Unit Objectives	Lesson 1 (Date:_____)	Lesson 2 (Date:_____)
STEP 1	• Identify syllable types: closed, **r**-controlled, open, final silent **e**, vowel digraph, final consonant + **le**, and diphthong. • Identify stress patterns.	❏ Exercise 1: Identify It: Syllable Types ❏ Review: Syllable Types	❏ Review: Stressed Syllables and Schwa ❏ Vowel Chart ❏ Exercise 1: Listening for Stressed Syllables and Schwa
STEP 2	• Read and spell multisyllable words. • Read and spell words composed of Greek combining forms.	❏ Exercise 2: Spelling Pretest 1	❏ Divide It: Unit Words ❏ Word Fluency 1
STEP 3	• Identify and define Greek combining forms. • Identify multiple meanings for words.	❏ Unit Words ❏ Review: Synonyms and Antonyms ❏ Word Wheel ❏ Expression of the Day	❏ Introduce: Additional Greek Combining Forms ❏ Exercise 2: Build It: Words with Greek Combining Forms
STEP 4	• Identify nominative, object, possessive, and demonstrative pronouns. • Identify correct pronoun usage in compounds. • Use transitional words and phrases for text coherence. • Identify sentences with complete comparative structure. • Identify and correct run-on sentences.	❏ Review: Nominative and Object Pronouns ❏ Exercise 3: Choose It: Nominative and Object Pronouns ❏ Pronoun Usage in Compounds ❏ Exercise 4: Choose It: Subject Pronoun or Object Pronoun ❏ Introduce: Avoiding Double Subjects	❏ Review: Possessive and Demonstrative Pronouns ❏ Exercise 3: Identify It: Possessive and Demonstrative Pronouns ❏ Text Coherence Through Transitional Words and Phrases ❏ Exercise 4: Identify It: Transitional Words and Phrases
STEP 5	• Use text features, such as tables and graphs, to understand informational text. • Use context-based strategies to define words. • Identify, understand, and answer questions that use different types of signal words. • Identify features of a personal essay. • Identify the elements of poetry in a poem.	❏ Independent Text: **"The Tech of Shrek: Imagination Animated"** ❏ Comprehend It: A Nonfiction Feature Article	❏ Passage Fluency
STEP 6	• Write responses to questions using their signal words. • Write an essay using a quick outline under timed conditions. • Write a compare and contrast literary analysis essay. • Write a persuasive essay incorporating key features. • Apply genre-specific Writer's Checklist to revise and edit a draft and final copy for a persuasive essay and a literary analysis essay.	❏ Exercise 5: Answer It: Using Graphics and Sidebar Information ❏ Review: Internet Search	❏ Exercise 5: How To: Write a Résumé ❏ Exercise 6: Write It: Résumé
	Self-Evaluation (5 is the highest) **Effort** = I produced my best work. **Participation** = I was actively involved in tasks. **Independence** = I worked on my own.	**Effort:** 1 2 3 4 5 **Participation:** 1 2 3 4 5 **Independence:** 1 2 3 4 5	**Effort:** 1 2 3 4 5 **Participation:** 1 2 3 4 5 **Independence:** 1 2 3 4 5
	Teacher Evaluation	**Effort:** 1 2 3 4 5 **Participation:** 1 2 3 4 5 **Independence:** 1 2 3 4 5	**Effort:** 1 2 3 4 5 **Participation:** 1 2 3 4 5 **Independence:** 1 2 3 4 5

Lesson 3 (Date:_____)	**Lesson 4** (Date:_____)	**Lesson 5** (Date:_____)
❑ Exercise 1: Listening for Stressed Syllables	❑ Exercise 1: Identify It: Syllable Types	❑ Content Mastery: Syllable Types
❑ Word Fluency 2 ❑ Instructional Text: **"The Raven: A Romantic Imagination"** Text Connection 9	❑ Exercise 2: Identify It: Spelling Rules	❑ Content Mastery: Spelling Posttest 1
❑ Instructional Text: **"The Raven: A Romantic Imagination"** Text Connection 9 ❑ Write It: Journal Entry	❑ Review: Greek Combining Forms ❑ Exercise 3: Choose It: Words with Greek Combining Forms	❑ Exercise 1: Choose It: Words with Greek Combining Forms
❑ Review: Text Coherence Through Transitional Words and Phrases ❑ Exercise 2: Rewrite It: Sentences with Transitional Words and Phrases	❑ Review: Degrees of Adjectives ❑ Review: Comparative Sentence Structure ❑ Exercise 4: Rewrite It: Comparative Sentences ❑ Exercise 5: Identify It: Transitional Words in Text	❑ Exercise 2: Identify It: Transitional Words in Text ❑ Review: Run-On Sentences ❑ Exercise 3: Choose It: Run-On Sentence Correction
❑ Instructional Text: **"The Raven: A Romantic Imagination"**	❑ Review: Six Elements of Poetry	❑ Prepare to Write: Timed Essay
❑ Comprehend It Text Connection 9	❑ Take Note: Elements of Poetry Text Connection 9 ❑ Exercise 6: Six Elements of Poetry ❑ Answer It: Using Signal Words	❑ Write It: Timed Essay
Effort: 1 2 3 4 5 **Participation:** 1 2 3 4 5 **Independence:** 1 2 3 4 5	**Effort:** 1 2 3 4 5 **Participation:** 1 2 3 4 5 **Independence:** 1 2 3 4 5	**Effort:** 1 2 3 4 5 **Participation:** 1 2 3 4 5 **Independence:** 1 2 3 4 5
Effort: 1 2 3 4 5 **Participation:** 1 2 3 4 5 **Independence:** 1 2 3 4 5	**Effort:** 1 2 3 4 5 **Participation:** 1 2 3 4 5 **Independence:** 1 2 3 4 5	**Effort:** 1 2 3 4 5 **Participation:** 1 2 3 4 5 **Independence:** 1 2 3 4 5

Check off the activities you complete with each lesson. Evaluate your accomplishments at the end of each lesson. Pay attention to teacher evaluations and comments.

Unit Objectives	Lesson 6 (Date:_____)	Lesson 7 (Date:_____)
STEP 1 • Identify syllable types: closed, **r**-controlled, open, final silent **e**, vowel digraph, final consonant + **le**, and diphthong. • Identify stress patterns.	❑ Content Mastery: Using Student Performance	❑ Exercise 1: Using a Dictionary: Diacritical Marks
STEP 2 • Read and spell multisyllable words. • Read and spell words composed of Greek combining forms.	❑ Exercise 1: Spelling Pretest 2 ❑ Word Fluency 3	❑ Exercise 2: Sentence Dictation ❑ Word Fluency 4
STEP 3 • Identify and define Greek combining forms. • Identify multiple meanings for words.	❑ Instructional Text: **"La Vida Robot: Imagination Rules!"** Text Connection 10 ❑ Use the Clues: Vocabulary Strategies ❑ Expression of the Day	❑ Review: Antonyms ❑ Exercise 3: Match It: Antonyms ❑ Expression of the Day
STEP 4 • Identify nominative, object, possessive, and demonstrative pronouns. • Identify correct pronoun usage in compounds. • Use transitional words and phrases for text coherence. • Identify sentences with complete comparative structure. • Identify and correct run-on sentences.	❑ Review: Run-On Sentences ❑ Exercise 2: Choose It: Run-On Sentence Correction ❑ Review: Comparative Sentence Structure ❑ Exercise 3: Rewrite It: Comparative Sentences	❑ Exercise 4: Rewrite It: Sentences
STEP 5 • Use text features, such as tables and graphs, to understand informational text. • Use context-based strategies to define words. • Identify, understand, and answer questions that use different types of signal words. • Identify features of a personal essay. • Identify the elements of poetry in a poem.	❑ Instructional Text: **"La Vida Robot: Imagination Rules!"**	❑ Instructional Text: **"La Vida Robot: Imagination Rules!"** Text Connection 10 ❑ Comprehend It
STEP 6 • Write responses to questions using their signal words. • Write an essay using a quick outline under timed conditions. • Write a compare and contrast literary analysis essay. • Write a persuasive essay incorporating key features. • Apply genre-specific Writer's Checklist to revise and edit a draft and final copy for a persuasive essay and a literary analysis essay.	❑ Review: Features of a Persuasive Essay ❑ Exercise 4: Analyze It: Persuasive Essay	❑ Review: Audience and Purpose ❑ Prepare to Write: Persuasive Essay Exercise 5: Choosing a Topic Exercise 6: Write It: Shaping the Topic
Self-Evaluation (5 is the highest) **Effort** = I produced my best work. **Participation** = I was actively involved in tasks. **Independence** = I worked on my own.	**Effort:** 1 2 3 4 5 **Participation:** 1 2 3 4 5 **Independence:** 1 2 3 4 5	**Effort:** 1 2 3 4 5 **Participation:** 1 2 3 4 5 **Independence:** 1 2 3 4 5
Teacher Evaluation	**Effort:** 1 2 3 4 5 **Participation:** 1 2 3 4 5 **Independence:** 1 2 3 4 5	**Effort:** 1 2 3 4 5 **Participation:** 1 2 3 4 5 **Independence:** 1 2 3 4 5

Lesson 8 (Date:_____)	Lesson 9 (Date:_____)	Lesson 10 (Date:_____)
	❑ Exercise 1: Listening for Word Parts: Greek Combining Forms	
❑ Exercise 1: Fill In: Homophones	❑ Exercise 2: Build It	❑ Content Mastery: Spelling Posttest 2
❑ Exercise 2: Choose It	❑ Content Mastery: Vocabulary; Antonyms; Morphology	❑ Content Mastery: Using Student Performance ❑ Find It: Words with Greek Combining Forms ❑ Write a Mini-Dialog: Idioms
❑ Review: Subject and Object Pronouns and Comparative Sentences	❑ Content Mastery: Nominative and Object Pronouns; Comparative Sentences	❑ Content Mastery: Using Student Performance
❑ Instructional Text: **"La Vida Robot: Imagination Rules!"** Text Connection 10	❑ Prepare to Write: Persuasive Essay	❑ Exercise 1: Answering Open-Ended Questions: Timed Writing
❑ Answer It: Using Signal Words	❑ Write It: Persuasive Essay	❑ Revise It: Persuasive Essay
Effort: 1 2 3 4 5 **Participation:** 1 2 3 4 5 **Independence:** 1 2 3 4 5	**Effort:** 1 2 3 4 5 **Participation:** 1 2 3 4 5 **Independence:** 1 2 3 4 5	**Effort:** 1 2 3 4 5 **Participation:** 1 2 3 4 5 **Independence:** 1 2 3 4 5
Effort: 1 2 3 4 5 **Participation:** 1 2 3 4 5 **Independence:** 1 2 3 4 5	**Effort:** 1 2 3 4 5 **Participation:** 1 2 3 4 5 **Independence:** 1 2 3 4 5	**Effort:** 1 2 3 4 5 **Participation:** 1 2 3 4 5 **Independence:** 1 2 3 4 5

Exercise 1 · Identify It: Syllable Types

▶ Read each word in the first column.

▶ Use what you know about prefixes, suffixes, and patterns for syllable division to identify the syllables in each word.

▶ Identify what type each syllable is, and write it in the correct column.

	Closed Syllable	r-Controlled Syllable	Open Syllable	Final Silent e Syllable	Vowel Digraph Syllable	Final Consonant + le Syllable	Vowel Diphthong Syllable
Example: conspicuous	con spic		u		ous		
1. accessible							
2. delineate							
3. investigate							
4. boisterous							
5. lackadaisical							
6. invincible							
7. manipulate							
8. equilibrium							
9. voluntary							
10. predominate							

Exercise 2 · Spelling Pretest 1

▸ Write the word your teacher repeats.

1. _____   6. _____   11. _____

2. _____   7. _____   12. _____

3. _____   8. _____   13. _____

4. _____   9. _____   14. _____

5. _____   10. _____   15. _____

Exercise 3 · Choose It: Nominative and Object Pronouns

▸ Read each sentence and the answer choices below it.

▸ Circle the correct pronoun and write the selected pronoun in the blank.

▸ Draw a line from the pronoun to its antecedent.

Note: Not every pronoun in this activity has an antecedent.

1. The filmmakers wanted a realistic environment, so _____ experimented with new animation techniques.

   a. them   b. me   c. they   d. I   e. it

2. To make the characters look real, they modeled _____ from the inside out.

   a. them   b. him   c. they   d. I   e. it

3. When Shrek was released to the movie theaters, _____ became a huge success.

   a. them   b. she   c. they   d. I   e. it

4. My brother took _____ to see the movie.

   a. we   b. me   c. she   d. I   e. he

5. The filmmakers told the students that _____ could see how the movie was made.

   a. them   b. her   c. they   d. him   e. us

Exercise 4 · Choose It: Subject Pronoun or Object Pronoun

▶ Read each sentence, including the pronoun choices in parentheses.

▶ Determine whether the pronoun is functioning as a subject or object.

▶ Select and circle the correct form.

▶ Read the sentence using the circled form to check your answer.

1. Shrek and (he, him) lived in the swamp.

2. The team of artists created Shrek and (she, her).

3. My friends and (I, me) learned about computer-generated animation.

4. (He and I, Him and me) saw the latest animated movie.

5. The animators sculpted statues of Fiona and (he, him).

Exercise 5 · Answer It: Using Graphics and Sidebar Information

▶ Use information from the selection **"The Tech of Shrek: Imagination Animated"** to answer each of these questions. Write complete sentences.

1. How is the Shrek character unlike a typical fairytale hero?

_____

_____

_____

_____

2. What does CG stand for?

_____

_____

_____

_____

3. How do the first three section headings in the article help readers follow the information that is presented in the article?

_____

_____

_____

_____

_____

(continued)

Unit 35 · Lesson 1

4. Read the information in the sidebar. Then explain how a **wireframe** is created.

_____

_____

_____

_____

_____

5. How did the animators of *Shrek* make fire look realistic?

_____

_____

_____

_____

_____

Exercise 1 · Listening for Stressed Syllables and Schwa

▸ Listen to each word as your teacher reads it.

▸ Repeat the word.

▸ Listen for the stressed syllable and underline it.

▸ Listen for the schwa in each unstressed syllable. Circle the vowel that is reduced to schwa, or the letter combination that produces the schwa sound.

(The schwa sound in final consonant + **le** syllables is not represented by a letter.)

1. ex ec u tive

2. i den ti fy

3. ac cess i ble

4. de riv a tive

5. trans par en cy

6. pro tag o nist

7. in vin ci ble

8. pre dom i nate

9. in del i ble

10. an tag on ist

Unit 35 · Lesson 2

Exercise 2 · Build It: Words with Greek Combining Forms

▸ Read each sentence.

▸ Fill in the blanks with Greek combining forms to create a word to fit the definition inside the quotation marks.

▸ Use the **Morphemes for Meaning Cards** as a reference as needed.

1. _____ _____ literally means "fear of water."

2. _____ _____ literally means "half circle."

3. _____ _____ literally means "animal study."

4. _____ _____ literally means "see water."

5. _____ _____ literally means "star study."

Exercise 3 · Identify It: Possessive and Demonstrative Pronouns

▸ Read each sentence.

▸ Underline the possessive pronoun or demonstrative pronoun.

▸ Circle the correct answer.

1. "I've lost my DVD of *Shrek*; do you have yours?"

    a. possessive pronoun   b. demonstrative pronoun

2. This is a film to remember.

    a. possessive pronoun   b. demonstrative pronoun

3. Ours is the large ogre statue over there.

    a. possessive pronoun   b. demonstrative pronoun

4. The producers of *Shrek* were pleased to learn that the Academy Award was theirs.

    a. possessive pronoun   b. demonstrative pronoun

5. That will not fit into the environment of this movie.

    a. possessive pronoun   b. demonstrative pronoun

Exercise 4 · Identify It: Transitional Words and Phrases

▸ Read each sentence.

▸ Underline the transitional word or phrase.

▸ Determine the relationship conveyed by the transitional term, using the list in the box.

Types of Relationships Conveyed by Transitional Words and Phrases

a. addition   d. example

b. cause–effect   e. time sequence

c. compare–contrast f. summary

▸ Write the relationship on the line.

▸ Refer to the **Transitional Words and Phrases** chart in the Handbook section of the *Student Text* as needed.

1. The filmmakers elaborated on the story and parodied traditional fairy tales.

   Relationship: _____

2. Many individuals contributed their special talents to the film, but everyone had to work together to create a great movie.

   Relationship: _____

3. Some cartoon movies, for example *Shrek*, are produced using computer-generated animation.

   Relationship: _____

4. The full effect of the animation was not seen until all the visual effects were in place.

   Relationship: _____

5. The animators wanted the fire to look realistic, so they studied many films of real fires.

   Relationship: _____

Exercise 5 · How To: Write a Résumé

This is the information you provide in a résumé:

- Your **name** and **address**.

- An **objective**: This is where you state the position you are interested in. Begin your objective with an infinitive such as **to gain employment**, or with a noun phrase such as **position as an animator**.

- A summary of **qualifications**: This is where you summarize your major achievements and the special skills you bring to a job.

- **Education**: This is where you summarize the education you have received. Be sure to list any classes that are related to the job you are seeking.

- **Employment**: This is where you list the jobs you have had and briefly describe your responsibilities there. List your jobs in reverse chronological order. Begin your job descriptions with action verbs such as **created** or **assisted**, or with noun phrases such as **Duties included**. Include volunteer positions as well as paid jobs.

(continued)

SUNG-MEI CHU
3115 32nd Avenue
Oakland, CA 94601
Home Phone (510) 555-2468
sungmei_chu@sungmei_cartoons.com

OBJECTIVE: To gain employment as an animator for an animated feature film

QUALIFICATIONS
- Animated Short Film Club President at State University
- Proficient in both PC and MAC computer software
- Volunteer at 2005 Adventure Animators Conference
- Experience in both print and film media
- Maintain personal Web site, which features animated film shorts and comic strips (http://www.sungmei_cartoons.com)

EDUCATION

2000–2004 Bachelor of Fine Arts in Graphic Design, State University. Coursework included focuses in computer animation, graphic design, and film.

1996–2000 Graduate of Central High School. Classes included art, journalism, and computer programming.

EMPLOYMENT

2005 *Lead animator, Baby Betty Doll commercial*
Duties included organizing and leading a team of designers to create an animated 30-second commercial for Baby Betty Dolls.

2004 *Special Effects Artist*, Pompeii: Countdown to Eruption
Duties included using computer animation software to simulate scenes from ancient Pompeii, scanning and touching up photographs, and creating animated graphics.

2000–2002 *Assistant Animator, State College News at Night*
Assisted lead animator in creating graphics for college nightly news program.

1998–2000 *Cartoonist, The Central High Bugle*
Created a comic strip, *High School Hijinks*, for the Central High School newspaper. Responsibilities included conceptualizing the strip, organizing its layout, and animating the strip on a weekly basis.

Exercise 6 · Write It: Résumé

▸ Think of a job you would like to have.

▸ Then complete the following résumé planner.

NAME: _____

ADDRESS: _____

PHONE: _____

E-MAIL ADDRESS: _____

OBJECTIVE: _____

QUALIFICATIONS

Special skills you bring to the job:

_____   _____

_____   _____

Include any awards you have won:

_____   _____

_____   _____

EDUCATION

Years at current school: _____

Name of school: _____

Classes you are taking, especially those that relate to your desired job:

_____   _____

_____   _____

(continued)

Exercise 6 (continued) · Write It: Résumé

EMPLOYMENT (Tip: If you have a mixture of paid and unpaid jobs, you might call this EXPERIENCE instead of EMPLOYMENT.)

_____   _____   _____

Year   Position   Company

Duties: _____

_____

_____

_____   _____   _____

Year   Position   Company

Duties: _____

_____

_____

_____   _____   _____

Year   Position   Company

Duties: _____

_____

_____

▶ Listen to each pair of words your teacher says.

▶ Repeat each word.

▶ Underline the stressed syllable in each word.

1. mod er ate   mod er a tion

2. re spon sib le   re spon si bil ity

3. in ter pret   in ter pre ta tion

4. man ip u late   man ip u la tion

5. i den ti fy   i den ti fi ca tion

6. ac cess   ac cess i bil ity

7. in ves ti gate   in ves ti ga tion

8. sen ti ment   sen ti men tal ity

9. mod er ate   mod er a tion

10. ir ri ta ble   ir ri ta tion

▶ When adding a suffix to a multisyllable word, what happens to the stressed syllable?

_____

_____

_____

Exercise 2 · Rewrite It: Sentences with Transitional Words and Phrases

▸ Combine each pair of sentences to create one sentence with the designated relationship.

▸ Refer to the **Transitional Words and Phrases** chart in the Handbook section of the *Student Text* as needed. **Note:** There is more than one way to combine each pair of sentences.

1. I have heard of the poem "The Raven." I have never read it. (compare-contrast relationship)

_____

_____

_____

_____

2. Poe's poem "The Raven" became instantly popular. It was published in 1845. (time sequence relationship)

_____

_____

_____

_____

3. Readers wonder if the raven in the poem is meant to be real. Could it be imaginary? (compare-contrast relationship)

_____

_____

_____

_____

(continued)

Exercise 2 *(continued)* · Rewrite It: Sentences with Transitional Words and Phrases

4. The poem has a dark, mysterious quality. It has an entrancing rhythm. (addition relationship)

_____

_____

_____

_____

5. Poe did not reveal who Lenore was. The reader is free to imagine. (cause-effect relationship)

_____

_____

_____

_____

Exercise 1 · Identify It: Syllable Types

▶ Read each item.

▶ Identify the designated syllable in the word.

▶ Write the syllable on the line.

1. Identify the closed syllable in **identify**. _____

2. Identify the final silent **e** syllable in **manipulate**. _____

3. Identify the **r**-controlled syllable in **exorbitant**. _____

4. Identify the final consonant + **le** syllable in **immutable**. _____

5. Identify the first open syllable in **protagonist**. _____

6. Identify the first open syllable in **degenerate**. _____

7. Identify the vowel diphthong syllable in **boisterous**. _____

8. Identify the vowel digraph syllable in **lackadaisical**. _____

9. Identify the **r**-controlled syllable in **interpretation**. _____

10. Identify the closed syllable in **temporary**. _____

Exercise 2 · Identify It: Spelling Rules

▶ Read each numbered word.

▶ Write its base word and suffix in the next two columns.

▶ Check the box that identifies the spelling rule used when adding the suffix to the base word.

	Base Word	Suffix	Change It	Drop It	No Rule
Example 1 sensible					
Example 2 arbitrarily					
1. physicist					
2. neurologist					
3. predominantly					
4. antibodies					
5. cyclones					
6. identifying					
7. identified					
8. ordinarily					
9. physically					
10. investigated					

Unit 35 · Lesson 4

Exercise 3 · Choose It: Words with Greek Combining Forms

▸ Read each sentence and the answer choices below.

▸ Select the correct answer and write it in the blank.

▸ Circle the Greek combining forms in the word.

▸ Use the **Morphemes for Meaning Cards** and a dictionary as needed for reference.

▸ Identify and underline clues in the sentence that helped you select the word.

1. Some people believe that the study of the meanings of the movements of the stars, or

   _____, produces useful information.

   a. astrophysics   b. astronaut   c. astrology   d. astrodome

2. _____ electricity is produced by harnessing the power of hot water gushing from the earth in volcanic areas.

   a. hydrologist   b. thermometer   c. hydrogen   d. hydrothermal

3. The United States is situated in the half of the world called the northern

   _____.

   a. hemisphere   b. hemitrope   c. hemicycle   d. hemihedron

4. She became a _____ because she is a lover of knowledge.

   a. sophomore   b. philosopher   c. philatelist   d. sophisticate

5. The person who appeared to have a morbid fear of water had contracted

   _____.

   a. hydrologist   b. hydrogen   c. hydrothermal   d. hydrophobia

Exercise 4 · Rewrite It: Comparative Sentences

▸ Read each sentence.

▸ Rewrite the sentence to complete the comparison.

▸ Underline each of the words used to create the comparison.

1. The poem "The Raven" is better known.

   _____

   _____

2. Some verses are not as long.

   _____

   _____

3. I like this poem better.

   _____

   _____

4. The tapping on the window is louder now.

   _____

   _____

5. Memorizing the poem "The Raven" was more difficult.

   _____

   _____

Unit 35 · Lesson 4

Exercise 5 · Identify It: Transitional Words in Text

▸ Read each sentence of this excerpt.

▸ Locate and underline transitional words and phrases in the text.

▸ List the words on the lines below.

▸ Identify the relationship created by each transitional word and write it beside the word.

▸ Refer to the **Transitional Words and Phrases** chart in the Handbook section of the *Student Text* as needed.

---

from "Blue Gold: Earth's Liquid Asset"

Major rivers such as the Ganges, the Yellow River, the Colorado, and the Nile are now so dammed, diverted, or oversubscribed for farm irrigation or industrial use that little is left to go out to sea. This can have serious knock-on consequences. The Indus feeds huge mangrove forests but irrigation schemes in its delta are drying up and killing the mangroves. Because mangroves are major fish breeding grounds, fishing villages lose their livelihoods and people have to move to overburdened cities which are desperately short of water themselves.

Example   **Relationship**

_____

_____

_____

_____

_____

_____

_____

Exercise 6 · Six Elements of Poetry

▶ Complete this chart with information you have learned and examples from **"The Raven: A Romantic Imagination."**

Element	Definition	Examples
form	The element that defines the poem's actual structure	
thought	The element that contains the poem's message	The theme of "The Raven" seems to be that _____.
imagery	The poem's creation of mental pictures, or images, for the reader	
mood		
melody		
rhyme	A regular correspondence of sounds, especially at the ends of lines	
alliteration	The repetition of the same sounds at the beginning of words	
consonance	The repetition of consonant sounds in words	
assonance	The repetition of vowel sounds in words	
meter		Each stanza has _____ lines. The first five lines have _____ stressed syllables. The last lines have _____ stressed syllables.

Exercise 1 · Choose It: Words with Greek Combining Forms

▸ Read the words in the **Word Bank**.

Word Bank

zoology	hydrology	biophysics	zooplankton
technophobic	pyromaniac	hemicycle	technical
astronauts	biosphere	physique	bibliomaniac

▸ Read each sentence and choose a word from the **Word Bank** to complete the sentence.

▸ Use the **Morphemes for Meaning Cards** and a dictionary as needed.

▸ Identify and underline clues in the sentence that helped you select the word.

1. The _____ in Apollo 13 were disappointed when their voyage to the stars was cut short.

2. The moon's full cycle is approximately thirty days; a _____ is half of that.

3. As the class was studying _____ they learned many things about the effects of water on the earth's surface.

4. Many older people are _____; they have a morbid fear of computers and other technology.

5. Because the student loved animals, she decided to study _____ in college.

(continued)

6. I think my father is a _____ as he is obsessed with books.

7. Scientists are constantly making new discoveries about _____, the nature and growth of life.

8. The _____ could not resist his obsession with fire.

9. In the desert, scientists tried to create a _____ with a controlled life environment inside a dome.

10. The assembly of the rocket required sophisticated _____ skills and abilities.

Exercise 2 · Identify It: Transitional Words in Text

▸ Read each sentence of the excerpt below.

▸ Locate and underline each transitional word and phrase in the text.

▸ List those terms on the lines below.

▸ Identify the relationship created by each transitional word or phrase and write it beside the term.

▸ Refer to the **Transitional Words and Phrases** chart in the Handbook section of the *Student Text* as needed.

---

from "Marjory Stoneman Douglas: Knowing the River of Life"

Long crucial years went by when not enough folks took notice, particularly those in Tallahassee and Washington. Meanwhile, the Everglades went from fire to flood to drought, and more and more of its water was siphoned for new cities, subdivisions and farms.

Douglas was discouraged, but never beaten. The older she got, the stronger and more insistent her voice became. Finally in the '70s, when water woes began to jeopardize development, politicians discovered the Everglades.

And here's what they learned: A broad and avid constituency already existed, thanks to some blunt-spoken, floppy-hatted old woman who wrote a book a long time ago. Lots of people, it seemed, already cared about the Everglades. They wanted very much to save it.

So suddenly every Tom, Dick, and Gomer who ran for office in Florida was waxing lyrical about Mrs. Douglas' river of grass. In shirtsleeves they pilgrimmed to Coconut Grove for a prized private audience and, if they were lucky, a photograph.

(continued)

> Because a photograph with the famous lady herself was worth votes. This they'd figured out, these genius politicians: People really loved those Everglades. How about that?

Example   **Relationship**

_____

_____

_____

_____

_____

_____

_____

Exercise 3 · Choose It: Run-On Sentence Correction

▸ Read each run-on sentence.

▸ Read the answer choices.

▸ Choose the answer that is a correct revision of the run-on sentence.

1. Many readers like joyful, light-hearted poems, "The Raven" is not that type of poem at all.

   a. Many readers like joyful, light-hearted poems "The Raven" is not that type of a poem at all.

   b. Many readers like joyful, light-hearted poems and "The Raven" is not that type of poem at all.

   c. Many readers like joyful, light-hearted poems, but "The Raven" is not that type of poem at all.

2. The poem has a dark, mysterious quality, it has an entrancing rhythm.

   a. The poem has a dark, mysterious quality it has an entrancing rhythm.

   b. The poem has a dark, mysterious quality. It has an entrancing rhythm.

   c. Although the poem has a dark, mysterious quality because it has an entrancing rhythm.

3. The identity of Lenore is a mystery, the reader is free to imagine her identity.

   a. The identity of Lenore is a mystery; the reader is free to imagine her identity.

   b. The identity of Lenore is a mystery. the reader is free to imagine her identity.

   c. The identity of Lenore is a mystery The reader is free to imagine her identity.

4. Many people have heard of "The Raven" not many have read it carefully

   a. Many people have heard of "The Raven," although not many have read it carefully.

   b. Since many people have heard of "The Raven," but not many have read it carefully.

   c. Many people have heard of "The Raven," not many have read it carefully.

5. We read "The Raven" in class, I found it fascinating.

   a. We read "The Raven" in class I found it fascinating.

   b. We read "The Raven" in class; I found it fascinating.

   c. We read "The Raven" in class and I found it fascinating.

Exercise 1 · Spelling Pretest 2

▸ Write the word your teacher repeats.

1. _____	6. _____	11. _____
2. _____	7. _____	12. _____
3. _____	8. _____	13. _____
4. _____	9. _____	14. _____
5. _____	10. _____	15. _____

Exercise 2 · Choose It: Run-On Sentence Correction

▸ Read each run-on sentence.

▸ Read the answer choices.

▸ Circle the answer that is correctly punctuated and makes sense.

1. The team from Carl Hayden entered the expert-level competition, they would be competing against teams from top colleges.

   The team from Carl Hayden entered the expert-level competition and they would be competing against teams from top colleges.

   Although the team from Carl Hayden entered the expert-level competition because they would be competing against teams from top colleges.

   The team from Carl Hayden entered the expert-level competition; they would be competing against teams from top colleges.

2. The Carl Hayden students were willing to work hard they were eager to show they could meet this challenge.

   The Carl Hayden students were willing to work hard because they were eager to show they could meet this challenge.

   The Carl Hayden students were willing to work hard They were eager to show they could meet this challenge.

   The Carl Hayden students were willing to work hard, they were eager to show they could meet this challenge.

(continued)

Exercise 2 *(continued)* · Choose It: Run-On Sentence Correction

3. The Carl Hayden team put their robot into the water, they found that its controls did not work properly.

   The Carl Hayden team put their robot into the water they found that its controls did not work properly.

   The Carl Hayden team put their robot into the water. they found that its controls did not work properly.

   When the Carl Hayden team put their robot into the water, they found that its controls did not work properly.

4. Oscar was tired and his vision was blurred he kept at the soldering task.

   Oscar was tired, and his vision was blurred he kept at the soldering task.

   Oscar was tired and his vision was blurred, but he kept at the soldering task.

   Oscar was tired and his vision was blurred and he kept at the soldering task.

5. An expert asked the team a technical question about their laser range finder, Cristian answered it perfectly.

   An expert asked the team a technical question about their laser range finder. Cristian answered it perfectly.

   An expert asked the team a technical question about their laser range finder Cristian answered it perfectly.

   An expert asked the team a technical question about their laser range finder and Cristian answered it perfectly.

Exercise 3 · Rewrite It: Comparative Sentences

▸ Read each sentence.

▸ Rewrite the sentence to complete the comparison.

▸ Underline the comparative words.

1. Assembling the robot was more challenging.

_____

_____

2. The Carl Hayden team spent less money.

_____

_____

3. The wires in their robot were slightly thicker.

_____

_____

4. The seven underwater tasks were more difficult.

_____

_____

5. The Carl Hayden team performed better.

_____

_____

Exercise 4 · Analyze It: Persuasive Essay

▸ Read the sample student essay below with your teacher.

▸ Number the paragraphs 1–5.

▸ Label the paragraphs in the margins: **Introduction**, **Body**, and **Conclusion**.

▸ Locate the thesis statement and underline it. Label the thesis in the margin.

▸ Look at paragraphs 2 and 3. In each paragraph, underline a reason that supports the thesis. Label each reason in the margin.

▸ Look at paragraph 4. Draw boxes around two objections that the writer expects other people to have. Label each objection in the margin.

▸ Look at paragraph 5. Circle the writer's call to action. Label the call to action in the margin.

▸ Use the **Persuasive Essay Writer's Checklist** to analyze the essay.

Danger Ahead: Cell Phones and Kids

1   Sixteen-year-old Tiffany is in a hurry to get to her friend's house. She gets into her dad's car and takes off down the street. Her cell phone rings, and she takes her eyes off the road for just a minute to reach over and find it. As she does this, her

5 car changes lanes and suddenly there is a loud bang when her car crashes into another one. Tiffany's cell phone is responsible for an accident with injuries. Every kid wants a cell phone, but no parent should buy one for his or her kid because they are distracting.

10   First, cell phones are distracting when teenagers drive. The National Highway Traffic Safety Administration did a study called "Driving While Distracted" that says there are between 4000 and 8000 crashes per day that are caused by driving when distracted. A teenager is distracted when talking on a cell phone.

15 Even if the teenager keeps her eyes on the road and thinks she's paying attention to her driving, some of her attention is going to the phone conversation or the text message. She is not as aware of the traffic around her as she should be.

      Second, cell phones are distracting in other ways. Kids don't

20 want a lame cell phone with basic service. They want a cool one that can text message, take pictures, and download music. All of

(continued)

this can mean that kids don't pay attention in school or in other important activities. Kids can silently text message friends or send them pictures during class. Outside of school, kids often
25 spend hours on their cell phones, talking or texting when they should be doing homework.

Some parents will say that kids should have cell phones. They say that kids should have phones because they are convenient and help when kids aren't in a safe situation. The
30 United States Census Bureau says one out of five children between the ages of 5 and 14 has no adult supervision for some of the day. Kids like that they can check in a lot with parents if they have cell phones. Children can also use cell phones to call parents in case they are sick or have an accident or get in some
35 other kind of trouble. Kids should definitely keep in touch with parents, but there are ways to do this other than a cell phone. Kids are supposed to be in school during the day. Kids whose parents work should be in daycare or an activity after school. A teacher, principal, or coach can call the parent if the child is sick
40 or in some kind of trouble. Police inform parents of teenagers who get in car accidents.

Cell phones are too distracting, sometimes in dangerous ways like driving and talking/texting, or in inappropriate ways, like using a cell phone when in school or doing homework.
45 No parent should buy a kid a cell phone. There are enough distractions in the world. Kids don't need a cell phone as an additional one.

Exercise 1 · Using a Dictionary

▶ Turn to the **Vocabulary** section (dictionary) in the back of the *Student Text*.

▶ Find the word **autonomous** and its pronunciation.

▶ Write the diacritical markings for that word on the line in item 1 below.

▶ Use the markings to read the word aloud.

▶ Complete numbers 2–5 using the same process.

Word	Pronunciation
1. autonomous	_____
2. rudimentary	_____
3. analytical	_____
4. chivalry	_____
5. intrinsically	_____

▶ Use a classroom dictionary or an online reference source to complete numbers 6–10.

6. derivative	_____
7. exorbitant	_____
8. fidelity	_____
9. hypocrisy	_____
10. pedestrian	_____

Exercise 2 · Sentence Dictation

▸ Write the sentences that your teacher dictates.

▸ Apply spelling rules when necessary.

1. _____

   _____

2. _____

   _____

3. _____

   _____

4. _____

   _____

5. _____

   _____

Exercise 3 · Match It: Antonyms

▶ Read both columns of words.

▶ Use morphology clues to identify an antonym for each word.

▶ Draw lines to match the antonyms.

▶ Circle the morpheme clue that helped you identify the antonym.

1.	protagonist	a.	photomania
2.	fidelity	b.	immutable
3.	characteristic	c.	disequalibrium
4.	photophobia	d.	hypnophobia
5.	sensible	e.	nontechnical
6.	technical	f.	infidelity
7.	hypnomania	g.	antagonist
8.	responsible	h.	uncharactistic
9.	equilibrium	i.	irresponsible
10.	mutable	j.	insensible

Exercise 4 · Rewrite It: Sentences

▶ Work with your teacher to identify the errors in the first two sentences, and then rewrite them as a single correctly written sentence.

▶ Identify and correct errors in the remainder of the paragraph.

▶ Pay special attention to:
- Incomplete comparisons
- Pronouns without antecedents
- Overuse of simple sentences
- Absence of transitional words and phrases to provide text coherence

▶ Fill in the problem and an explanation of the revision in the chart.

---

1. They made a robot. 2. They entered it in a competition. 3. It cost less. 4. The others were built by students from universities. 5. They were surprised and impressed by their knowledge of laser technology. 6. The boys were a bit disappointed. 7. They were awarded a special prize. 8. Their attitude changed. 9. They won the design award and the technical award. 10. They were announced as the overall winners. 11. The boys must have been speechless with joy.

_____

_____

_____

_____

_____

_____

_____

_____

_____

(continued)

Unit 35 · Lesson 7

Sentence #	Trait(s)	Problem(s)	Revision

Exercise 5 · Choosing a Topic

▶ Read the following topics.

▶ Discuss each with a partner.

▶ Think about which side you would take on the issue.

▶ Then circle the topic that you feel most strongly about and about which you think you have the most to say.

1. Some parents and educators feel that students would benefit from performing community service and therefore students should be required to complete 75 hours of community service as part of their graduation requirements. Others feel that students should stick to their core curriculum and spend all their time in class studying. State your own position on the issue and give at least two reasons to support that position.

2. Your school is considering eliminating study hall from the school schedule. While this would allow you to take another class and earn additional credits, it would eliminate time to study. In a persuasive essay, either persuade the school board to eliminate study hall or keep study hall on the schedule. Include at least two reasons to support your position.

3. Your school board is thinking of establishing career-oriented clubs at your school. Through these clubs, students would spend time working with people in various professions. Identify a profession for which you think a club would be valuable. State your position on this issue, and give at least two reasons to support your position.

Unit 35 · Lesson 7

Exercise 6 · Write It: Shaping the Topic

▶ Use the activity below to generate ideas to support the position you chose.

What is your position?

_____

Who is your audience?

_____

What is your purpose for writing?

_____

Reasons to Support Your Position

1. Make a list of reasons to support your position.

   _____

   _____

   _____

2. Look at the reasons you listed in 1 above. Which is the strongest? Put an X next to the strongest reason.

Anticipated Objections

3. List at least one reason why some people may disagree with your position.

   _____

   _____

4. What could you say to convince people that the reason in 3 above is either illogical or unimportant?

   _____

Exercise 1 · Fill In: Homophones

▶ Read each homophone pair.

▶ Read the sentence.

▶ Fill in each blank with the homophone that makes sense in that place.

1. bear   bare

I could see the _____ through the _____ trees.

2. here   hear

Did you _____ that we have to return _____ to catch the bus?

3. vary   very

It is _____ important to _____ the types of food you eat.

4. lose   loose

It is easy to _____ _____ change.

5. through   threw

She _____ out the catalogs before I could sort _____ them.

Unit 35 · Lesson 8

Exercise 2 · Choose It

▸ Read each confusing triplet.

▸ Read the definition under each blank line.

▸ Choose the word that matches the definition.

▸ Write the word on the line above its definition.

1. **they're**   **their**   **there**

   _____   _____   _____
   location   they are   possessive form of **they**

2. **we're**   **were**   **where**

   _____   _____   _____
   at which place   past tense form of **be**   we are

3. **desert**   **desert**   **dessert**

   _____   _____   _____
   hot, dry, sandy region   sweet food   leave, abandon

4. **too**   **to**   **two**

   _____   _____   _____
   toward   number   also

5. **you're**   **your**   **yours**

   _____   _____   _____
   you are   belonging to you   belongs to you
                          (usually precedes a noun) (usually follows a linking
                                                    verb)

Exercise 1 · Listening for Word Parts: Greek Combining Forms

▸ Listen as your teacher reads a set of three words.

▸ Repeat the words.

▸ Listen for a Greek combining form contained in all three words.

▸ Write the Greek combining form in the space provided.

▸ Repeat this process with the remaining trios of words.

1. _____　　4. _____

2. _____　　5. _____

3. _____　　6. _____

7. _____　　8. _____

9. _____　　10. _____

Exercise 2 · Build It

▸ Read the word parts in each table.

▸ Combine two or three word parts to build words. Build as many words as you can.

▸ Record the words on the lines below the table.

▸ Check a dictionary to verify that the words you have written are real words.

1.

in	sense	access	ible	

_____ _____ _____ _____

_____ _____ _____ _____

2.

zoo	phobia	mania	pyro	photo

_____ _____ _____ _____

_____ _____ _____ _____

3.

techno	phobia	logy	logist	chrono

_____ _____ _____ _____

_____ _____ _____ _____

4.

hemi	strato	sphere	atmos	thermos

_____ _____ _____ _____

_____ _____ _____ _____

5.

tech	non	al	ly	nic

_____ _____ _____ _____

_____ _____ _____ _____

Exercise 1 · Answering Open-Ended Questions

▶ In this assessment, you will have 30 minutes to read an article and answer a question about it. Your answer must be in the form of a paragraph.

▶ Carefully read the passage and the question that follows. Think about your answer and make a quick map or outline of points to include in your paragraph. Then write your paragraph. Be sure to proofread your answer.

Aim for the Stars
By Barbara Krasner-Khait

Her father once told her, "Aim for the stars, so that you can reach the treetops, and at least you'll get off the ground." Shirley Ann Jackson, president of Rensselaer Polytechnic Institute in Troy, New York, has used these words successfully throughout her life.

Jackson has achieved a steady stream of "first." She was the first African American woman to receive a doctorate from Massachusetts Institute of Technology (MIT) in any subject. She was also one of the first two African American women to receive a doctorate in physics. She was both the first woman and the first African American to serve as chairman of the Nuclear Regulatory Commission (NRC). In 1999, she became the first African American woman to preside over a national research university. In February 2004, she became the president of the American Association for the Advancement of Science, the world's largest scientific society. She also has held senior positions in industry and research as a theoretical physicist at Bell Laboratories (now part of Lucent Technologies), and in academia as professor of theoretical physics at Rutgers University. It is no wonder that Jackson was named to the National Women's Hall of Fame in 1998 and named one of the Top 50 Women in Science in *Discover* magazine in 2002.

Her passion for science, knowledge, and achievement began by the time she was eight. "As I was growing up, I became fascinated with the notion that the physical

---

(continued)

Exercise 1 (continued) · Answering Open-Ended Questions

world around me was a world of secrets," Jackson said. She decided to enter that world. "I recall one three-year period when I was fascinated with bees," she said. "During this time, I collected and experimented on live bees of all sorts—bumblebees, yellow jackets, and wasps. I adjusted their habitats, their diets, their exposure to light and heat, all the while keeping a detailed log of my observations of their behavior." She created her own laboratory under the back porch of her house.

Her parents and her teachers encouraged her. At Roosevelt High School in Washington, D.C., she took college-level classes in math and biology and graduated as valedictorian of her class.

She arrived at MIT in 1964 and found herself alone. "I was cut out of study groups until people found out what I could do and that I was as serious as they were," Jackson said. One professor told her, "Colored girls should learn a trade." Jackson decided her trade was physics. Inspired by the Rev. Dr. Martin Luther King, Jr., she pursued graduate work at MIT. She organized the Black Student Association and increased the number of minority students at MIT from two to 57 in just one year.

At MIT and throughout her life, Jackson has found strength from her family, her church, her teachers, and her community. She has sought mentors and others from whom she could learn, believing that education multiplies options and opportunities in life.

She asks, "Why limit your possibilities in life when there is an exciting world out there waiting for your brainpower?" Heed the same advice she was given, and aim for the stars.

Question: Shirley Ann Jackson's father once told her to "aim for the stars." What is your opinion? Do you think it is important to aim high? Or do you think it is better to set goals that are easier to achieve in order to avoid disappointment? Support your answer with your own examples or evidence from the selection.

Plan your answer here:

(continued)

Exercise 1 (continued) · Answering Open-Ended Questions

Write your paragraph here:

_____

_____

_____

_____

_____

_____

_____

_____

_____

_____

_____

_____

_____

_____

Trait	Point
Ideas/Content	
Organization	
Word Choice	
Sentence Fluency	
Conventions	

Total Number Correct _____ /5

Check off the activities you complete with each lesson. Evaluate your accomplishments at the end of each lesson. Pay attention to teacher evaluations and comments.

Unit Objectives	Lesson 1 (Date:_____)	Lesson 2 (Date:_____)
STEP 1 • Identify syllable types: closed, **r**-controlled, open, final silent **e**, vowel digraph, final consonant + **le**, and diphthong. • **End-of-Book Content Mastery: Phonemic Awareness and Phonics**	❏ Review: Decoding Tools ❏ Present It: Using Decoding Tools	❏ Present It: Using Decoding Tools
STEP 2 • Read and spell multisyllable words. • Read and spell words composed of Greek combining forms. • **Progress Indicator: Test of Silent Contextual Reading Fluency** • **Progress Indicator: Test of Written Spelling-4**	❏ Exercise 1: Spelling Pretest 1	❏ Divide It: Unit Words ❏ Word Fluency 1
STEP 3 • Identify and define Greek combining forms. • Identify multiple meanings for words. • **End-of-Book Content Mastery: Vocabulary and Morphology**	❏ Unit Words ❏ Review: Synonyms and Antonyms ❏ Word Wheel ❏ Expression of the Day	❏ Exercise 1: Choose It: Words with Greek Combining Forms
STEP 4 • Identify nominative and object pronouns. • Identify correct pronoun usage in compounds. • Identify adverbial, adjectival, and noun clauses. • Identify transitional words and phrases used for text cohesion. • Identify and correct run-on sentences. • Identify correct punctuation use. • **End-of-Book Content Mastery: Grammar and Usage**	❏ Review: Adverbial, Adjectival, and Noun Clauses ❏ Exercise 2: Identify It: Adverbial, Adjectival, and Noun Clauses ❏ Review: Run-On Sentences ❏ Exercise 3: Choose It: Run-On Sentence Correction	❏ Review: Nominative and Object Pronouns ❏ Exercise 2: Choose It: Subject Pronoun or Object Pronoun
STEP 5 • Use text features, such as tables and graphs, to understand informational text. • Use context-based strategies to define words. • Identify, understand, and answer questions that use different types of signal words. • Identify the elements of drama. • **Progress Indicator: _LANGUAGE!_ Reading Scale**	❏ Independent Text: **"Brilliance Through Time and Space"**	❏ Passage Fluency
STEP 6 • Write responses to questions using their signal words. • Edit and revise writing using a checklist based on the Six Traits of Effective Writing. • Develop an informal outline to prepare to write a personal essay. • Write a personal essay. • Apply a genre-specific Writer's Checklist to revise and edit a personal essay. • **Progress Indicator: Writing**	❏ Exercise 4: Answer It: Using Signal Words ❏ Exercise 5: Answer It: Using Diagrams	❏ Exercise 3: How To: Read an Application ❏ Exercise 4: Write It: Complete an Application ❏ Exercise 5: Revise It: Using the Six Traits
Self-Evaluation (5 is the highest) **Effort** = I produced my best work. **Participation** = I was actively involved in tasks. **Independence** = I worked on my own.	Effort: 1 2 3 4 5 Participation: 1 2 3 4 5 Independence: 1 2 3 4 5	Effort: 1 2 3 4 5 Participation: 1 2 3 4 5 Independence: 1 2 3 4 5
Teacher Evaluation	Effort: 1 2 3 4 5 Participation: 1 2 3 4 5 Independence: 1 2 3 4 5	Effort: 1 2 3 4 5 Participation: 1 2 3 4 5 Independence: 1 2 3 4 5

Lesson 3 (Date:_____)	Lesson 4 (Date:_____)	Lesson 5 (Date:_____)
❏ Present It: Using Decoding Tools	❏ Present It: Using Decoding Tools	❏ Present It: Using Decoding Tools
❏ Word Fluency 2 ❏ Instructional Text: **"Sequoyah: Brilliant Code-Maker"** Text Connection 11	❏ Exercise 1: Sentence Dictation: Homophones	❏ Content Mastery: Spelling Posttest 1
❏ Instructional Text: **"Sequoyah: Brilliant Code-Maker"** Text Connection 11 ❏ Write It: Journal Entry	❏ Exercise 2: Choose It: Words with Number Prefixes	❏ Exercise 1: Identify It: Greek Combining Forms
❏ Review: Transitional Words and Phrases ❏ Instructional Text: **"Sequoyah: Brilliant Code-Maker"** Text Connection 11	❏ Review: Punctuation ❏ Exercise 3: Choose It: Correct Punctuation	❏ Review: Text Cohesion ❏ Exercise 2: Rewrite It: Sentences with Transitional Words and Phrases
❏ Instructional Text: **"Sequoyah: Brilliant Code-Maker"**	❏ Instructional Text: **"Sequoyah: Brilliant Code-Maker"** ❏ Review: Main Ideas and Details Text Connection 11	❏ Answer It: Using Signal Words
❏ Introduce: Personal Essay Writer's Checklist ❏ Exercise 1: Analyze It: Personal Essay	❏ Analyze It: Structure of Body Paragraphs	❏ Review: Ways to Introduce a Topic
Effort: 1 2 3 4 5 **Participation:** 1 2 3 4 5 **Independence:** 1 2 3 4 5	**Effort:** 1 2 3 4 5 **Participation:** 1 2 3 4 5 **Independence:** 1 2 3 4 5	**Effort:** 1 2 3 4 5 **Participation:** 1 2 3 4 5 **Independence:** 1 2 3 4 5
Effort: 1 2 3 4 5 **Participation:** 1 2 3 4 5 **Independence:** 1 2 3 4 5	**Effort:** 1 2 3 4 5 **Participation:** 1 2 3 4 5 **Independence:** 1 2 3 4 5	**Effort:** 1 2 3 4 5 **Participation:** 1 2 3 4 5 **Independence:** 1 2 3 4 5

Check off the activities you complete with each lesson. Evaluate your accomplishments at the end of each lesson. Pay attention to teacher evaluations and comments.

	Unit Objectives	Lesson 6 (Date:_____)	Lesson 7 (Date:_____)
STEP 1	• Identify syllable types: closed, **r**-controlled, open, final silent **e**, vowel digraph, final consonant + **le**, and diphthong. • **End-of-Book Content Mastery: Phonemic Awareness and Phonics**	❏ Present It: Decoding Tools	❏ Exercise 1: Using a Dictionary: Word Pronunciation
STEP 2	• Read and spell multisyllable words. • Read and spell words composed of Greek combining forms. • **Progress Indicator: Test of Silent Contextual Reading Fluency** • **Progress Indicator: Test of Written Spelling-4**	❏ Exercise 1: Spelling Pretest 2 ❏ Word Fluency 3	❏ Word Fluency 4 ❏ Exercise 2: Fill In: Homophones
STEP 3	• Identify and define Greek combining forms. • Identify multiple meanings for words. • **End-of-Book Content Mastery: Vocabulary and Morphology**	❏ Instructional Text: **"The Miracle Worker: Dawning of Brilliance"** Text Connection 12 ❏ Expression of the Day	❏ Exercise 3: Choose It ❏ Expression of the Day
STEP 4	• Identify nominative and object pronouns. • Identify correct pronoun usage in compounds. • Identify adverbial, adjectival, and noun clauses. • Identify transitional words and phrases used for text cohesion. • Identify and correct run-on sentences. • Identify correct punctuation use. • **End-of-Book Content Mastery: Grammar and Usage**	❏ Review: Quotation Marks ❏ Instructional Text: **"The Miracle Worker: Dawning of Brilliance"** Text Connection 12	❏ Review: Sentence Fragments ❏ Review: Run-On Sentences ❏ Exercise 4: Rewrite It: Sentences
STEP 5	• Use text features, such as tables and graphs, to understand informational text. • Use context-based strategies to define words. • Identify, understand, and answer questions that use different types of signal words. • Identify the elements of drama. • **Progress Indicator: *LANGUAGE!* Reading Scale**	❏ Instructional Text: **"The Miracle Worker: Dawning of Brilliance"**	❏ Take Note: **"The Miracle Worker: Dawning of Brilliance"** Text Connection 12 ❏ Comprehend It
STEP 6	• Write responses to questions using their signal words. • Edit and revise writing using a checklist based on the Six Traits of Effective Writing. • Develop an informal outline to prepare to write a personal essay. • Write a personal essay. • Apply a genre-specific Writer's Checklist to revise and edit a personal essay. • **Progress Indicator: Writing**	❏ Prepare to Write: Personal Essay	❏ Write It: Personal Essay
	Self-Evaluation (5 is the highest) **Effort** = I produced my best work. **Participation** = I was actively involved in tasks. **Independence** = I worked on my own.	**Effort:** 1 2 3 4 5 **Participation:** 1 2 3 4 5 **Independence:** 1 2 3 4 5	**Effort:** 1 2 3 4 5 **Participation:** 1 2 3 4 5 **Independence:** 1 2 3 4 5
	Teacher Evaluation	**Effort:** 1 2 3 4 5 **Participation:** 1 2 3 4 5 **Independence:** 1 2 3 4 5	**Effort:** 1 2 3 4 5 **Participation:** 1 2 3 4 5 **Independence:** 1 2 3 4 5

Lesson 8 (Date:_____)	**Lesson 9** (Date:_____)	**Lesson 10** (Date:_____)
❑ Exercise 1: Listening for Word Parts: Greek Combining Forms		❑ End-of-Book Content Mastery: Phonemic Awareness and Phonics
❑ Progress Indicator: Test of Silent Contextual Reading Fluency (TOSCRF)	❑ Progress Indicator: Test of Written Spelling-4	❑ Content Mastery: Spelling Posttest 2
❑ Exercise 2: Define It: Words with Greek Combining Forms		❑ End-of-Book Content Mastery: Vocabulary and Morphology
❑ Review: Grammar	❑ Exercise 1: Identify It: Usage Issues	❑ End-of-Book Content Mastery: Grammar and Usage
❑ Comprehend It: **"The Miracle Worker: Dawning of Brilliance"** ❑ Answer It: Using Signal Words		❑ Progress Indicator: *LANGUAGE!* Reading Scale (LRS)
❑ Revise It: Personal Essay	❑ Progress Indicator: Writing	
Effort: 1 2 3 4 5 **Participation:** 1 2 3 4 5 **Independence:** 1 2 3 4 5	**Effort:** 1 2 3 4 5 **Participation:** 1 2 3 4 5 **Independence:** 1 2 3 4 5	**Effort:** 1 2 3 4 5 **Participation:** 1 2 3 4 5 **Independence:** 1 2 3 4 5
Effort: 1 2 3 4 5 **Participation:** 1 2 3 4 5 **Independence:** 1 2 3 4 5	**Effort:** 1 2 3 4 5 **Participation:** 1 2 3 4 5 **Independence:** 1 2 3 4 5	**Effort:** 1 2 3 4 5 **Participation:** 1 2 3 4 5 **Independence:** 1 2 3 4 5

Exercise 1 · Spelling Pretest 1

▶ Write the word your teacher repeats.

1. _____   6. _____   11. _____

2. _____   7. _____   12. _____

3. _____   8. _____   13. _____

4. _____   9. _____   14. _____

5. _____   10. _____   15. _____

Exercise 2 · Identify It: Adverbial, Adjectival, and Noun Clauses

▶ Read each sentence.

▶ Identify and circle the word that introduces the dependent clause.

▶ Draw two lines under the dependent clause.

▶ Determine whether the dependent clause is an adverbial clause, an adjectival clause, or a noun clause.

▶ Circle the correct answer.

1. When a star burns up all its fuel, the outer layer collapses into its core.

    a. adverbial   b. adjectival   c. noun

2. That star, which has such brilliance, is not far from earth.

    a. adverbial   b. adjectival   c. noun

3. The astronomers who had followed the course of the star witnessed its final collapse and explosion.

    a. adverbial   b. adjectival   c. noun

4. Whoever studies the stars is awed by the order in the universe.

    a. adverbial   b. adjectival   c. noun

5. Although astronomers know much about the origin of stars, new discoveries are being made all the time.

    a. adverbial   b. adjectival   c. noun

Exercise 3 · Choose It: Run-On Sentence Correction

▸ Read each run-on sentence.

▸ Read the choices for how it could be rewritten.

▸ Underline the answer that is correctly punctuated and makes sense.

1. The sun is a medium-sized star, it is close to the earth.

   The sun is a medium-sized star it is close to the earth.

   The sun is a medium-sized star. It is close to the earth.

   Although the sun is a medium-sized star; however, it is close to the earth.

2. A chemical change occurs continuously at the center of a star, this produces heat and light.

   A chemical change occurs continuously at the center of a star, and this produces heat and light.

   A chemical change occurs continuously at the center of a star but this produces heat and light.

   A chemical change occurs continuously at the center of a star this produces heat and light.

3. The brightness of stars varies it is dependent on the size and distance of each from earth.

   The brightness of stars varies, it is dependent on the size and distance of each from earth.

   The brightness of stars varies. Dependent on the size and distance of each from earth.

   The brightness of stars varies; it is dependent on the size and distance of each from earth.

4. The sun is close to earth, we feel its heat.

   The sun is close to earth we feel its heat.

   Because the sun is close to earth, we feel its heat.

   The sun is close to earth. we feel its heat.

5. That massive star exhausted its fuel its outer layer collapsed.

   That massive star exhausted its fuel then its outer layer collapsed.

   That massive star, exhausted its fuel, its outer layer collapsed.

   After that massive star exhausted its fuel, its outer layer collapsed.

Exercise 4 · Answer It: Using Signal Words

▶ Use information from the selection **"Brilliance Through Time and Space"** in the *Student Text* to answer each of these questions. Write complete sentences.

1. What are stars composed of?

_____

_____

_____

_____

2. List two factors that affect a star's brilliance as seen from Earth.

_____

_____

_____

_____

3. Summarize how scientists measure distance in outer space.

_____

_____

_____

_____

(continued)

Exercise 4 *(continued)* · **Answer It: Using Signal Words**

4. Explain what causes a supernova.

_____

_____

_____

_____

_____

_____

_____

_____

5. Look at the diagram on page 183. What is the purpose of the diagram? Judge whether or not you think the diagram is effective in meeting its purpose.

_____

_____

_____

_____

Exercise 5 · Answer It: Using Diagrams

▸ Use information from the diagram in **"Brilliance Through Time and Space"** in the *Student Text* to complete the chart below.

Stars of the Big Dipper (from closest to farthest from Earth)	Approximate Distance from Earth (in light-years)
1 (closest to Earth)	
2	
3	
4	
5	
6	
7 (farthest from Earth)	

Exercise 1 · Choose It: Words with Greek Combining Forms

▸ Read the words in the **Word Bank**.

Word Bank

hydroplane	psychologist	bibliography	microscope
hydrogen	biography	perimeter	metropolis
democracy	democratic	anthropology	geopolitics

▸ Read each sentence, and then choose a word from the Word Bank to complete the sentence.

▸ Underline one or more clues in the sentence that helped you select the word.

▸ Use the **Morphemes for Meaning Cards** and a dictionary as needed.

1. The United States has a _____ form of government in which the people have power.

2. I listed all the books I had used for my research in the _____ at the end of the report.

3. I was driving too fast and my car began to _____ when it hit the water on the road.

4. The student had always been interested in different peoples and societies, so she

   decided to study _____ in college.

5. In order to see the small details better, the doctor examined the specimen under the

   _____.

6. The measured distance around an area is called the _____.

(continued)

Exercise 1 (continued) · Choose It: Words with Greek Combining Forms

7. A doctor who studies people's behavior and emotions is a _____.

8. In the large _____, a citywide emergency plan was made ready for use in case of disaster.

9. Each presidential library has at least one _____ giving the details of that president's life in writing.

10. _____ is politics that involve large parts of the earth.

Unit 36 · Lesson 2

Exercise 2 · Choose It: Subject Pronoun or Object Pronoun

▸ Read each pair of sentences and the answer choices below them.

▸ Fill in the blank in the first sentence with the correctly written phrase.

▸ Find and underline the pronoun in the second sentence.

▸ Draw an arrow from the pronoun to its antecedent in the first sentence.

1. Our teacher gave _____ a chance to look through the telescope. We found different constellations.

   a. me and Carlos   b. Carlos and me   c. Carlos and I

2. _____ are going to the planetarium. It is not far from our school.

   a. Me and her   b. I and she   c. She and I

3. _____ found the seven stars in the Big Dipper. They were shining brightly in the night sky.

   a. Oscar and she   b. Her and Oscar   c. Oscar and her

4. _____ could feel the sun's heat. We tried to find a shady place to stand.

   a. Me and my sister   b. My sister and me   c. My sister and I

5. The telescope stood between _____. It was pointed toward the planet Saturn.

   a. Julio and I   b. Julio and me   c. me and Julio

Exercise 3 · How To: Read an Application

Tips for Reading an Application

To fill out an application correctly, you must first learn to read it carefully. Here are some tips that will help you read and understand an application:

- Survey the application. Read headings, identify the different sections, and think about what kind of information is being asked for in each section.
- Read the directions. There are usually instructions for completing the application at the very beginning of the application or at the top of each section.
- Note any sections to be filled in by others. Some forms will ask for a signature, or request information to be provided by another person, such as a parent or guardian. Sometimes there are spaces you should leave blank. They will often be labeled **Do Not Write Below This Line or For Office Use Only**.
- Read the entire application.
- Look for abbreviations. Because there is not a lot of space on an application form, abbreviations such as these are often found on applications: St. (Street), Apt. (Apartment), Zip (Zip Code), and SSN (Social Security Number).

Activity Directions

▶ Look at the example application on page 208 of the *Interactive Text*.

▶ Follow each of the tips listed above as you read it.

▶ Then complete the following:

1. How many sections are there are on the application? _____

2. What parts of the application are to be completed by people other than the applicant?

   _____

3. Circle the directions for completing the application. What are you asked to mail in

   along with the completed application? _____

4. Draw a box around any abbreviations you find on the application.

5. Read the paragraph right above the signature line on the application. By signing your

   name on the line, what are you promising? _____

   _____

   _____

   _____

Exercise 4 · Write It: Complete an Application

▶ Read and complete the following application for a library card.

Oakville Public Library
Library Card Application

Photo identification and proof of address are required for all registrants. If you are 12 years of age or under, your parent/guardian must sign the application form.

PLEASE PRINT

Last Name   First Name   Middle

Mailing Address   Apt. #

City   County   State   ZIP

_____/_____/_____
Date of Birth: Month   Day   Year   Age (circle one)   0–12 years   13–17   18–64   65 and over

E-mail   Telephone 1   Telephone 2

Driver's License/Student ID

I agree to abide by library rules and to pay for any loss of, or damage to, library materials and to pay for overdue fines accumulated on this card. I understand I am responsible for notifying the library in case of loss or theft of this card. Failure to do so will result in my being held liable for materials on this card and for fines incurred on the card. I also agree to inform the library of any street address or e-mail changes or change in the status of parent/guardian.

Your Signature

Signature of Parent/Guardian (if applicant is 12 years of age or younger)

PLEASE DO NOT WRITE BELOW THIS LINE

Type: JV   YA   AD   SR   ST   BU   RC   VC   Agency _____

PID# 21223 _____   Initials _____

Exercise 5 · Revise It: Using the Six Traits

▸ Read this paragraph from a literary analysis essay.

▸ Then, review the **Persuasive Essay Writer's Checklist** on the next page.

▸ Put a check next to each item the author did correctly.

▸ For each item with no check, use the editor's marks to identify the needed revisions.

In 2004, a group of high school students from Phoenix, Arizona, one a contest. Teachers helped them build a robot that beat other robots around the country. Their story is vary inspiring. Whats more, they show the value of supporting clubs in high schools. I feel that our school, too, should go for a robotics club that participate in engineering competitions. A robotics club would give students a chance. To discover engineering as a possible career. Their are many reasons that sponsoring a robotics club would benefit our school. Also, working in teams and participating in competitions, the school would learn teamwork and bring pride to our school.

Editor's Marks

∧	add or change text
ℓ	delete text
◯→	move text
¶	new paragraph
≡	capitalize
/	lowercase
⊙	insert period
◯	check spelling or spell out word

(continued)

Exercise 5 (continued) · Revise It: Using the Six Traits

Persuasive Essay Writer's Checklist

Trait	Did I...?	Unit
Ideas and Content	❏ Clearly state my position on an issue	29
	❏ Focus the content of each paragraph on the topic	7
	❏ Include examples, evidence, and/or explanations that are logically, emotionally, or ethically compelling	29
	❏ When necessary, include recent, relevant, reliable research to validate my position	29
	❏ Create a title	20
Organization	❏ Write an introductory paragraph that captures the reader's interest and contains a clear thesis statement that serves as a "map" for my essay	29
	❏ Sequence body paragraphs logically and use transition sentences that make clear the relationship between my ideas	7
	❏ Write a concluding paragraph that restates my position and issues a call to action	29
Voice and Audience Awareness	❏ Write in a voice that is confident and reasonable*	35
	❏ Write in a tone of voice that suits my audience and my purpose for writing	35
	❏ Demonstrate that I have considered the beliefs and opinions that others might have on the topic*	29
	❏ Acknowledge one or more objections that others may make to my own position*	29
Word Choice	❏ Use words that are lively, accurate, specific to the content, and convey authority	2
	❏ Vary the words so that my writing does not sound repetitive	13
Sentence Fluency	❏ Write complete sentences	1
	❏ Expand some of my sentences by painting the subject and predicate	3, 6
	❏ Write complex sentences	28
	❏ Avoid sentence fragments	29
	❏ Avoid run-on sentences	25

Conventions	❏ Edit my work for:
	    ❏ Capitalization
	    ❏ Punctuation
	    ❏ Grammar and usage
	    ❏ Spelling
	
	For specific rules governing any of these items, refer to the Handbook section of the *Student Text*.	

Exercise 1 · Analyze It: Personal Essay

▸ Read the sample student essay below with your teacher.

▸ Number the paragraphs 1–4.

▸ Label the paragraphs in the margins **Introduction**, **Body**, and **Conclusion**.

▸ Locate the thesis statement and draw two lines under it. Label it **thesis**.

▸ Look at paragraphs 2 and 3. In each paragraph, underline a main idea that supports the thesis. Label it **transition topic sentence**. Then bracket { } the details that support that main idea. Label them **elaborations**.

How I Got Involved in Community Art

Walk into the lobby of my apartment building and you'll find a wall of portraits drawn in pencil. There is a portrait of each resident in the building—even Grouch, the pug who lives with his owner on the third floor. For the last two years, I have been drawing the residents of Parkway Apartments, where my family has lived since I was born. There is a portrait of Casey Cisneros, who owns the taquería on the corner. There is one of Anabelle, who just started kindergarten, and one of Melissa Lee, who takes care of senior citizens. Working on this project taught me that not only am I a talented artist, but also that I can use my artistic talents to bring people together.

I always liked to draw when I was younger, but I did not know how much I loved art or how skilled I was at drawing until I worked on the Parkway Apartments portraits. My portrait project began with a sad event. Mr. Jones, my neighbor, retired and then moved across the country. Mr. Jones spent his life working as a newspaper cartoonist. I love him because he taught me how to draw. He told me that art is important because it shows you a different way to see your world and the people in it. When he moved away, my mom encouraged me to hang my best portrait of Mr. Jones in the lobby for everyone to enjoy. Soon, I realized that many of my neighbors never got to know Mr. Jones. That gave me the idea to begin sketching portraits of all the residents of Parkway Apartments. I could see my drawing skills improve with each portrait I made. When people saw my pictures, they told me they were really impressed by my work.

Since I finished my project, I've learned that community art is something that artists can do professionally. Some artists work on public murals. Others design public sculptures or landscape community gardens. Community artists work with architects to design community buildings, or they help organize festivals and concerts. After high school, I plan on studying art in college. I want to improve my technical artistic skills. I also would like to study art history, a subject I know very little about. When I graduate from college, I plan on creating community art in my neighborhood. I would also like to teach other young people how to get involved.

(continued)

Exercise 1 (continued) · Analyze It: Personal Essay

To celebrate the completed portraits, we threw a small "art party" in the lobby of my building. Casey brought delicious tamales, and my mom made fresh lemonade. Everyone in the building attended! This project taught me many things. It made me want to become the best artist I can be. Also, I learned that art is a wonderful way to bring people together. Now everyone in my building knows each other. We have a community that makes us proud. I hope that one day I will be able to use my art to help others develop a deeper appreciation of their own communities.

Exercise 1 · Sentence Dictation: Homophones

▶ Write the sentences that your teacher dictates.

1. _____

_____

2. _____

_____

3. _____

_____

4. _____

_____

5. _____

_____

Unit 36 · Lesson 4

Exercise 2 · Choose It: Words with Number Prefixes

▶ Read each sentence and the answer choices below.

▶ Select the correct answer and write it in the blank.

▶ Circle the number prefix or prefixes in the word.

▶ Identify and underline clues in the sentence that helped you select the word.

▶ Use the **Morphemes for Meaning Cards** and a dictionary as references.

1. It is not often that a principal serves for a _____, but our principal now has been the head of our school for ten years.

   a. decathlon   b. decade   c. century

2. The U.S. Department of Defense has its offices in a five-sided building; that is why it

   is called the _____.

   a. Octagon   b. Hexagon   c. Pentagon

3. Three times around the track is equal to one thousand meters, or one

   _____.

   a. centimeter   b. kilometer   c. millimeter

4. The one-wheeled bike that the clown rode was a very large _____.

   a. tricycle   b. bicycle   c. unicycle

5. A space that has four sides and four angles is called a _____.

   a. triangle   b. polygon   c. quadrangle

(continued)

6. The _____ celebration in 1976 marked the two hundredth anniversary of the signing of the Declaration of Independence.

   a. Tricentennial   b. Bicentennial   c. Centennial

7. The photographer placed his camera on a three-legged stand, or

   _____ .

   a. tripod   b. pedestal   c. triangle

8. The gold dust weighed a thousand grams, or one _____ .

   a. centigram   b. milligram   c. kilogram

9. The reader's voice had only one tone; I found her _____ boring.

   a. duotone   b. monotone   c. quartet

10. _____ is a conversation between two people.

    a. monologue   b. dialog   c. digraph

Unit 36 · Lesson 4

Exercise 3 · Choose It: Correct Punctuation

▸ Read each sentence.

▸ Identify and circle each punctuation element used.

▸ Select a reason for its use from the menu of options, and write the number over the circled punctuation mark.

Menu of Options for Punctuation Marks

1. A period, question mark, or exclamation mark to indicate the end of a sentence
2. A comma to separate a clause or phrase from the rest of the sentence
3. A comma to separate two items in a series
4. A comma to separate an appositive from the rest of a sentence
5. A comma to separate dialog from the rest of a sentence
6. A quotation mark to indicate exact words spoken
7. A colon to introduce a list

---

1. The teacher asked, "Which of the following systems do you think is most efficient: alphabetic, syllabic, or hieroglyphic?"

2. When pictographs did not work, Sequoyah turned to symbols to represent words.

3. As they had never used written language, the tribal leaders did not believe their words could be recorded this way.

4. His daughter entered the tent and asked, "Would you like me to read this message?"

5. In developing his language, Sequoyah used symbols similar to those in the Roman, Greek, and Hebrew alphabets.

Exercise 1 · Identify It: Greek Combining Forms

▸ Read each sentence.

▸ Underline each word that contains a Greek combining form you have studied.

▸ Write the word on the line and circle each Greek combining form in it.

▸ Give the meaning of each combining form, using the **Morphemes for Meaning Cards** as a reference.

1. Without stopping to think about it, you automatically, rapidly, and fluently associate the symbols you see with the phonemes those sounds represent.

   _____

   _____

2. His people's language had been spoken for millennia.

   _____

   _____

3. At first, Sequoyah set out to devise a set of pictographs.

   _____

   _____

4. A long-standing theory of left hemispheric damage has found support in these imaging studies.

   _____

   _____

5. The speed of light is about 186,000 miles (300,000 kilometers) per second.

   _____

   _____

Unit 36 · Lesson 5

Exercise 2 · Rewrite It: Sentences with Transitional Words and Phrases

▸ Combine each pair of sentences to create one sentence with the designated relationship.

▸ Refer to the **Transitional Words and Phrases** chart in the Handbook section of the *Student Text* as needed.

Note: There is more than one way to combine each pair of sentences.

1. Combine these sentences to show a **time sequence** relationship.

   Sequoyah tried developing a written language using pictographs. Sequoyah tried assigning symbols to every sound.

   _____

   _____

   _____

   _____

2. Combine these sentences to show a **contrast** relationship.

   Sequoyah's symbols were not easy to memorize. Thousands of Cherokees studied them and learned to read their language

   _____

   _____

   _____

   _____

3. Combine these sentences to show an **addition** relationship.

   Some symbols resembled letters in the Roman alphabet. Other symbols resembled letters in the Greek alphabet.

   _____

   _____

   _____

   _____

(continued)

Exercise 2 (continued) · Rewrite It: Sentences with Transitional Words and Phrases

4. Combine these sentences to show an **example** relationship.

   Many alphabets use letters that represent phonemes. Letters in the Greek, Roman, Hebrew, and Cyrillic alphabets represent phonemes.

   _____

   _____

   _____

   _____

5. Combine these sentences to show a **cause-effect** relationship.

   Sequoyah's written language was effective. It became popular and is still used today.

   _____

   _____

   _____

   _____

Exercise 1 · Spelling Pretest 2

▸ Write the word your teacher repeats.

1. _____   6. _____   11. _____

2. _____   7. _____   12. _____

3. _____   8. _____   13. _____

4. _____   9. _____   14. _____

5. _____   10. _____   15. _____

Exercise 1 · Using a Dictionary

▸ Turn to the **Vocabulary** section (dictionary) of the *Student Text*.

▸ Find the word **commodity** and its pronunciation.

▸ Write the diacritical markings for that word on the line in item 1 below.

▸ Use the markings to read the word aloud.

▸ Complete numbers 2–5 using the same process.

Word	Pronunciation
1. commodity	_____
2. entrepreneur	_____
3. audible	_____
4. renowned	_____
5. juxtaposition	_____

▸ Use a classroom dictionary or online reference source to complete numbers 6–10.

6. mischievous	_____
7. requisite	_____
8. miser	_____
9. prevalent	_____
10. prodigious	_____

Exercise 2 · Fill In: Homophones

▶ Read each homophone pair.

▶ Read the sentence.

▶ Fill in each blank with the homophone that makes sense in that place.

1. **berry**   **bury**

   I like to _____ each _____ in corn flakes.

2. **eight**   **ate**

   She _____ _____ pieces of pizza!

3. **pole**   **poll**

   The sign on the telephone _____ said the _____, or voting place, closes at nine.

4. **tolled**   **told**

   The bell _____ at noon, as I _____ you it would.

5. **roll**   **role**

   I played the _____ of a rock and _____ star.

6. **side**   **sighed**

   We _____ with relief when the judge took our _____.

7. **right**   **write**

   I _____ with my _____ hand.

8. **knot**   **not**

   I am _____ able to tie a square _____.

9. **wrote**   **rote**

   I _____ the words by _____.

10. **night**   **knight**

    The _____ traveled through the _____ to reach the castle.

Exercise 3 · Choose It

▸ Read each confusing set of triplets.

▸ Read the definition under each blank line.

▸ Choose the word that matches the definition.

▸ Write the word on the line above its definition.

1. **buy**   **by**   **bye**

   _____   _____   _____

   near   to purchase   farewell

2. **sight**   **site**   **cite**

   _____   _____   _____

   to quote or refer to   ability to see   a place or setting

3. **weight**   **wait**   **weigh**

   _____   _____   _____

   to stay or remain   unit of measure   to determine the mass

4. **ring**   **wring**   **rung**

   _____   _____   _____

   to twist or squeeze   a chime   past tense of **ring**

5. **knew**   **know**   **no**

   _____   _____   _____

   to be acquainted with   past tense of **know**   a negative word

Exercise 4 · Rewrite It: Sentences

▸ Read the paragraph.

▸ Do the first sentence with your teacher.

▸ Identify and correct errors in each remaining sentence or fragment in the paragraph.

▸ Pay special attention to:
Correcting run-on sentences and sentence fragments
Using correct pronoun forms
Correcting punctuation

▸ Fill in the problem and an explanation of the revision in the chart.

---

1. Helen Keller became ill, she lost her ability to see and hear at 19 months.

2. Helen's parents were kind to her, they were not able to teach her to behave. 3. Annie Sullivan was hired. 4. To work with Helen. 5. She was only twenty, she was an exceptional teacher. 6. Annie eventually taught she the meanings of words. 7. By spelling them into her hands. 8. Helens first word was water. 9. She had a brilliant mind. 10. She learned to read and write she went on to college.

_____

_____

_____

_____

_____

_____

_____

_____

(continued)

Exercise 4 (continued) · Rewrite It: Sentences

Sentence #	Trait(s)	Problem(s)	Revision

Exercise 1 · Listening for Word Parts: Greek Combining Forms

▶ Listen as your teacher reads each set of three words.

▶ Repeat the words.

▶ Listen for a Greek combining form contained in all three words.

▶ Write the Greek combining form in the space provided.

▶ Repeat this process with the remaining sets of words.

1. _____   6. _____

2. _____   7. _____

3. _____   8. _____

4. _____   9. _____

5. _____   10. _____

Exercise 2 · Define It: Words with Greek Combining Forms

▶ Read each word.

▶ Circle each word part in it.

▶ Use what you know about the meanings of the word parts in this word to select the correct meaning of the word.

▶ Refer to the **Morphemes for Meaning Cards** and a dictionary as references as needed.

1. dermatologist
   a. a person who demolishes things
   b. the study of the earth
   c. a person who studies the skin

2. demographer
   a. a written demonstration
   b. a person who studies statistics of populations
   c. a picture of people

3. hydrophobia
   a. a fear of heights
   b. a fire hydrant
   c. a disease whose victims appear to fear water

4. chronometer
   a. an instrument to measure time
   b. a color chart
   c. a parking meter

5. polygon
   a. frequent departures
   b. a many-angled figure
   c. a type of gown

Exercise 1 · Identify It: Usage Issues

▶ Read each sentence, identify the usage error, and circle the answer.

▶ Rewrite the sentence to correct the error.

1. Captain Keller did not want no one to contradict him.

   a. sentence fragment   b. double negative   c. inappropriate use of passive voice

   _____

   _____

2. While working with Annie, great gains were made by Helen.

   a. run-on sentence   b. inappropriate use of passive voice   c. dangling participle

   _____

   _____

3. James sat and watched Helen's outburst, he thought she had reverted to her old behavior.

   a. run-on sentence   b. sentence fragment   c. inappropriate use of passive voice

   _____

   _____

4. Running out of the pump, Annie held Helen's hand under the water.

   a. run-on sentence   b. sentence fragment   c. dangling participle

   _____

   _____

5. Listening in amazement as Helen spoke her first word.

   a. run-on sentence   b. sentence fragment   c. inappropriate use of passive voice

   _____

   _____

Text Connections

Dear Rosita

by Nash Candelaria

Dear Rose,

See, I remember to call you Rose instead of Rosita. Now that you left New Mexico to go to that Eastern university I guess you need a name that fits. So I'll write Rose from now
5 on. Tho your old papá will always think of you as his Rosita.

Mamá says hi. Says now she wished she had gone to school so she could write to you. Except times were hard then. She had to go to work almost as soon as she learned to walk. But she's glad times are better now and *you* can go.
10 The first one in the family to go to college. She's very proud of you. With your scholarship [1] and everything. She shake her fist and say, "Show 'em, Rosie. Show 'em what kind of stuff Sandoval women are made of."

Sometimes at night I catch her leaning on the adobe
15 wall staring out the window with tears in her eyes. "Where's Massachusetts?" she says. "Do the pilgrims still live there? And how about the madam on the boat?" she say. "The *Mayflower*. Mrs. González told me about that. That's not very nice."
20 I tell her not to worry. You're not going on any boat. You're at the university.

Your little brothers and sisters say hello and send you kisses. They say to send them a souvaneer from back East. They ask, "Is your university in one of those tall buildings
25 like on TV? Do the people live in those tall buildings too? Where do they keep the children and the goats? (Hah!) And how can you get any sunshine if you're always indoors and there are no fields?"

The kids have been very good since you've been gone. The
30 corn crop was so big that they worked extra hard this year.

---

[1] **scholarship:** money awarded for educational purposes

(continued)

Preview the Text

Read the highlighted words. Write the words you cannot pronounce in the margin or on a self-stick note. Circle words that you can't define.

Comprehend It

How do Rosita's parents feel about her going away to college?

_____

_____

_____

_____

_____

_____

_____

Text Connection 1 (continued)

Comprehend It

Using your own words, explain the mistake the postal worker made.

_____

_____

_____

_____

_____

Take Note

Read lines 51–61. Underline details that show what Rosita's life is like in college.

Panchito picked more than anybody. Almost as much as a man. And he sold at our stand all by himself when I had to take Mamá to the doctor.

Well, that's all for now. I got to go to the corral and feed
35 the animals.

> Love,
> Papá

Dear Rose,

We receive your letter. We think it very funny that the
40 woman at the university post office said you had to pay extra
to send T-shirts because she didn't think New Mexico was
in the United States. At least I think it funny. Mamá got
mad. "What kind of dumb university is that where they don't
know their states?" she say. "How they are going to teach our
45 daughter anything?"

Panchito's teacher say there is a magazine here called
New Mexico. The state prints it. Every month there is a page
called "One of Our Fifty Is Missing." It tells about other
dumb people who don't know where New Mexico is. They
50 think it Old Mexico which is another country.

The kids are crazy for the T-shirts with the university
name on the front. Everybody at their school is jealous [2].
Sometimes they play like they go to university like their big
sister. It must cost a lot to buy eight T-shirts. I know you have
55 this job in the Affirmative Action [3] office at school. But you
say you have to read six hours a day for your homework. So
either you can't work too much and earn money. Or you don't
sleep enough which is not healthy. Or those smart professors
found how to stretch the day to 28 hours. Anyway, there was
60 lots of corn this year. We earned a little extra so I am sending
you a money order to help with the T-shirts.

How was your Thanksgiving there in the land of the
pilgrims? Around here the Indians don't eat much turkey

---

[2] **jealous:** envious

[3] **affirmative action:** policies for improving the employment and educational opportunities of minorities

(continued)

but corn and chile and frijoles[a] like us. Or cabrito. There
65 is nothing so good as bar-b-q goat. But we roasted some
chickens this year. And the corn was so sweet and so tender.

I am so sorry you can't come home for Xmas. It will be
the first time ever we won't be all together. We'll hang out
your stocking and save it for you when you come home next
70 summer. Santa won't forget his Rose.

Well, time to open the sluice[4] gate to the acequia[b]. It has
been dry so we need to fill the ditch with more water from
the Río Grande.

                                    Love,
75   Papá

Comprehend It

Read lines 77–86. Make an inference about what Rosita may have told her father in her last letter.

_____

_____

_____

_____

_____

Find It: Use of Capital Letters

• Reread the second letter.

• Find an example of each of the following uses of capital letters.

• Write each one on the appropriate line.

1. A person's name: _____

2. A specific name of a place: _____

3. A title: _____

4. The greeting of a letter: _____

5. The salutation of a letter: _____

Dear Rose,

What's all this about I'm not supposed to eat meat? All
my life I was too poor to buy much meat. I mean like round
steak or roast. Now that things are better and we can afford
80 beef, there's all this worry about your heart. Don't eat meat!
You say we suppose to eat fish. But tell me. You grew up

---

[4] **sluice:** an artificial channel or canal for moving water, with a gate to regulate the flow

[a] **frijoles:** beans

[b] **acequia:** an irrigation canal

(continued)

here in Los Rafas. You know it's desert. Where you going
to get fish in the desert? Sure, we could go up north in the
mountains and fish for trout. It's only an hour by car. But
85 who has the time even if your car is running OK? There's too
much to do on our little plot of ground.

Not only that. Now I hear that beans are *good* for you.
Lots of protein. Very high fiber too. So you can go to the
excusado^c regular. Any fool could have told you that. Then
90 some smart doctor says that chile is good for the blood.
Cleans out the fat or something. Another smarty doctor
says we need more exercise. More exercise? I bet he never
did anything harder than push pills. Just send him down to
the country to work the land for a summer. He'll know what
95 exercise is. Who needs to go out and run on purpose? Or
sweat and breathe hard on purpose? Man, that's the way we
live—sweating and breathing hard.

So here I am. Practically an old man who spent his life on
the land, one of the working poor. I've had a little luck so I
100 can enjoy my old age, and now what? They tell me: Don't give
up chile and beans for steak and potatoes. Continue to work
like a dog in the fields. Do all that and you live longer. Maybe
not happier but longer. Like the Bible says, if you wait long
enough the seasons change and everything comes back to
105 you. Who needs it?

Anyway, I got to go out in the field and sweat again so I
can live to a ripe old age.

Love,
Papá

110 Dear Rose,

What's all this about bail⁵? I didn't tell your mamá
because I knew it would break her heart. Not only are you the
first in the family to go to college, you are the first to need bail.

I don't understand why anybody has to take over the
115 university president's office. Any fool knows that those big
shots got the cops on their side. The little guy hasn't got

---

⁵ **bail:** money left with a court of law when a person awaiting trial
is released from jail

^c **excusado:** a bathroom

(continued)

Text Connection 1 (continued)

a chance. If the cops aren't enough, they can call out the marines. Or—like Panchito say—they nuke 'em.

Anyway, it didn't make the newspapers here so you don't
120 have to worry about that. Nobody knows but me, and I won't tell even if they cut my tongue off.

I know I'm not an educated man. But there's some things I learn just by living. And one of them is never bite the hand that feed you. I mean I like the scholarships and things.
125 Another is, you can't fight city hall. Which means don't take over the president's office.

Sure. I know that you feel that there aren't enough Chicano and Black and Chinese professors. Everybody like to see some of their own kind make good. Have a professor who
130 understands what you come from and how hard you worked for it. How much you want a chance like everybody else. But Rose, you got to do things the right way.

What you do now, Rose, is make an appointment with the president. Go see him and have a nice talk. Be honest
135 with him. If he is the right kind of guy, he will understand. If he don't understand, do what we did in the fields when a skinflint farmer didn't pay a living wage. The crops, they just come up once a year. You don't pick at the right time—boom! There goes every red cent you planned to harvest. Well,
140 colleges are like that too. Only their crops are students. They're student farmers. And if a farm don't turn out crops, they don't make money. If they don't make money, they get a new farmer or the banks take over the farm. I don't want to sound like no revolutionary, but that's how I see it.
145 It worked in the fields. Maybe it will work in the colleges. It's something you can do without staying arrested. Which means you don't have to pay bail.

Anyway, the goats are making a racket in the corral. They say they go on strike if I don't feed them. Everybody wants
150 something from somebody. That's all for now.

Love,

Papá

Take Note

Read lines 114–132. Underline clues that suggest why Rosita needs bail.

Comprehend It

How does Rosita's father react to the news that she needs bail?

_____

_____

_____

_____

Comprehend It

Read lines 133–147. Rosita's father makes a comparison between farm workers and students. Describe the approach he suggests students take when they want to get the president to listen to them.

_____

_____

_____

_____

_____

_____

(continued)

Text Connection 1 (continued)

Comprehend It

Why do you think Rosita's father writes that lots of good people have been put in jail?

_____

_____

_____

_____

Comprehend It

What message might Rosita's father be sending her by telling the story of Dolores the cow?

_____

_____

_____

_____

_____

Dear Rose,

I been thinking about bail since the last time I wrote.
155 Lots of good people been put in jail. Jesus. That Indian man
Gandhi. I don't remember who else, but lots of good people. I
don't know if George Washington ever got arrested, but I bet
if those red coats had got him they'd have locked him up for
life plus a hundred years.

160   What reminded me was cleaning out the old shed. You
didn't know but we going to make a room from it and cut a
door into the rest of the house. We need another room to
separate the boys and the girls. They getting older, and it's
the right thing to have a room for the boys and another for
165 the girls.

Anyway, I found these old newspapers. Some of them go
way back. This was before your time, and I'm sure you don't
remember it. But there was that big land problem up north in
Tierra Amarilla maybe 20, 25 years ago. The people they got
170 into a—I don't know what you call it. Maybe a war. With the
government. About who the land belong to and who can do
what to it.

Anyway. There on the front page is this big picture. This
paisano with his cow. The cow is staring over the barb wire
175 fence. And the farmer, he got tears in his eyes and he say:
"My cow, she arrested." Alongside the cow—her name was
Dolores—was this government chota[d], shiny badge, holster
with a gun and all, holding a rope. The other end was around
Dolores's neck.

180   Seems like Dolores, she's a naughty girl. She go through
a broken place in the fence into this field that say "U.S.
Government. No Trespassing." But Dolores, she can't read.
So this cop, he tie a rope around her neck and arrest her. I
wonder if he read her her rights? And the poor old farmer, he
185 has to pay the bail. Or maybe it was a fine. Anyway, I wonder
if they really put that cow in a cell? Sounds pretty silly to me.

_____

[d] **chota:** slang for "police"

(continued)

Specially since the fence was broke, and how's a cow supposed to know? Just one of God's dumb creatures.

So I guess you are not in bad company. Jesus. Gandhi.
190   Maybe George Washington. And Dolores the cow. Only don't let it happen again if you can help it. Someday somebody may not have bail.

That's all for now. I promised to take Mamá to church tonight. We say a prayer for you.

195   Love,
                                  Papá

Dear Rose,

Oh, how sad we all are that you may stay and work back East this summer. It seems so long since we see you. Tina
200   start to cry, and then your mamá. Pretty soon everybody. So it was like a flood in the house. The linoleum in the front room had tear spots all over. We hardly talked. Just worked. At supper we could not look in each other's eyes. Then your next letter came that said you were coming home. Everybody
205   start to smile and laugh again.

Don't worry about the money. If you don't find a job here, we will help you. Money isn't everything. I mean you need enough to get along. But whether you eat beans or steak don't matter as long as you eat. (And I learn from you this year that
210   beans are better.) Money you can always earn. But not seeing your friends, not seeing your family. That's something if you miss, you never get back. Your little brothers and sisters grow so much since you went away. You'd hardly know them. Now Panchito, he say he going to college too. They all so proud of
215   their big sister and want so much to see you.

Your mamá have this fear. She say, "How am I going to talk to her? I never talk to no college person except when I go to the doctor. What am I going to say? What if she's changed? Is she going to be ashamed of her mamá who can't
220   even write her a letter? Oh, I'm so worried."

Take Note

Underline a clue that suggests why Rosita was considering staying in Massachusetts for the summer.

Comprehend It

What is Rosita's mother worried about?

_____

_____

_____

_____

_____

(continued)

Unit 31

Take Note

Underline lines 229–231. Rosita's father is making a reference to a famous Greek myth. Even if you don't know the story told in that myth, try to infer what Papá is trying to tell Rosita.

Comprehend It

Identify this form of writing. What is the author's purpose?

_____

_____

_____

_____

_____

_____

_____

_____

_____

Worry, worry, worry. She worry you don't come. She worry you *do* come. I just say, "Relax. Just tell her you love her. She the same daughter you used to nurse and change diapers and all that. She still learn a thing or two from you.
225 So don't worry. It'll be fine. Besides. I bet she can't cook like you. Not yet."

But the truth is, I worry a little too. We are so proud of you. And want you not to be ashamed of us poor country folks. You are going up in the world. Only like the old story:
230 Don't get too close to the sun or it melt your wings and down you go.

Look for us at the station when your bus comes in. Panchito nags [6] his sisters and brothers to wash and iron their university T-shirts. That's so you can tell who they are
235 because they grown so much since you gone. They think you be a grown lady like a princess in the movies now that you been in the university one year. They are so excited.

God love you and speed you home safely. We are so excited our hearts will burst. So hurry home. We can hardly
240 wait to see you next week.

> With love from all,
> Papá

Excerpted with permission from Bilingual Press/Editorial Bilingüe

---

[6] **nags:** repeatedly reminds someone to do something; pesters

The Tell-Tale Heart

by Edgar Allan Poe

Who Was Edgar Allan Poe?

1 Edgar Allan Poe is dead. He died in Baltimore the day before yesterday. This announcement will startle many, but few will be grieved by it. The poet was known, personally or by reputation, in all this country; he had readers in England, and

5 in several of the states of Continental Europe; but he had few or no friends; and the regrets for his death will be suggested principally by the consideration that in him literary art has lost one of its most brilliant but erratic stars.
(From the Evening Edition of the *New York Tribune*,

10 October 9, 1849.)

These are the words of Rufus Wilmot Griswold, a literary rival and secret enemy of Poe. After Poe's death, he wrote a memoir about Poe that tied Poe's fascination with horror and mystery stories to claims that Poe was an alcoholic, a drug

15 *addict, and possibly insane. This was the only biography of Poe's life for over thirty years. It caused readers to focus on the events of Poe's life as an explanation for his work. Today, we realize that Poe's work was influenced by much more than the events of his life.*

20 *So who was Edgar Allan Poe (1809–1849)? Poe was an American poet, fiction writer, and literary critic. He wrote during a time known as the Romantic period, a literary and artistic movement of the late eighteenth and nineteenth centuries. Romantic literature is characterized by an interest*

25 *in nature and a fascination with an idealized past of mystery and adventure. It also focuses on an individual's imagination and powerful emotions. Two of the poets we study in Unit 31, Emily Dickinson and William Wordsworth, are also considered Romantic poets.*

Comprehend It

Identify and describe the literary and artistic period during which Poe wrote.

_____

_____

_____

_____

_____

_____

_____

_____

_____

_____

(continued)

Comprehend It

What did Poe's stories focus on?

_____

_____

_____

_____

Comprehend It

How is Poe's writing viewed today?

_____

_____

_____

_____

_____

_____

30   *Influenced by the Romantic movement, Poe wrote poems and short stories that revealed the dark inner thoughts and feelings of his characters. The publication of his poem, "The Raven" in 1845 earned him the respect of his peers. His stories, including "The Tell-Tale Heart," were not acclaimed during*
35 *his lifetime.*

Today, Poe is considered the father of the detective story. When we read "The Tell-Tale Heart" we can understand why. In this story, Poe reveals to us the extreme thoughts and feelings of the criminal mind. Poe is now widely regarded not
40 *just as an expert horror story writer, but a superb craftsman of the psychological thriller. During his lifetime, he worked as an editor and literary critic. Poe believed all good literature should create a unity of effect on the reader that reveals fundamental truth and deep emotion. His creative work*
45 *and literary criticism went on to influence numerous writers around the world, including poets, mystery writers, and Hollywood horror filmmakers.*

(continued)

True!— nervous [1]—very, very dreadfully nervous I had been and am; but why *will* you say that I am mad? The
50 disease had <u>sharpened</u> my senses—not destroyed—not dulled them.

Use the Clues A: Vocabulary Strategies

- Read lines 48–51. Use contrast clues and knowledge of antonyms to determine the meaning of the word **sharpened**, and put a check by the correct answer.

- **Sharpened** means:

  a) made thin for cutting

  b) made more keen

  c) destroyed

  d) made less sensitive

  Underline the contrast clues that helped you determine your answer. Circle the transition words that signal the contrast.

Above all was the sense of hearing acute [2]. I heard all things in the heaven and in the earth. I heard many things in hell. How, then, am I <u>mad</u>? Hearken! and observe how healthily—
55 how calmly I can tell you the whole story.

Use the Clues B: Vocabulary Stragegies

- Read lines 52–55. The meaning of **mad** in this context is "crazy." Identify the word or words that contrast with the word **mad** from the following list, and put a check by the correct answer.

  a) healthy

  b) sane

  c) calm

  d) all of the above

Comprehend It

The narrator assumes that his audience, or the people he is telling his story to, believe him to be mad. List the line that shows this.

_____

_____

Comprehend It

What details in the second paragraph suggest that the narrator is indeed mad? Include two quotations from the story in your response.

_____

_____

_____

_____

_____

_____

_____

[1] **nervous:** easily upset; worried and tense

[2] **acute:** highly sensitive

(continued)

Take Note

Draw a box around the event that causes the rest of the story to unfold. In the right margin, label this **initiating event**. Hint: In this case, the initiating event is simply a decision.

Comprehend It

What is the narrator's motive, or reason, for wanting to kill the old man?

_____

_____

_____

_____

_____

_____

_____

_____

It is impossible to say how first the idea entered my brain; but once <u>conceived</u>, it haunted me day and night.

> ### Use the Clues C: Vocabulary Strategies
>
> - Read lines 56–57. Use substitution clues to determine the meaning of the word **conceived**. Put a check by the correct answer.
> - In this context, **conceived** means:
>
>   a) scared
>
>   b) thought of
>
>   c) constructed
>
>   d) rejected
>
> Underline the synonym or phrase that helped you determine your answer.

Object there was none. Passion there was none. I loved the old man. He had never wronged me. He had never given me
60 insult. For his gold I had no desire. I think it was his eye! yes, it was this! One of his eyes resembled that of a vulture—a pale blue eye, with a film over it. Whenever it fell upon me, my blood ran cold; and so by degrees—very gradually—I made up my mind to take the life of the old man, and thus
65 rid myself of the eye for ever.

   Now this is the point. You fancy me mad. Madmen know nothing. But you should have seen *me*. You should have seen how wisely I proceeded—with what caution—with what foresight—with what dissimulation I went to work!
70 I was never kinder to the old man than during the whole week before I killed him. And every night, about midnight, I turned the latch of his door and opened it—oh; so gently! And then, when I had made an opening sufficient for my head, I put in a dark lantern, all closed, closed, so that no
75 light shone out, and then I thrust in my head. Oh, you would have laughed to see how cunningly I thrust it in! I moved it slowly—very, very slowly, so that I might not disturb the old man's sleep. It took me an hour to place my whole head

(continued)

within the opening so far that I could see him as he lay upon
80 his bed. Ha!—would a madman have been so wise as this?
And then, when my head was well in the room, I undid the
lantern cautiously—oh, so cautiously—cautiously (for the
hinges creaked)—I undid it just so much that a single thin
ray fell upon the vulture eye. And this I did for seven long
85 nights—every night just at midnight—but I found the eye
always closed; and so it was impossible to do the work; for
it was not the old man who vexed [3] me, but his Evil Eye.
And every morning, when the day broke, I went boldly into
the chamber, and spoke courageously to him, calling him
90 by name in a hearty tone, and inquiring how he had passed
the night. So you see he would have been a very profound
old man, indeed, to suspect that every night, just at twelve, I
looked in upon him while he slept.

Upon the eighth night I was more than usually cautious
95 in opening the door. A watch's minute hand moves more
quickly than did mine. Never before that night had I *felt* the
extent of my own powers—of my sagacity [4]. I could scarcely
contain my feelings of triumph. To think that there I was,
opening the door, little by little, and he not even to dream of
100 my secret deeds or thoughts. I fairly chuckled at the idea; and
perhaps he heard me; for he moved on the bed suddenly, as
if startled. Now you may think that I drew back—but no. His
room was as black as pitch with the thick darkness (for the
shutters were close fastened, through fear of robbers), and so
105 I knew that he could not see the opening of the door, and I
kept pushing it on steadily, steadily.

I had my head in, and was about to open the lantern,
when my thumb slipped upon the tin fastening, and the old
man sprang up in the bed, crying out—"Who's there?"
110 I kept quite still and said nothing. For a whole hour I did
not move a muscle, and in the meantime I did not hear him
lie down. He was still sitting up in the bed listening;—just
as I have done, night after night, hearkening to the death
watches in the wall.

[3] **vexed:** irritated

[4] **sagacity:** keen perception, with foresight and judgment

Comprehend It

Why does the narrator shine a lantern into the old man's room for seven nights?

_____

_____

_____

_____

_____

Take Note

Draw an X in the margin next to what the narrator does for seven nights.

(continued)

Unit 31

Comprehend It

• Why does the narrator recognize the old man's groan as a groan of terror?

_____

_____

_____

_____

• Make a generalization about the narrator based on this information.

_____

_____

_____

Find It: Nouns With Articles and Adjectives

• Read lines 94–114 to find five examples of a noun modified by an article and at least one adjective.

• Underline each of these noun phrases.

• Write each one on a line below. Answers may vary.

1. _____

2. _____

3. _____

4. _____

5. _____

115   Presently I heard a slight groan, and I knew it was the groan of mortal terror. It was not a groan of pain or of grief—oh, no!—it was the low stifled sound that arises from the bottom of the soul when overcharged with awe. I knew the sound well. Many a night, just at midnight, when all the
120 world slept, it has welled up from my own bosom, deepening, with its dreadful echo, the terrors that distracted me. I say I knew it well. I knew what the old man felt, and pitied him, although I chuckled at heart. I knew that he had been lying awake ever since the first slight noise, when he had turned
125 in the bed. His fears had been ever since growing upon him. He had been trying to fancy them causeless, but could not. He had been saying to himself—"It is nothing but the wind in the chimney—it is only a mouse crossing the floor," or "it is merely a cricket which has made a single chirp." Yes, he
130 has been trying to comfort himself with these suppositions; but he had found all in vain. *All in vain*; because Death, in approaching him, had stalked with his black shadow before him, and enveloped the victim. And it was the mournful influence of the unperceived shadow that caused him to
135 feel—although he neither saw nor heard—to *feel* the presence of my head within the room.

(continued)

Text Connection 2 (continued)

When I had a waited a long time, very patiently, without hearing him lie down, I resolved to open a little—a very, very little crevice in the lantern. So I opened it—you cannot
140 imagine how stealthily, stealthily—until, at length, a single dim ray, like the thread of the spider, shot from out the crevice and full upon the vulture eye.

It was open—wide, wide open—and I grew furious as I gazed upon it. I saw it with perfect distinctness—all a dull
145 blue, with a hideous veil over it that chilled the very marrow in my bones; but I could see nothing else of the old man's face or person: for I had directed the ray as if by instinct, precisely upon the damned spot.

And now have I not told you that what you mistake
150 for madness is but over-acuteness of the senses?—now, I say, there came to my ears a low, dull, quick sound, such as a watch makes when enveloped in cotton. I knew *that* sound well too. It was the beating of the old man's heart. It increased my fury, as the beating of a drum stimulates the
155 soldier into courage.

But even yet I refrained and kept still. I scarcely breathed. I held the lantern motionless. I tried how steadily I could maintain the ray upon the eye. Meantime the hellish tattoo of the heart increased. It grew quicker and quicker,
160 and louder and louder every instant. The old man's terror *must* have been extreme! It grew louder, I say, louder every moment!—do you mark me well? I have told you that I am nervous: so I am. And now at the dead hour of the night, amid the dreadful silence of that old house, so strange a
165 noise as this excited me to uncontrollable terror. Yet, for some minutes longer I refrained and stood still. But the beating grew louder, louder! I thought the heart must burst. And now a new anxiety seized me—the sound would be heard by a neighbor! The old man's hour had come! With a
170 loud yell, I threw open the lantern and leaped into the room. He shrieked [5] once—once only. In an instant I dragged him to the floor, and pulled the heavy bed over him. I then smiled gaily, to find the deed so far done. But, for many minutes, the

---

[5] **shrieked:** screamed loudly in a high pitch

Take Note

Draw an X in the margin next to the event that happens on the eighth night, after the narrator shines the light on the old man.

Comprehend It

According to the narrator, what is making a sound "such as a watch when enveloped in cotton"?

_____

_____

_____

_____

Take Note

Draw an X in the margin next to what happens when the narrator can no longer bear hearing the heartbeat.

(continued)

Comprehend It

What causes the police officers to come to the narrator's home?

_____

_____

_____

_____

Take Note

• Draw an X in the margin next to what the narrator does after killing the old man.

• Draw an X by the next exciting event.

175 heart beat on with a muffled sound. This, however, did not vex me; it would not be heard through the wall. At length it ceased. The old man was dead. I removed the bed and examined the corpse. Yes, he was stone, stone dead. I placed my hand upon the heart and held it there many minutes. There was no pulsation. He was stone dead. His eye would

180 trouble me no more.

If still you think me mad, you will think so no longer when I describe the wise precautions I took for the concealment of the body. The night waned, and I worked hastily, but in silence. . . .

185 I then took up three planks from the flooring of the chamber, and deposited all between the scantlings. I then replaced the boards so cleverly, so cunningly, that no human eye—not even *his*—could have detected any thing wrong. There was nothing to wash out—no stain of any kind—no

190 blood-spot whatever. I had been too wary for that. A tub had caught all—ha! ha!

When I had made an end of these labors, it was four o'clock—still dark as midnight. As the bell sounded the hour, there came a knocking at the street door. I went down

195 to open it with a light heart,—for what had I *now* to fear? There entered three men, who introduced themselves, with perfect suavity, as officers of the police. A shriek had been heard by a neighbor during the night; suspicion of foul play had been aroused; information had been lodged at the police

200 office, and they (the officers) had been deputed to search the premises.

I smiled,—for *what* had I to fear? I bade the gentlemen welcome. The shriek, I said, was my own in a dream. The old man, I mentioned, was absent in the country. I took

205 my visitors all over the house. I bade them search—search *well*. I led them, at length, to *his* chamber. I showed them his treasures, secure, undisturbed. In the enthusiasm of my confidence, I brought chairs into the room, and desired them *here* to rest from their fatigues, while I myself, in the wild

210 audacity of my perfect triumph, placed my own seat upon the very spot beneath which reposed the corpse of the victim.

(continued)

The officers were satisfied. My *manner* had convinced them. I was singularly at ease. They sat, and while I answered cheerily, they chatted familiar things. But, ere long, I felt
215 myself getting pale and wished them gone. My head ached, and I fancied a ringing in my ears: but still they sat and still chatted. The ringing became more distinct:—it continued and became more distinct: I talked more freely to get rid of the feeling: but it continued and gained definitiveness—until,
220 at length, I found that the noise was *not* within my ears.

No doubt I now grew *very* pale;—but I talked more fluently, and with a heightened voice. Yet the sound increased—and what could I do? It was *a low, dull, quick sound—much such a sound as a watch makes when enveloped*
225 *in cotton.* I gasped for breath—and yet the officers heard it not. I talked more quickly—more vehemently; but the noise steadily increased. I arose and argued about trifles, in a high key and with violent gesticulations, but the noise steadily increased. Why *would* they not be gone? I paced the floor
230 to and fro with heavy strides, as if excited to fury by the observation of the men—but the noise steadily increased. Oh God! what *could* I do? I foamed—I raved—I swore! I swung the chair upon which I had been sitting, and grated it upon the boards, but the noise arose over all and continually
235 increased. It grew louder—louder—*louder*! And still the men chatted pleasantly, and smiled. Was it possible they heard not? Almighty God!—no, no! They heard!—they suspected!— they *knew*!—they were making a mockery of my horror!— this I thought, and this I think. But any thing was better than
240 this agony! Any thing was more tolerable than this derision! I could bear those hypocritical smiles no longer! I felt that I must scream or die!—and now—again!—hark! louder! louder! louder! *louder*!

"Villains!" I shrieked, " dissemble [6] no more! I admit the
245 deed!—tear up the planks!—here, here!—it is the beating of his hideous heart!"

---

[6] **dissemble:** to hide the truth, pretend

Comprehend It

Read the description set in italics in lines 223–225. Why do you think Poe chose to put the description in lines 223–225 in italics?

_____

_____

_____

_____

_____

Take Note

• Draw an X in the margin next to the description of the sound the narrator hears.

• Draw a box around the confession the narrator makes. Label this **climax**.

Comprehend It

Identify this form of writing. What is the author's purpose?

_____

_____

_____

_____

_____

_____

Preview the Text

Read the highlighted words. Write the words you cannot pronounce in the margin or on a self-stick note. Circle words that you can't define.

Comprehend It

Reread lines 18–28. Then complete this sentence:

Even though Robert Frost wrote short poems about simple things,

_____

_____

_____

Nothing Gold Can Stay

Who Was Robert Frost?

"My definition of poetry (if I were forced to give one) would be this: words that become deeds."—Robert Frost

For the American poet Robert Frost (1874–1963), the sounds of words—especially the sounds of the plain and
5 *simple language that he had heard growing up in New England—had everything to do with creating meaning in his poetry. He wanted to write poems that sounded like people talking. He worked to make his poems sound real and be meaningful—not just to another poet, critic, or scholar, but to*
10 *the average person. And he succeeded very well. In the latter[1] part of his career, audiences packed lecture halls to hear "the gentle-farmer" poet read his poetry. In his career, Frost won four Pulitzer Prizes and received 44 honorary degrees, a host of government tributes, and an invitation from John F.*
15 *Kennedy to read a poem at his presidential inauguration[2]. Frost is still considered one of the greatest American poets of the twentieth century.*

At first glance, Frost's poems may seem to be simple descriptions of personal experiences from everyday life in New
20 *England. Frost moved to New England when he was 11 and lived there on farms most of his life. Frost often wrote poems about common things, such as "The Woodpile," "The Oven Bird," and "The Mending Wall." However, Frost used these simple things to explore the complexities of life with what*
25 *some have called a "deep and mysterious tenderness."*

---

[1] **latter:** near the end

[2] **inauguration:** an induction into office by a formal ceremony

(continued)

Text Connection 3 (continued)

Nothing Gold Can Stay

"Nothing Gold Can Stay" is one of Frost's most famous poems and a perfect example of how Frost could condense [3] profound meaning into a few short lines of verse. The poem contains a paradox, a statement that contains a contrary
30 statement that nevertheless seems to be true. How can green be gold? When the trees in New England sprout their first leaves, do they appear to be gold instead of green? Or does Frost mean that the first green is as valuable as gold? Or is he trying to suggest that the green color of the leaves inevitably
35 will turn to gold?

NOTHING GOLD CAN STAY
by Robert Frost

Nature's first green is gold,
Her hardest hue [4] to hold.
40 Her early leaf's a flower;
But only so an hour.
Then leaf subsides [5] to leaf.
So Eden sank to grief [6],
So dawn goes down to day.
45 Nothing gold can stay.

Take Note

Reread lines 28–30. Circle the word **paradox** and underline its definition. Then define **paradox** using your own words.

_____

_____

_____

_____

[3] **condense:** to shorten; make compact
[4] **hue:** a shade of color
[5] **subsides:** lessens
[6] **grief:** profound sadness

(continued)

Take Note

1. Underline one metaphor in line 1 of the poem, and another in line 3.

2. Read line 2 of the poem. Find all the words in that line that start with the same letter. Circle that same first letter in each word of the line.

3. Repetition of the same first sound in a word is known as:

   ____ alliteration   ____ consonance

4. Draw lines connecting each pair of final words that rhyme. This pattern is known as AABBCCDD.

5. Place an accent mark over each stressed syllable in the poem. Which describes the meter of this poem?

   ____ It is regular—the lines have the same number of stresses.

   ____ It is not regular—the lines do not all have the same number of stresses.

6. Closed form poems have regular rhyme and meter, and open form poems do not. The form of this poem is:

   ____ closed   ____ open

From *The Poetry of Robert Frost*, edited by Edward Connery Lathem

Reprinted by permission of Henry Holt and Company, LLC

The Treasure of the Sierra Madre

Screenplay by John Huston from the novel by B. Traven

"I've dug in Alaska and in Canada and Colorado. I was
with the crowd in British Honduras where I made my fare
back home and almost enough over to cure me of the [gold]
fever I'd caught. I've dug in California and Australia, all
5 over the world practically. Yeah, I know what gold does to
men's souls. . . . Aw, as long as there's no find, the noble
brotherhood will last, but when the piles of gold begin to
grow, that's when the trouble starts."—Howard, the old
<u>prospector</u> from *The Treasure of the Sierra Madre*

Use the Clues A: Vocabulary Strategies

- Read lines 1–9.

- Reread the underlined word, **prospector**.

- Write the meaning of the root **spect**: _____

  _____

- Write the meaning of the suffix **-or**: _____

- Use morpheme clues and context clues to define

  prospector: _____

  _____

  _____

10   *For its dramatic portrayal of the pitfalls of human greed,*
The Treasure of the Sierra Madre endures as one of the most
popular Hollywood movies ever made. The screenplay, written
by John Huston, was based upon a 1936 novel by B. Traven,
a mysterious and <u>elusive</u> individual who wrote novels under

Comprehend It

Reread lines 1–9. Paraphrase
what Howard means. Be careful
to use your own words.

_____

_____

_____

_____

_____

_____

_____

(continued)

Text Connection 4 (continued)

Take Note

Underline lines 25–30 and lines 37–39. Use the information to predict what will happen to the three miners.

_____

_____

_____

_____

_____

_____

_____

15 *an <u>assumed</u> name and who lived <u>incognito</u> in Mexico in the 1920s. John Huston, a well-known American film director, actor, and screenwriter, won an Academy Award in 1948 for his screenplay version of the novel.*

Use the Clues B: Vocabulary Strategies

- Read lines 10–18.
- Reread the underlined words: **elusive, assumed,** and **incognito.**
- Use context clues to help you figure out the meaning of each word.
- Match the word with its definition below.
- Use a dictionary for help if needed.

    a. elusive   in disguise

    b. assumed   false or temporary, alias

    c. incognito   hard to describe

- Reread the paragraph substituting the matched words.
- Finish this sentence: B. Traven was mysterious because

_____

What question do these adverbs answer?

This classic film tells a gripping story of three men—
20 *Dobbs, Curtin, and Howard—who join forces to prospect for gold in the mountain range known as the Sierra Madre of northeastern Mexico. Dobbs and Curtin have separately traveled to Mexico in search of an opportunity to make a fortune. They meet each other during a brief stint at working*
25 *in the oilfields. Still down on their luck in Tampico, they meet Howard, an old prospector, who tells them that there is gold to be found in the Sierra Madre. There may be enough gold to make them all rich. But he also warns them that gold prospecting and the greed that comes with it can change men*
30 *and can lead to madness and even murder.*

In their eagerness for wealth, Dobbs and Curtin ignore Howard's warnings. The three men decide to pool their

(continued)

resources to buy prospecting gear, and Howard agrees to lead Dobbs and Curtin to where the gold might be. They make a

35 difficult journey through jungles, over mountains, and across deserts, but they find a remote place—home to wild animals and bandits—that is rich with gold. The scene that follows shows how prophetic [1] Howard has been about what the discovery of gold can do to friendship.

40 CAMERA PANS UP to a high mountain peak, wearing in its majesty a crown of clouds.

DISSOLVE TO:

33.   INSERT: OF A PAN
the water turning in it. CAMERA PULLS BACK to show Howard

45 panning dirt. They are near the crest of the mountain now, at the place Howard pointed to in the previous scene. Dobbs and Curtin look on at what Howard is doing, their faces sober [2] and intent.

DOBBS:

50 So that's the way the stuff looks, is it...not much different from sand...plain sand.

HOWARD:

1. Gold ain't like stones in a riverbed. 2. It don't call out to be picked up. You got to know how to recognize it. And the

55 finding ain't all. Not by a long shot. You got to know how to tickle it so it comes out laughing. (*Sifting some dirt through his fingers.*) Mighty rich dirt. It'll pay good.

DOBBS:

How good?

60 HOWARD:

Oh, this dirt ought to run about twenty ounces to the ton.

---

[1] **prophetic:** related to predicting the future
[2] **sober:** serious; solemn

Comprehend It

- Reread line 62. How many ounces of gold does Howard think there will there be in one ton of dirt?

_____

- How much money will one ton of dirt yield if each ounce of gold is worth $20?

_____

(continued)

Text Connection 4 (continued)

Comprehend It

Why does Howard want to pitch camp a mile or two from where they are mining for gold?

_____

_____

_____

_____

_____

_____

_____

Comprehend It

When miners file a claim, they notify the local authorities that they are mining for gold in a certain area. Why does Howard not want to file a claim?

_____

_____

_____

_____

_____

_____

_____

CURTIN:
At some twenty dollars an ounce...!

The old man nods.

65 DOBBS:
How many tons will we be able to handle a week?

HOWARD:
That depends on how hard we work... We better pitch our camp a mile or two away.

70 DOBBS:
Why, if here is where we're goin' to dig?

HOWARD:
In case anybody happens by, we can tell 'em we're hunters and get away with it maybe... 3. We'll cut bushes and pile 'em
75 around the mine itself so it can't be spotted from below.

DOBBS:
I'd sure hate to play poker with you, old-timer.

HOWARD:
Every so often one of us will have to go to the nearest village
80 after provisions. Whoever goes first ought to go all the time.
4. That way they'll figure only one man's up here. If they find out there's more than one they're liable to get suspicious. Hunters usually work alone.

CURTIN:
85 Wouldn't it be a lot easier to file a claim ³?

HOWARD:
Easier, maybe, but not very profitable. 5. It wouldn't be no time till an emissary from one of the big mining companies

---

³ **claim:** the title or legal right to a piece of land

(continued)

turned up with a paper in his hand showing we haven't any
90 right to be here. (*Squatting there, he picks up some of the dirt,
sifts it through his fingers. Then he grins at Dobbs and Curtin.)
How does it feel, you fellers, to be men of property...?

FADE OUT

Find It: Errors in Grammar and Subject-Verb Agreement

• Read each item below.

• Locate the sentence in the text with the corresponding number.

• Respond to each question by writing the answer on the line.

1. What grammatically correct word could be used instead of **ain't**?_____

2. Name the type of error in this sentence. _____

_____

3. What person and what tense are the underlined subject and verb in this sentence? _____

4. What person and what tense are the underlined subject and verb in this sentence? _____

5. Name the type of error in this sentence. _____

FADE IN
95 *33A.   FULL SHOT WATER WHEEL*
*A construction designed to draw water from a tank and,
by means of cans and cases, raise it to an upper tank from
whence, upon opening a lock, the water is to run back down a
wooden sluice to the original tank. The power that turns the*
100 *wheel is a burro. The final nail has just been driven and the
moment has arrived when the handiwork of the three partners
is to be tested. Howard harnesses the burro to the wheel and
kicks it in the rear, setting the wheel and system of tin cans
and boxes into motion. Curtin climbs to the upper tank,*
105 *pacing himself according to the speed of the crude machine.*

(continued)

Comprehend It

Read lines 95–108. Then make an inference about why Dobbs shakes Howard's hand and says "My hat's off to you."

_____

_____

_____

_____

Comprehend It

Reread lines 112–127. Why might there be irony in Howard's telling Dobbs, "Pretty soon I won't be able to tell you anything. You'll know it all"?

_____

_____

_____

_____

_____

_____

DOBBS: (*pumps Howard's hand*):

My hat's off to you. From now on it's your show, old-timer. Whatever you say goes far as I'm concerned.

HOWARD:

110 The tanks'll leak some at first till the boards swell and close the seams.

DOBBS:

I sure had some cockeyed ideas about prospecting for gold. It was all in the finding I thought. Once you found it you just

115 picked it up and put it into sacks and carried it to the nearest bank. (*He laughs uproariously at his former innocence.*)

HOWARD:

We might burn some lime out of the rocks and build a tank that wouldn't lose a drop of water.

120 DOBBS: (laughing):

I'd hate to think what would've happened to Curtin and me if we'd gone it alone. Even if we'd found the stuff we wouldn't have known how to get it out.

HOWARD:

125 You're learning. Pretty soon I won't be able to tell you anything. You'll know it all.

If there is any irony [4] *in Howard's voice it escapes Dobbs.*

HOWARD (*to Curtin*):

Tank full yet?

130 CURTIN:

Right to the top.

---

[4] **irony:** the use of words or actions that mean the opposite of what is meant literally

(continued)

HOWARD:

Then open up the sluice gate.

CURTIN:

135 Right.

He obeys and the water starts running down the sluice.
Following Howard's lead, Dobbs begins to wash the sand,
trying his best to imitate the actions of the old man.

HOWARD:

140 Like this—do it.

DOBBS:

I get it.

Curtin joins them.

DOBBS (*to Curtin*):

145 This is how it's done—see.

CURTIN:

Yeah—I get it.

34. *INDIVIDUAL CLOSE-UPS OF THE THREE MEN*
    as they separate the sand from the gold.

150 35. *TINY FLAKES OF GOLD*
    as the sand is washed away.

                    DISSOLVE TO NIGHT:

36. *CAMP CLOSE-UP OF DOBBS*

155 *His eyes, reflecting the light of the campfire, glitter in their*
sockets. He leans forward and we see a Mexican calendar
tacked to the wall. Lines have been drawn across all the dates
up to October 21.

Take Note

Reread lines 155–156. Underline the detail that suggests that Dobbs may be catching "gold fever."

Comprehend It

What does the fact that Dobbs wants to divide up the gold and Curtin does not suggest about each man's character?

_____

_____

_____

_____

_____

_____

(continued)

37.   CLOSE-UP OF A SCALE

160   *as the proceeds of the day's work are weighed.* CAMERA PULLS BACK TO A CLOSE SHOT OF THE THREE MEN. *Howard measures dust onto the scale.*

CURTIN:
How much do you figure it is now?

165   HOWARD:
Close on to five thousand dollars worth.

DOBBS:
When're we going to start dividing it?

Howard looks at him keenly.

170   HOWARD:
Any time you say.

CURTIN:
Why divide it at all? I don't see any point. We're all going back together, when the time comes. Why not wait until we get paid
175 for the stuff, then just divide the money?

HOWARD:
Either way suits me. You fellers decide.

DOBBS:
I'm for dividing it up as we go along and leaving it up to each
180 man to be responsible for his own goods.

HOWARD:
I reckon I'd rather have it that way, too. I haven't liked the responsibility of guarding your treasure any too well.

DOBBS:
185 Nobody asked you.

(continued)

HOWARD (*smilingly*):

That's right—you never asked me. I only thought I was the most trustworthy among us three.

DOBBS:

190 You? How come?

HOWARD:

I said the most trustworthy. As for being the most honest, no one can say.

DOBBS:

195 I don't get you.

HOWARD:

Well, let's look the thing straight in the face. Suppose you were charged with taking care of the goods. All right, I'm somewhere deep in the brush one day getting timber and

200 Curtin here is on his way to the village for provisions. That'd be your big chance to pack up and leave us in the cold.

DOBBS:

Only a guy that's a thief at heart would think me likely to do a thing like that!

205 HOWARD:

Right now it wouldn't be worthwhile. But when our pile has grown to let's say three hundred ounces, think of such things, you will...

CURTIN:

210 How's about yourself?

HOWARD:

I'm not quick on my feet any longer. You fellers are a lot tougher than when we started out. And by the time the pile is big enough to be really tempting I won't be able to run half

215 as fast as either one of you. You'd get me by the collar and

Take Note

Find and underline Howard's explanation for why he is the most trustworthy of the three men.

Comprehend It

Why do you think Howard says that once they divide up the gold, each man will have to hide his share?

_____

_____

_____

_____

_____

(continued)

string me up in no time. And that's why I think I'm the most trustworthy in this outfit.

Curtin grins.

CURTIN:

220 Looking at it that way I guess you're right. But perhaps it would be better to cut the proceeds three ways every night. It'd relieve you of a responsibility you don't like.

HOWARD:

Swell by me. After we've gotten more than a couple hundred
225 ounces it'll be a nuisance to carry it around in little bags hanging from our necks, so each of us will have to hide his share of the treasure from the other two. And having done so he'll have to be forever on the watch in case his hiding place is discovered.

230 DOBBS:

What a dirty filthy mind you have.

HOWARD:

Not dirty, baby. No, not dirty. Only I know what sort of ideas even supposedly decent people can get in their heads when
235 gold's at stake.

▲ ● ▲ ● ▲

47.   NIGHT
        *Howard is measuring out the yellow sand into three
        equal parts. Curtin and Dobbs follow his every move.
        Presently it is divided.*

▲ ● ▲ ● ▲

(continued)

240 HOWARD:

You know what. We ought to put some kind of limit on our take. Agree between ourselves that when we get exactly so much we pull up stakes and beat it.

CURTIN:

245 What do you think the limit ought to be?

HOWARD:

Oh, say twenty-five thousand dollars worth apiece.

DOBBS:

Twenty-five thousand? That's small potatoes.

250 CURTIN:

How much do you say?

DOBBS:

Fifty thousand anyway. Seventy-five's more like it.

HOWARD:

255 That'd take another year at least…if the vein held out, which wouldn't be likely.

DOBBS:

What's a year more or less when that kind of dough's to be made?

260 HOWARD:

Twenty-five's plenty far as I'm concerned. More'n enough to last me out my lifetime.

DOBBS:

Sure, you're old. But I'm still young. I need dough and plenty 265 of it.

CURTIN:

Twenty-five thousand in one piece is more'n I ever expected to get my hands on.

(continued)

Comprehend It

Compare and contrast the views that Howard and Dobbs hold on how much money they should make apiece before quitting the mine.

_____

_____

_____

_____

_____

_____

Comprehend It

Do you think Dobbs is justified in saying that he has a right to demand half again what Curtin makes? Why or why not?

_____

_____

_____

_____

Take Note

Underline lines 293–296. This is another example of **irony**. Howard is saying the opposite of what he believes. He thinks that Dobbs is putting too much emphasis on the money he loaned Curtin, and not valuing all of the work that Curtin is doing.

Comprehend It

Why do you think that Dobbs flings the gold dust into the fire when Curtin pays him?

_____

_____

_____

_____

_____

DOBBS (*snorts*):
270   Small potatoes!

CURTIN:
No use making hogs of ourselves.

DOBBS:
Hog am I! Why, I'd be within my rights if I demanded half
275   again what you get.

CURTIN:
How come?

DOBBS:
There's no denying, is there, I put up the lion's share of the
280   cash?

CURTIN:
So you did, Dobbsie—and I always meant to pay you back.

DOBBS (*pointedly*):
In civilized places the biggest investor [5] always gets the
285   biggest return.

HOWARD:
That's one thing in favor of the wilds.

DOBBS:
Not that I intend to make any such demand, you understand,
290   but I'd be within my rights if I did. Next time you go calling
me a hog, remember what I could'a done if I'd'a wanted…

HOWARD:
I think you're wise not to put things on a strictly money
basis, partner. Curtin might take it into his head he was a

---

[5] **investor:** a person who puts money into a business idea in hopes of making a profit from its success

(continued)

Text Connection 4 (continued)

295 capitalist instead of a guy with a shovel and just sit back and take things easy and let you and me do all the work.

While the old man talks, Curtin uses the scales to weigh out a portion of his dust.

HOWARD (*continuing*):

300 He'd stand to realize a tidy sum on his investment without so much as turning his hand over. If anybody's to get more, I reckon it ought to be the one who does the most work.

CURTIN (*giving the dust to Dobbs*):
There you are, Dobbsie. What I owe you with interest.

305 DOBBS (*he takes the dust, weighs it in his hand, then, with a sudden gesture, flings it away so that it falls, a little shower, into the fire*):
I just don't like being told I'm a hog, that's all.

HOWARD (*addressing Dobbs*):

310 Other things aside, there's a lot of truth in what you were saying about being younger than me and needing more dough. Therefore, I'm willing to make it forty thousand apiece. (*To Curtin.*) What do you say, partner?

CURTIN:

315 How long will it take?

HOWARD:
Oh, another six months, I reckon.

CURTIN (*after a moment's debate*):
Make it forty thousand or six months.

320 HOWARD:
Suits me. Okay, Dobbs?

Comprehend It

Make an inference about where Dobbs thinks Howard has been.

_____

_____

_____

_____

_____

(continued)

DOBBS (*sourly*):
Okay.

HOWARD:
325 Let's shake on it then.

The three men shake hands solemnly. Then Curtin gets up, starts away from the fire to hide his goods.

DISSOLVE TO:

NIGHT

330 *48.* INT. TENT CLOSE SHOT ON DOBBS
sleeping, a bar of moonlight across his face. OVER SCENE *the* SCREAM *of a tiger. He stirs, turns over. The* SCREAM *is repeated. Dobbs opens his eyes. Then he sits up, leaning on an elbow.*

335 *49.* HOWARD'S BLANKETS
They're empty. CAMERA PULLS BACK TO FULL SHOT INTERIOR TENT. *Curtin is in his blankets sound asleep. Dobbs frowns. After a moment Dobbs sits all the way up, throws back his blankets, reaches for his shoes, and*
340 *puts them on. Then, picking up his revolver, he moves silently out of the tent and heads across the campsite. He's gone perhaps a dozen steps when he hears Howard coming. He draws back into the shadows. When Howard is scarcely three feet away, Dobbs steps out,*
345 *suddenly confronting him.*

DOBBS:
That you, Howard?

HOWARD (*startled*):
You oughtn't to go jumping out at me like that. I might've let
350 you have it.

DOBBS:
Out for a midnight stroll?

(continued)

HOWARD:

There's a tiger around. I went to see if the burros were all
355 right.

DOBBS (*grunts skeptically, then*):
So!

HOWARD:

What's the matter, Dobbsie?

360 DOBBS:

Think I'll make *sure* the burros are all right.

HOWARD:

Help yourself.

He walks away in the direction of the tent.

365 *50.   INT. TENT*
as Howard enters. Curtin stirs.

CURTIN (*to Howard, sleepily*):
What's up?

HOWARD:

370 Nothing's up.

Curtin sees that Dobbs's blankets are empty.

CURTIN:

Where's Dobbs?

HOWARD:

375 Poking around in the dark out there.

51.   DOBBS
taking sacks of the precious dust out of his hiding
place—a hole underneath a rock. He is counting the
sacks aloud.

(continued)

Take Note

Draw a box around the lines in which Howard teases Dobbs and Curtin about anxiously checking their gold.

Comprehend It

What can you infer about why Dobbs is talking to himself?

_____

_____

_____

_____

_____

_____

380 DOBBS:

Three—four—five—six.

He gives a satisfied grunt, then starts putting them back.

52.   INT. TENT
       Howard has got back in his blankets.

385 CURTIN:

He's sure taking a long time…

Curtin throws his blankets off, puts on his shoes.

CURTIN (*continuing*):

I'm going to have a look-see.

390 53.   EXT. TENT
       CAMERA PANS *with Curtin to his hiding place—a hollow tree. He begins to pick out his sacks of gold.*

54.   INT. TENT
       as Dobbs enters. He starts to take his shoes off, then
395   *notices Curtin's absence.*

DOBBS (*sharply*):
Where's Curtin?

HOWARD:
Out there some place. He said something about having a
400 look-see.

Again Dobbs's brow becomes furrowed with suspicion. He puts his shoe back on, gets up, and is about to leave the tent when Curtin enters. He and Dobbs survey each other wordlessly.

HOWARD:
405 It's come around to me again, but I won't take my turn if you guys'll quit worrying about your goods and go to bed. We got work to do tomorrow.

(continued)

Dobbs grunts, turns back into the tent. Curtin drops down on his blankets.

410   DISSOLVE TO:

55.   *EXT. THE MINE CLOSE SHOT DOBBS*
        at the sluice, washing sand and talking to himself.

DOBBS:
You can't catch me sleeping....Don't you ever believe that. I'm
415 not so dumb. The day you try to put anything over on me will
be a costly one for both of you.

At the OVER SCENE SOUND *of hoofs on rock, Dobbs stops
talking.* CAMERA PULLS BACK *to show Curtin driving two of
the burros. Dobbs keeps his face* averted[6] *and Curtin passes*
420 *without any words being exchanged. As the sound of the hoofs
fades, Dobbs resumes his monologue.*

DOBBS:
Any more lip out of you and I'll pull off and let you have it.
If you know what's good for you, you won't monkey around
425 with Fred C. Dobbs.

56.   CURTIN
        *at a turn of the trail. He comes upon the old man
repairing a tool.*

CURTIN:
430 You ought to get a load of Dobbsie. He's talking away to
himself a mile a minute.

HOWARD (*shaking his head*):
Something's eating him. I don't know what. He's spoiling for
trouble.

435 *Curtin grunts, proceeds on down the trail.*

---

[6] **averted:** turned aside or away

(continued)

Comprehend It

What does Dobbs accuse
Howard and Curtin of?

_____

_____

_____

_____

_____

57.   DOBBS (*mimicking Howard's voice*):

We're low on provisions, Dobbsie. How about you going to
the village. (*Then as Dobbs again.*) Who does Howard think
he is, ordering me around?

440 HOWARD'S VOICE (*OVER SCENE*):
What's that, Dobbsie?

Dobbs looks up in surprise. CAMERA PULLS BACK TO A CLOSE
SHOT *of Howard and Dobbs.*

DOBBS:
445 Nothing.

HOWARD:
Better look out. It's a bad sign when a guy starts talking to
himself.

DOBBS (*angrily*):
450 Who else have I got to talk to? Certainly not you or Curtin.
Fine partners, I must say.

HOWARD:
Got something up your nose?

Dobbs doesn't answer.

455 HOWARD:
Blow it out. It'll do you good.

DOBBS (*shouts suddenly*):
Don't get the idea you two are putting anything over on me.

HOWARD:
460 Take it easy, Dobbsie.

DOBBS (*still louder*):
I know what your game is.

(continued)

Text Connection 4 (continued)

HOWARD:

Then you know more than I do.

465 DOBBS (*railing*):

Why am I elected to go to the village for provisions—why me instead of you or Curtin? Don't think I don't see through that. I know you've thrown together against me. The two days I'd be gone would give you plenty of time to discover where my dust 470 is, wouldn't it?

HOWARD:

If you have any fears along those lines, why don't you take your dust along with you?

DOBBS:

475 And run the risk of having it taken from me by bandits.

HOWARD:

If you were to run into bandits, you'd be out of luck anyway. They'd kill you for the shoes on your feet.

DOBBS:

480 So that's it. Everything is clear now. You're hoping bandits'll get me. That would save you a lot of trouble, wouldn't it? And your consciences wouldn't bother you either!

HOWARD:

Okay, Dobbs, you just forget about going. Curtin or I'll go.

485 *Dobbs turns on his heel, stalks off.*

58.   *PAN SHOT OF CURTIN*
      Something he sees out of scene causes him to stop.

59.   *A GILA MONSTER*
      Curtin picks up a rock, but before he can heave it the
490   *big yellow and black lizard has disappeared under*
      a boulder. Curtin drops the rock, picks up a piece of

Take Note

A **gila monster** is a poisonous lizard that lives in the southwestern United States and northern Mexico. Underline the text that describes where the gila monster hides.

(continued)

Text Connection 4 (continued)

Comprehend It

Why does Dobbs threaten to shoot Curtin?

_____

_____

_____

_____

_____

timber, runs one end underneath the rock making a lever. He leans his weight on the end of the timber.

DOBBS' VOICE (OVER SCENE):

495 Just like I thought.

Curtin turns. CAMERA PULLS BACK *to show Dobbs covering Curtin with his gun.*

CURTIN:

What's the idea?

500 DOBBS:

Put your hands up.

Curtin obeys. Dobbs takes Curtin's gun away from him.

DOBBS:

I got a good mind to pull off and pump you up, chest and
505 belly alike.

CURTIN:

Go ahead and pull, but would you mind telling me first what it's all about?

DOBBS:

510 It won't get you anywhere playin' dumb.

CURTIN (*comprehension dawning on his face*):
Well, I'll be—so that's where your dust is hidden, Dobbsie?

Howard comes up.

HOWARD:

515 What's all the hollerin' for?

CURTIN:

Seems like I stumbled accidentally on Dobbs's treasure.

(continued)

Text Connection 4 (continued)

DOBBS (*snorts*):

Accidentally! What were you trying to pry up that rock for?
520 Tell me that!

CURTIN:

I saw a gila monster crawl under it.

DOBBS:

Brother, I got to hand it to you. You can sure think up a good
525 story when you need one.

CURTIN:

Okay. I'm a liar. There isn't any gila monster under there.
Let's see you stick your hand in and get your goods out. Go
ahead.

530 DOBBS:

Sure I will. But don't you make a move or I'll...

CURTIN:

Don't worry. I'll stand right where I am. I want to see this.

Dobbs goes down on one knee beside the boulder. He starts
535 *to put his hand in, hesitates, then bends forward to look into*
the hole.

CURTIN:

Reach right in and get your goods. If you don't we'll think
you're plain yellow, won't we, Howard?

540 *Dobbs sneaks his hand forward toward the opening beneath*
the rock.

CURTIN:

They never let go, do they, Howard, once they grab onto
you—gila monsters. You can cut' em in half at the neck and
545 their heads'll still hang on till sundown, I hear, but by that
time the victim don't usually care anymore because he's
dead. Isn't that right, Howard?

Comprehend It

Hypothesize why Curtin might be daring Dobbs to put his hand beneath the rock.

_____

_____

_____

_____

_____

_____

_____

(continued)

Unit 32

Comprehend It

What might the gila monster standing on top of Dobbs's treasure symbolize?

_____

_____

_____

_____

_____

_____

HOWARD:

I reckon.

550 CURTIN:

What's the matter, Dobbs, why don't you reach your hand right in and get your treasure? It couldn't be you're scared to, could it, after the way you shot off your mouth. Show us you aren't yellow, Dobbsie. I'd hate to think my partner had a
555 yellow streak up his back.

DOBBS (*sweat showing on his face—the sweat of fear; he springs to his feet, aims wildly at Curtin, shouting*):
I'll kill you, you dirty, thieving...

But before he can pull the trigger Howard has knocked up his
560 *arm. Then both men close in on him. Curtin gets the gun away from him.*

CURTIN:

Okay, Howard, I got him covered. Dobbs, another bad move out of you, and I'll blow you to kingdom come. Hey, Howard,
565 turn that rock over, will you.

Howard obeys, leaning his weight on one end of the timber until the rock rolls over. CAMERA MOVES INTO A CLOSE-UP of *a gila monster, its body arched, hissing, atop Dobbs's treasure.* OVER SCENE *the* SOUND *of a shot. The slug bores through the*
570 *lizard's head, its body rises, its tail threshes.*

60.   CLOSE-UP DOBBS
      his face is white, his eyes are staring.

CUT BACK TO:

61.   CLOSE-UP THE GILA MONSTER
575   *lying belly up on Dobbs's treasure, his arms clawing at the air.*

Reprinted from *The Treasure of the Sierra Madre* by James Naremore by permission of The University of Wisconsin Press

The First Amendment

by Lucy Bledsoe

"Congress shall make no law respecting an establishment of religion, or prohibiting the free exercise thereof; or abridging the freedom of speech, or of the press; or the right of the people peaceably to assemble, and to petition the government
5 for a redress of grievances."[1]

These are the exact words of the First Amendment to the United States Constitution, and their purpose is to guarantee American citizens five basic freedoms: religion, speech, press, assembly, and petition. These rights are at the heart
10 of American democracy. Though they were written over 200 years ago, they still protect every citizen today.

Use the Clues: Vocabulary Strategies

- Read lines 1–11.
- Reread the underlined pronoun **these** in line 6.
- Highlight the exact words that **these** in line 6 refers to.
- Reread the underlined possessive pronoun **their** on Line 7.
- Identify the noun that the pronoun is replacing.
- Draw an arrow to show the link between the pronoun and the noun it replaced. Write the noun here:

_____

_____

- Reread the underlined pronoun **these** in Line 9.
- Draw an arrow to show the link between the pronoun and the nouns it replaced. Write the nouns here:

_____

_____

Take Note

Reread lines 1–5. Notice that this text is in quotation marks. Circle the number 1 following the text. Then read the footnote at the bottom of the page. Circle the source of the quoted text.

Comprehend It

List the five basic freedoms guaranteed in the First Amendment:

_____

_____

_____

_____

_____

[1] Constitution for the United States of America, Amendment I

(continued)

Unit 33

Comprehend It

What are two things that Thomas Jefferson believed about religion as it relates to government?

_____

_____

_____

_____

_____

_____

_____

Take Note

Underline the quotations by Thomas Jefferson. It is from a letter. A letter is an example of a **primary source**.

Underline the second heading on this page. Based on the heading, what information will the section under the heading provide?

_____

_____

_____

_____

_____

Definition of the First Amendment

The First Amendment is one long sentence. The first part of the sentence deals with religious freedom. It says that the government cannot establish an official national religion, and

15 it also says that people have the right to practice any religion they choose.

In 1802, when he was president, Thomas Jefferson wrote in a letter to the Danbury Baptists that "religion is a matter which lies solely between Man & his God, that he owes

20 account to none other for his faith or his worship, that the legitimate powers of government reach actions only, & not opinions," and that there should be "a wall of separation between Church & State."[2] The first part of the First Amendment erects this wall of separation between church

25 and state.

The next part of the First Amendment addresses the right to free expression. The right to freedom of speech means citizens may express any opinion they want. They can be critical [a] of the government without being punished for

30 doing so. Freedom of the press means that people have the right to research and write about whatever they choose. They just need to print what is true.

The last part of the First Amendment presents two more rights. The right to assemble means that people can

35 get together in groups. They can talk about ideas, and they can peaceably protest the actions of other people or the government. The right to petition the government means that citizens can ask the government to correct injustices.

Historical Purpose for the First Amendment

Most early American colonists came from Europe. Kings

40 and queens had unlimited power in many of these countries. 1 Expressing an idea or practicing a religion different from the official ruler's ideas and religion could be dangerous.

---

[2] Freedman, *In Defense of Liberty: The Story of America's Bill of Rights*, 45.

[a] **critical:** judgmental; having tendency to look for and point out faults

(continued)

2 It could be punished by fines, prison, and even death. For example, Catholic Queen Mary I reigned over England from
45 1553 until 1558. Known as "Bloody Mary," she had hundreds burned at the stake because of their religious beliefs.

3 Many early colonists came to America to escape religious **persecution** [b], but some of the new colonies also had state-sponsored churches. Massachusetts, for example,
50 allowed only Puritans to vote or hold public office. **4** In Virginia, the Church of England was supported by public taxes. Catholics, Baptists, and Jews could be punished for practicing their religions.

As more and more settlers came to America, they brought
55 a wider variety of religions. **5** Maintaining state-sponsored religions became difficult. The idea that people should have the liberty to practice whatever religion they chose grew popular.

Take Note

Reread lines 47–53. Underline the topic sentence in this paragraph. Then mark X in the right margin next to two examples that the writer provides to support her point.

Identify It: Gerunds, Gerund Phrases, and Active and Passive Voice

- Read the text, lines 39–60.
- Read each item below.
- Locate the sentence in the text with the corresponding number to each question.
- Respond to each question by writing its answer on the line.

1. What are the gerund phrases in this sentence?

   _____

2. Does this sentence have an active or passive verb?

   _____

3. Does this sentence have an active or passive verb?

   _____

4. Does this sentence have an active or passive verb?

   _____

5. Copy the gerund or gerund phrase

   _____

[b] **persecution:** the act of harassing or punishing based on a person's beliefs

(continued)

Text Connection 5 (continued)

Comprehend It

Seditious means relating to rebellion against the state. **Libel** refers to a false publication that damages a person's reputation. Who was charged with seditious libel and why?

_____

_____

_____

_____

_____

_____

How did Zenger's lawyer lay the foundation for the freedom of the press?

_____

_____

_____

_____

How does a free press benefit democracy?

_____

_____

_____

_____

_____

By the time the Bill of Rights was written, religious freedom was considered very important. Therefore, it was mentioned first in
60 the First Amendment to the Constitution.

Meanwhile, some colonists were also championing [c] the ideas of freedom of speech and the press. Even in colonial America, many states did not allow criticism of the British king or the local government. Doing so was called "seditious
65 libel." A German immigrant named John Peter Zenger challenged this idea. He published a newspaper called the *New-York Weekly Journal*. In 1734, he was thrown in jail for writing a harsh criticism of New York's colonial governor. He was held in jail for months without a trial. His wife continued
70 publishing the paper in his absence. When Zenger finally was allowed a trial, his lawyer presented a whole new idea. The lawyer argued that printed criticism that was in fact *true* wasn't libel. The lawyer convinced the jury of this new idea. He also convinced them that what Zenger wrote about the
75 governor was true. Zenger was set free. He became famous for helping to establish the idea of a free press. In fact, one of the authors of the American Constitution, Gouverneur Morris, praised the outcome of Zenger's trial. He said it was "the germ of American freedom—the morning star of that
80 liberty which subsequently revolutionized America."[3]

The early American leaders knew that a free press supported democracy. Citizens needed information to make educated choices about their leaders and laws. A free press, one not restricted by the government, could gather and
85 present this information.

The original United States Constitution, drafted in 1787, did not include a bill of rights. Some of the authors thought it was unnecessary because the states' constitutions had bills of rights. Others worried that spelling out specific
90 individual rights would leave the wrong impression. Some might conclude that all *other* rights were left to the federal

---

[3] Dueland, "A Voice From Paris," 36.

[c] **championing:** supporting; advocating

(continued)

government. So the Constitution was signed without a bill of rights, including, of course, the First Amendment.

95   Thomas Jefferson was particularly unhappy about the omission [d] of a bill of rights. He convinced James Madison that this was a grave error.[4] In the first United States Congress, Madison proposed that a bill of rights be added to the constitution. He drafted the amendments. Madison drew inspiration from the English Bill of Rights and the Virginia

100 Declaration of Rights.[5] The amendments were eventually passed by Congress and ratified by the states.

Relevance in Today's World

    Most people today consider the First Amendment to be the cornerstone of American democracy. Religious freedom means that Muslims, Jews, Christians, and people of all

105 faiths can vote and run for public office. It also means that people are allowed to practice their religions freely. Freedom of expression means that every point of view is allowed to be heard. The First Amendment encourages people from diverse [e] backgrounds to work together for the good of one nation.

110   The relevance of the First Amendment today is demonstrated by how often it is challenged. It is the job of the Supreme Court to uphold the Constitution, including the First Amendment.

    For example, in 1962, some parents objected to a New

115 York State law that allowed daily teacher-led prayer in the schools. The Supreme Court ruled that organized prayer in public schools violated the students' First Amendment rights to religious freedom. Some people said that the ruling was antireligious. But Supreme Court Justice Hugo L. Black

120 wrote that in fact the opposite was true. He wrote that the

---

[4] Carey, "Declaration Hits the Road."

[5] Freedman, *In Defense of Liberty: The Story of America's Bill of Rights*, 35.

[d] **omission:** something left out or neglected

[e] **diverse:** varied; different from one another

(continued)

Comprehend It

Why were the rights outlined in the First Amendment not included in the United States Constitution of 1787?

_____

_____

_____

_____

_____

Take Note

Circle the word **ratified** in line 101. Based on context cues, **ratified** probably means

❏ rejected

❏ approved

Look up **ratified** in a dictionary and confirm (or correct) your definition.

Comprehend It

Read lines 110–113. Then paraphrase them it in your own words.

_____

_____

_____

_____

_____

_____

_____

_____

_____

Unit 33

Take Note

Underline the quotation in lines 127–129. Who first wrote these words?

❏ Justice Anthony M. Kennedy

❏ Russell Freedman

Comprehend It

Identify this form of writing. What is the author's purpose.

_____

_____

_____

_____

_____

_____

ruling showed great respect for religion. The ruling actually supported the right for people to worship as they chose. The Supreme Court has continued to uphold this ruling in subsequent ᶠ cases. In 1992, for example, the Court said
125 that prayers couldn't be said at a graduation exercise. Justice Anthony M. Kennedy wrote the Court's response. He said that the Constitution "forbids the State to exact religious conformity from a student as the price of attending his or her own high school graduation."
130   The First Amendment grants all Americans the rights to five freedoms: religion, speech, press, assembly, and petition. These ideas were revolutionary in the late eighteenth century. Even today, in many parts of the world, people do not have such freedoms. They are not allowed to speak freely, gather
135 in groups, or worship according to their own beliefs. In the United States, the First Amendment guarantees these precious rights to all citizens.

ᶠ **subsequent:** happening later; succeeding

(continued)

Text Connection 5 (continued)

Bibliography

About the First Amendment. First Amendment Center. August 10, 2005. http://www.firstamendmentcenter.org/about.aspx?item=about_firstamd (accessed August 10, 2005).

140

America's Historical Documents. The National Archives. August 10, 2005. http://www.archives.gov/historical-docs/ (accessed August 10, 2005).

145 Blohm, Craig E. "The Road to Rights." *Cobblestone* Sept. 1991, Vol. 12 Number 9, p. 6.

Calkins, Virginia. "Mr. Madison Keeps His Promise." *Cobblestone* Sept. 1991: 24.

Carey, George. "Declaration Hits the Road." 2002. *Scholastic* http://teacher.scholastic.com/scholasticnews/indepth/declaration_independence/bill.htm (accessed August 10, 2005).

150

Dueland, Joy. "A Voice From Paris." *Cobblestone* Sept. 1982: 36.

Farish, Leah. *The First Amendment: Freedom of Speech, Religion, and the Press.* Berkeley Heights, NJ: Enslow Publishers, Inc. 1998.

155

Freedman, Russell. *In Defense of Liberty: The Story of America's Bill of Rights.* New York: Holiday House. 2003.

160 Jefferson, Thomas. Letter to the Danbury Baptists. 1 Jan. 1802. *LC Information Bulletin*, Library of Congress. June 1998. http://www.loc.gov/loc/lcib/9806/danpre.html (accessed August 5, 2005).

Levy, Leonard W. *Origins of the Bill of Rights.* New Haven: Yale University Press. 1999

165

Schilder, Rosalind. "Know Your Rights!" *Cobblestone* Sept. 1982: 26.

Take Note

- Write **I** in the margin next to Internet sources. (Hint: Look for the URL.)
- Write **M** in the margin next to magazine sources. (Hint: *Cobblestone* is a magazine.)
- The rest of the sources in this bibliography are books. Write **B** in the margin next to these.

Unit 33

Preview the Text

Read the highlighted words. Write the words you cannot pronounce in the margin or on a self-stick note. Circle words that you can't define.

Take Note

Reread lines 1–28.

• Circle each date.

• Underline each event that occurred on or by that date.

Underline the four major events that the printer will write about in his journal.

A Printer's Journal in Revolutionary America

On July 4, 1776, when American leaders signed the Declaration of Independence, the American Revolution already had been going on for a year. It would be another seven years before the British were finally defeated in 1783.
5 After that, the states carried on as best they could under the Articles of Confederation, which linked the states but did not make them one nation, until a Constitutional Convention was called in 1787. The summer of that year, delegates from states all over America wrote the Constitution of the United
10 States, forming a single, cohesive [1] nation. In 1791, the Bill of Rights was added as ten amendments.

The American Revolution may never have happened without the development of printing technology, particularly the printing press. The first regularly published American
15 newspaper, *The Boston News-Letter*, appeared in 1704. Fifty years later, only four newspapers were being published in New England. But by 1790, there were well over 100 newspapers in America! This explosion in communication technology was key in allowing the American revolutionaries
20 to spread their messages throughout the colonies.

Journalists in colonial times often made partnerships with those people who owned printing presses. The journal entries below are written by a fictional character, a young journalist living in a small town who chronicles
25 his experiences over four major events: the Declaration of Independence, July 4, 1776; the Revolutionary War, 1775–1783; the Constitutional Convention, 1787; and the passage of the Bill of Rights, 1791.

March 15, 1776
As anyone reading my journal (some day in the future)
30 knows, it has saddened my heart considerably that my bad leg has prevented me from taking part in the colonists' fight

---

[1] **cohesive:** united and working together effectively

(continued)

for our rights against the British. However, I've just read the
most extraordinary pamphlet, called *Common Sense*, written
by Thomas Paine and published on January 10 of this year.
35 Paine argues brilliantly for the American colonies to declare
their independence from Britain. Now I know what I want
more than anything: Like Paine, I want to use my pen to help
this cause.

July 1, 1776

This is the most exciting day of my life! Mr. Hatherbury
40 has acquired a printing press and he has hired me to be his
apprentice. I can hardly believe that my dreams are coming true.

July 10, 1776

1 After a year of <u>fighting</u> the British, we Americans have
declared ourselves independent! A rider came into town this
morning, his horse and he both perspiring profusely from
45 the long hard ride. He threw himself off the horse and ran
up the steps of town hall to read the declaration aloud to all
listeners. Mr. Hatherbury shoved me out the door and told
me to memorize his words!

The man read, "We hold these truths to be self-evident,
50 that all men are created equal, that they are endowed by their
Creator with certain unalienable Rights, that among these
are Life, Liberty, and the pursuit of Happiness."

Imagine! Rights that cannot be taken away, even by a
government!

55 Luckily, the man had printed copies of the extraordinary
Declaration of Independence, so I didn't have to memorize
the whole thing. 2 I understand that Thomas Jefferson wrote
it and that the Continental Congress adopted it, after <u>making</u>
changes, on July 4. The document is wonderful. 3 Besides
60 <u>declaring</u> our independence, it spells out the abuses of the
British government.

And such abuses! In 1765, there was the heinous Stamp
Act, which required colonists to pay a tax on newspapers,
among other things. We will not stand for taxation without

Comprehend It

What does the printer have in
common with Thomas Paine?

_____

_____

_____

_____

Read lines 49–52. From what
document is this quotation
taken?

_____

_____

Take Note

Underline the date on which the
Declaration of Independence
was adopted.

(continued)

Comprehend It

Reread lines 72–78. What passage drafted by Thomas Jefferson was left out of the Declaration of Independence?

_____

_____

_____

_____

_____

65 representation! The act was repealed [2] in 1766, but in 1767, the British placed a tax on many goods imported into the colonies. We objected so much that this too was repealed, all except for the tax on tea. Ha! **4** The Bostonians took care of that in 1773, by <u>boarding</u> the British ships in Boston Harbor

70 and dumping their cargoes of tea overboard. And now finally we have declared our independence from Britain altogether.

There is, however, one disappointing note: I understand that Jefferson had included a passage condemning King George for encouraging the slave trade. The delegates struck

75 that passage and I feel as discouraged as Jefferson must feel. **5** <u>Accepting</u> that compromise is a bitter pill, and yet my excitement for the birth of our new nation cannot be extinguished.

On another note, now that I have secured employment,

80 Virginia Smith has accepted my proposal of marriage.

Identify It: Functions of Gerunds

- Locate each numbered sentence in the text.
- Identify the function of the underlined gerund in each sentence and write the function on the line with the corresponding number.

1. _____

2. _____

3. _____

4. _____

5. _____

November 30, 1783

We have received word that the last British troops left New York City five days ago. What a great day this is. Of course, the war was truly won nearly two years ago at Yorktown. How I wish I could have seen the end of that

85 battle. The French soldiers, lead by Lieutenant General Jean Rochambeau, joined forces with the Americans, led of course

---

[2] **repealed:** cancelled; revoked

(continued)

by General George Washington, and closed in on Cornwallis. As the British general made a desperate attempt to ferry his men across the York River, a storm swept in to aid the

90 Americans. The British were not allowed to flee across the river.

What a sight that must have been on October 19, 1781, when 8,000 English soldiers laid down their guns. We'd surrounded them and they had nowhere to go. It was over.

95 We can now get down to the business of building our democracy. Like Thomas Jefferson wrote, a country where "All men are created equal." It's a new idea and we *will* make it work.

Five-year-old Catherine announced today that she will

100 be a printer, too, when she grows up. Mr. Hatherbury told her that perhaps she might. Later, when the child was out of earshot, I asked him to please not give the girl ideas. He scolded me, saying that as a thinker and journeyman printer, I should not close off channels to my daughters. Next, he'll be

105 encouraging three-year-old Elizabeth to be a doctor!

October 1, 1787

What a thrilling job I have. Today I wrote up the news about the new American Constitution, and Mr. Hatherbury is printing my story as quickly as he can.

When the Constitutional Convention began meeting in

110 May, the idea was to alter [3] the Articles of Confederation. But the states have been having so many problems. There are a dozen currencies [4] circulating, most of them nearly worthless. Trade is difficult, even between states. And just last year that group of farmers in western Massachusetts,

115 under Captain Shays, rose up against the state government. It is time for the states to join together, and so the delegates have written an entirely new document.

The new constitution divides the power between the national and state governments. Then, too, it divides the

---

[3] **alter:** to modify; change
[4] **currencies:** monies used in exchange for goods and services

(continued)

Comprehend It

Use what you know about life in colonial America to draw a conclusion about why the printer doesn't think Mr. Hatherbury should give Catherine ideas about becoming a printer.

_____

_____

_____

_____

_____

Take Note

Underline each of the rights and powers addressed in the Constitution.

Unit 33

Comprehend It

What important part was left out of the Constitution?

_____

Take Note

- Circle the date when the Bill of Rights became part of the U.S. Constitution.

- Find and circle the date of the previous journal entry.

How much time passed between the adoption of the Constitution and the ratification of the Bill of Rights?

_____

120 national government into three independent branches: executive, legislative, and judicial. The idea of the three branches is to spread the power and maintain balance. The executive branch, headed by the president, enforces the law. The legislative branch, meaning Congress, makes the law.
125 The judicial branch, led by the Supreme Court, explains the law.

The constitution gives the government the right to collect taxes, declare war, and regulate trade. It gives people the right to own property and have a trial by a jury of peers. I do
130 strongly agree, however, with Mr. Jefferson and Mr. Madison that the document is incomplete without a bill of rights. After all, several of the states have such rights as parts of their constitutions. Indeed, even the British have a Bill of Rights.
135 Now we must wait to see if all the states ratify [5] the new constitution.

December 20, 1791

What a glorious time to be living! Five days ago, on December 15, 1791, the Bill of Rights became an official part of the United States Constitution. I've asked Virginia to cook
140 a special celebration dinner.

It was a long process, getting the amendments passed by Congress and ratified by the States. To think that now Mr. Hatherbury's newspaper, and the words he and I write, are protected by our country's constitution. In the new United
145 States, the press will be allowed to seek out and publish truthful information, wherever we might find it, without recrimination [6].

Additionally, the Bill of Rights grants every American the rights to religious freedom, free speech, and much more.
150 It gives my heart great comfort to know that Catherine, Elizabeth, and now baby Thomas are coming into a world where their rights are protected.

_____

[5] **ratify:** to make into law; approve formally

[6] **recrimination:** a responding accusation

(continued)

February 5, 1792

    How can I possibly describe the dual emotions of grief and gratitude I am experiencing today. My good, hard-
155 working employer, Mr. Hatherbury, has fallen prey to a severe influenza and died. I fear I shall never get over the loss of this good man who gave me my life's vocation.

    Where possibly could the gratitude be, you might ask. I was astonished to be called upon to attend the reading of his
160 will. This good man, who has no children of his own, has left me his printing press. I shall take over the newspaper.

Comprehend It

Identify this form of writing. What is the author's purpose?

_____

_____

_____

_____

_____

_____

_____

_____

Take Note

Underline the term **Renaissance woman** in line 4. A Renaissance person is a person who is very knowledgeable and who has many talents and abilities.

Maya Angelou: A Love of Knowledge

Who Is Maya Angelou?

A bird doesn't sing because it has an answer; it sings because it has a song.
—Maya Angelou

American poet Maya Angelou has been called a Renaissance woman, and for good reason. Born Marguerite
5 Johnson in St. Louis, Missouri, in 1928, her life has been rich with experiences. Her accomplishments are many and cover a wide range including author, poet, historian, songwriter, playwright, producer and director, performer, and civil rights activist. She has written ten best-selling books and numerous
10 magazine articles. Her work has earned her Pulitzer Prize and National Book Award nominations. At President Clinton's invitation, she wrote and delivered a poem on the occasion of his 1993 inauguration. Her passion for languages is reflected in the fact that, in addition to her native English,
15 she speaks French, Spanish, Italian, and West African Fanti.

What drives Angelou, and how does she do it all? Her work and life are energized by an honest look at life's pretensions [1] and a strong conviction that courage is the most important virtue. Angelou advocates passionately for young
20 people to seek an education and the knowledge that breaks down false barriers of gender and race. "How important it is for us to recognize and celebrate our heroes and she-roes!" she declares. "It is time," she adds, "for parents to teach young people early on that in diversity there is beauty and there is
25 strength."

The story "Mrs. Flowers" is an excerpt from Angelou's autobiographical novel, I Know Why the Caged Bird Sings. It recounts an experience she had as a child living with her grandmother in rural Stamps, Arkansas. Mrs. Flowers, a

---

[1] **pretensions:** false appearances, actions, or statements

(continued)

30 *friend of her grandmother's, took a special interest in Maya*
and read poetry and fiction to her. In tribute to Mrs. Flowers,
Angelou says, "Most of the things I do now come out of what
that understanding woman read to me and got me to reading
as a child." Angelou's poem "I Love the Look of Words" was
35 *inspired by the hours she spent reading with Mrs. Flowers.*

Mrs. Flowers
by Maya Angelou

For nearly a year, I sopped around the house, the Store, the school and the church, like an old biscuit, dirty and inedible. Then I met, or rather got to know, the lady who threw me my first <u>life line</u>.

Use the Clues A: Vocabulary Strategies

- Read lines 36–39.
- Use context clues to figure out the meaning of the compound word **life line** in the first paragraph.
- Underline the correct answer below:

  a) a rope that saves lives

  b) a sense of hope

  c) a float attached by a rope

  d) a crease on the palm

40 Mrs. Bertha Flowers was the aristocrat [2] of Black Stamps. She had the grace of control to appear warm in the coldest weather, and on the Arkansas summer days it seemed she had a private breeze which swirled around, cooling her. She was thin without the <u>taut</u> look of <u>wiry</u> people, and her
45 printed voile dresses and flowered hats were as right for her as denim overalls for a farmer. She was our side's answer to the richest white woman in town.

[2] **aristocrat:** a member of a ruling class or nobility

(continued)

Take Note

Reread lines 40–60. Underline details that characterize Mrs. Flowers.

Use the Clues B: Vocabulary Strategies

- Read lines 40–47. Reread line 44 and the words **taut** and **wiry**.
- Use a dictionary to locate the meanings of each word. Select a meaning that fits this context.
- Complete each definition below.

Taut means _____.

Wiry means _____.

- Use the dictionary definitions and the context to select the words that best describe Mrs. Flowers. Write the numbers of these words on the lines below.

1) elegant   2) scrawny   3) poised   4) well-dressed

_____

Her skin was a rich black that would have peeled like a plum if snagged, but then no one would have thought of
50 getting close enough to Mrs. Flowers to ruffle her dress, let alone snag her skin. She didn't encourage familiarity. She wore gloves too.

I don't think I ever saw Mrs. Flowers laugh, but she smiled often. A slow widening of her thin black lips to show
55 even, small white teeth, then the slow effortless closing. When she chose to smile on me, I always wanted to thank her. The action was so graceful and inclusively benign[3].

She was one of the few gentlewomen I have ever known, and has remained throughout my life the measure of what a
60 human being can be.

Momma had a strange relationship with her. Most often when she passed on the road in front of the Store, she spoke to Momma in that soft yet carrying voice, "Good day, Mrs. Henderson." Momma responded with "How you, Sister
65 Flowers?"

Mrs. Flowers didn't belong to our church, nor was she Momma's familiar. Why on earth did she insist on calling

_____

[3] **benign:** harmless; gentle

(continued)

her Sister Flowers? Shame made me want to hide my face. Mrs. Flowers deserved better than to be called Sister. Then,
70 Momma left out the verb. Why not ask, "How *are* you, *Mrs. Flowers?*" With the unbalanced passion of the young, I hated her for her showing ignorance to Mrs. Flowers. It didn't occur to me for many years that they were as alike as sisters, separated only by formal education.

75   Although I was upset, neither of the women was in the least shaken by what I thought an unceremonious greeting. Mrs. Flowers would continue her easy gait up the hill to her little bungalow, and Momma kept on shelling peas or doing whatever had brought her to the front porch.

80   Occasionally, though, Mrs. Flowers would drift off the road and down to the Store and Momma would say to me, "Sister, you go on and play." As I left I would hear the beginning of an intimate conversation. Momma persistently using the wrong verb, or none at all.

85   "Brother and Sister Wilcox is sho'ly the meanest—" "Is," Momma? "Is"? Oh, please, not "is," Momma, for two or more. But they talked, and from the side of the building where I waited for the ground to open up and swallow me, I heard the soft-voiced Mrs. Flowers and the textured voice of my
90 grandmother merging and melting. They were interrupted from time to time by giggles that must have come from Mrs. Flowers (Momma never giggled in her life). Then she was gone.

    She appealed to me because she was like people I had
95 never met personally. Like women in English novels who walked the moors (whatever they were) with their loyal dogs racing at a respectful distance. Like the women who sat in front of roaring fireplaces, drinking tea incessantly from silver trays full of scones and crumpets. Women who walked
100 over the "heath" and read morocco-bound books and had two last names divided by a hyphen. It would be safe to say that she made me proud to be Negro, just by being herself.

    She acted just as refined as whitefolks in the movies and books and she was more beautiful, for none of them could
105 have come near that warm color without looking gray by comparison.

(continued)

Comprehend It

How might Mrs. Henderson and Mrs. Flowers be alike, despite the difference in their education?

_____

_____

_____

_____

_____

Text Connection 7 (continued)

Take Note

Reread the dialogue in lines 116–123. Underline the words that Mrs. Henderson says. Draw a box around what Mrs. Flowers says. Take note of how Maya Angelou wrote these lines.

It was fortunate that I never saw her in the company of powhitefolks. For since they tend to think of their whiteness as an evenizer, I'm certain that I would have had to hear her
110 spoken to commonly as Bertha, and my image of her would have been shattered like the unmendable Humpty-Dumpty.

One summer afternoon, sweet-milk fresh in my memory, she stopped at the Store to buy provisions. Another Negro woman of her health and age would have been expected to
115 carry the paper sacks home in one hand, but Momma said, "Sister Flowers, I'll send Bailey[a] up to your house with these things."

She smiled that slow dragging smile, "Thank you, Mrs. Henderson. I'd prefer Marguerite, though." My name was
120 beautiful when she said it. "I've been meaning to talk to her, anyway." They gave each other age-group looks.

Momma said, "Well, that's all right then. Sister, go and change your dress. You going to Sister Flowers's."

The chifforobe was a maze. What on earth did one put
125 on to go to Mrs. Flowers' house? I knew I shouldn't put on a Sunday dress. It might be sacrilegious. Certainly not a house dress, since I was already wearing a fresh one. I chose a school dress, naturally. It was formal without suggesting that going to Mrs. Flowers' house was equivalent to attending
130 church.

I trusted myself back into the Store.

"Now, don't you look nice." I had chosen the right thing, for once.

"Mrs. Henderson, you make most of the children's
135 clothes, don't you?"

"Yes, ma'am. Sure do. Store-bought clothes ain't hardly worth the thread it take to stitch them."

"I'll say you do a lovely job, though, so neat. That dress looks professional."

140 Momma was enjoying the seldom-received compliments. Since everyone we knew (except Mrs. Flowers, of course) could sew competently, praise was rarely handed out for the commonly practiced craft.

"I try, with the help of the Lord, Sister Flowers, to finish
145 the inside just like I does the outside. Come here, Sister."

(continued)

[a] **Bailey**—Maya Angelou's brother

I had buttoned up the collar and tied the belt, apron-like, in back. Momma told me to turn around. With one hand she pulled the strings and the belt fell free at both sides of my waist. Then her large hands were at my neck, opening the
150 button loops. I was terrified. What was happening?

"Take it off, Sister." She had her hands on the hem of the dress.

"I don't need to see the inside, Mrs. Henderson, I can tell…" But the dress was over my head and my arms were
155 stuck in the sleeves. Momma said, "That'll do. See here, Sister Flowers, I French-seams around the armholes." Through the cloth film, I saw the shadow approach. "That makes it last longer. Children these days would bust out of sheet-metal clothes. They so rough."

160 "That is a very good job, Mrs. Henderson. You should be proud. You can put your dress back on, Marguerite."

"No ma'am. Pride is a sin. And 'cording to the Good Book, it goeth before a fall."

"That's right. So the Bible says. It's a good thing to keep in
165 mind."

I wouldn't look at either of them. **1** Momma hadn't thought that taking off my dress in front of Mrs. Flowers would kill me stone dead. If I had refused, she would have thought I was trying to be "womanish" and might have
170 remembered St. Louis. **2** Mrs. Flowers had known that I would be embarrassed and that was even worse. I picked up the groceries and went out to wait in the hot sunshine. It would be fitting if I got a sunstroke and died before they came outside. Just dropped dead on the slanting porch.

175 There was a little path beside the rocky road, and Mrs. Flowers walked in front swinging her arms and picking her way over the stones.

She said, without turning her head, to me, "I hear you're doing very good school work, Marguerite, but that it's all
180 written. **3** The teachers report that they have trouble getting you to talk in class." We passed the triangular farm on our left and the path widened to allow us to walk together. I hung back in the separate unasked and unanswerable questions.

Comprehend It

Why does Momma want to show Mrs. Flowers the inside of Marguerite's dress?

_____

_____

_____

_____

Comprehend It

Why is it ironic that Momma says "Pride is a sin"?

_____

_____

_____

Infer why Marguerite does not talk much in class.

_____

_____

_____

_____

(continued)

Unit 34

Comprehend It

Why does Marguerite think "Death would be too kind and brief" if she damaged one of Mrs. Flowers' books?

_____

_____

_____

_____

_____

_____

185 "Come and walk along with me, Marguerite." I couldn't have refused even if I wanted to. She pronounced my name so nicely. Or more correctly, she spoke each word with such clarity [4] that I was certain a foreigner who didn't understand English could have understood her.

190 "Now no one is going to make you talk—possibly no one can. But bear in mind, language is man's way of communicating with his fellow man and it is language alone which separates him from the lower animals." That was a totally new idea to me, and I would need time to think about it.

195 "Your grandmother says you read a lot. Every chance you get. That's good, but not good enough. Words mean more than what is set down on paper. It takes the human voice to infuse them with the shades of deeper meaning."

200 I memorized the part about the human voice infusing words. It seemed so valid and poetic.

She said she was going to give me some books and that I not only must read them, I must read them aloud. **4** She suggested that I try to make a sentence sound in as many different ways as possible.

Identify It: Noun Clauses

- Locate the first numbered sentence in the text.
- Reread the sentence.
- Identify the noun clause in the sentence and underline it.
- Complete the rest of the numbered sentences in the same way.

205 "I'll accept no excuse if you return a book to me that has been badly handled." My imagination boggled at the punishment I would deserve if in fact I did abuse a book of Mrs. Flowers.' Death would be too kind and brief.

210 The odors in the house surprised me. Somehow I had never connected Mrs. Flowers with food or eating or any

---

[4] **clarity:** clearness of thought or style

(continued)

other common experience of common people. There must have been an outhouse, too, but my mind never recorded it.

The sweet scent of vanilla had met us as she opened the door.

215 "I made tea cookies this morning. You see, I had planned to invite you for cookies and lemonade so we could have this little chat. The lemonade is in the icebox."

It followed that Mrs. Flowers would have ice on an ordinary day, when most families in our town bought ice late
220 on Saturdays only a few times during the summer to be used in the wooden ice-cream freezers.

She took the bags from me and disappeared through the kitchen door. I looked around the room that I had never in my wildest fantasies imagined I would see. Browned
225 photographs leered or threatened from the walls and the white, freshly done curtains pushed against themselves and against the wind. I wanted to gobble up the room entire and take it to Bailey, who would help me analyze and enjoy it.

"Have a seat, Marguerite. Over there by the table." She
230 carried a platter covered with a tea towel. Although she warned that she hadn't tried her hand at baking sweets for some time, I was certain that like everything else about her the cookies would be perfect.

They were flat round wafers, slightly browned on
235 the edges and butter-yellow in the center. With the cold lemonade they were sufficient for childhood's lifelong diet. Remembering my manners, I took nice little lady-like bites off the edges. She said she had made them expressly for me and that she had a few in the kitchen that I could take home
240 to my brother. So I jammed one whole cake in my mouth and the rough crumbs scratched the insides of my jaws, and if I hadn't had to swallow, it would have been a dream come true.

5   As I ate she began the first of what we later called "my lessons in living." She said that I must always be intolerant [5]
245 of ignorance but understanding of illiteracy. That some people, unable to go to school, were more educated and even

---

[5] **intolerant:** unwilling to accept; disapproving of

(continued)

Comprehend It

Reread line 243–250. Infer why Mrs. Flowers teaches Marguerite this lesson, before teaching her anything else.

_____

_____

_____

_____

_____

_____

_____

_____

Comprehend It

Predict how her relationship with Mrs. Flowers will affect Marguerite's learning.

_____

_____

_____

_____

_____

more intelligent than college professors. She encouraged me to listen carefully to what country people called mother wit. That in those homely sayings was couched the collective
250 wisdom of generations.

When I finished the cookies she brushed off the table and brought a thick, small book from the bookcase. I had read *A Tale of Two Cities* and found it up to my standards as a romantic novel. She opened the first page and I heard poetry
255 for the first time in my life.

"It was the best of times and the worst of times..." Her voice slid in and curved down through and over the words. She was nearly singing. I wanted to look at the pages. Were they the same that I had read? Or were there notes, music,
260 lined on the pages, as in a hymn book? Her sounds began cascading gently. I knew from listening to a thousand preachers that she was nearing the end of her reading, and I hadn't really heard, heard to understand, a single word.

"How do you like that?"
265 It occurred to me that she expected a response. The sweet vanilla flavor was still on my tongue and her reading was a wonder in my ears. I had to speak.

I said, "Yes, ma'am." It was the least I could do, but it was the most also.
270 "There's one more thing. Take this book of poems and memorize one for me. Next time you pay me a visit, I want you to recite."

I have tried often to search behind the sophistication of years for the enchantment I so easily found in those gifts.
275 The essence [6] escapes but its aura remains. To be allowed, no, invited, into the private lives of strangers, and to share their joys and fears, was a chance to exchange the Southern bitter wormwood for a cup of mead with Beowulf or a hot cup of tea and milk with Oliver Twist. When I said aloud, "It is a far,
280 far better thing that I do, than I have ever done..." tears of love filled my eyes at my selflessness.

On that first day, I ran down the hill and into the road (few cars ever came along it) and had the good sense to stop running before I reached the Store.

---

[6] **essence:** the true substance or nature of something   *(continued)*

285   I was liked, and what a difference it made. I was respected not as Mrs. Henderson's grandchild or Bailey's sister but for just being Marguerite Johnson.

    Childhood's logic never asks to be proved (all conclusions are absolute). I didn't question why Mrs. Flowers had singled
290 me out for attention, nor did it occur to me that Momma might have asked her to give me a little talking to. All I cared about was that she had made tea cookies for *me* and read to *me* from her favorite book. It was enough to prove that she liked me.

I Love the Look of Words
by Maya Angelou

Popcorn leaps, popping from the floor
295 of a hot black skillet
and into my mouth.
Black words leap,
snapping from the white
page. Rushing into my eyes. Sliding
300 into my brain which gobbles them
the way my tongue and teeth
chomp the buttered popcorn.

When I have stopped reading,
ideas from the words stay stuck
305 in my mind, like the sweet
smell of butter perfuming my
fingers long after the popcorn
is finished.

I love the book and the look of words
310 the weight of ideas that popped into my mind.
I love the tracks
Of new thinking in my mind.

"Mrs. Flowers" excerpted from *I Know Why the Caged Bird Sings* by permission of Random House, Inc.

"I Love the Look of Words" used by permission of Dial Books for Young Readers, a member of Penguin Group (USA) Inc.

Take Note
• Underline a metaphor in lines 297–299.
• Underline a simile in lines 305–308.

Comprehend It
Identify the form of writing. What is the author's purpose?

_____

_____

_____

_____

_____

_____

Text Connection 8

Take Note

Underline the names of the three crew members. (As you read, note that the nickname for **James** is **Jim** and the nickname for **John** is **Jack**.)

Apollo 13: Ingenuity Saves the Mission

by Jim Lovell and Jeffrey Kluger

Propelled by the tremendous power of a Saturn V *booster rocket, the* Apollo 13 *spacecraft lifted off from the Kennedy Space Center at 2:13 p.m. on April 11, 1970. Its destination was the Fra Mauro highlands of the moon; it was to be the*
5 *third <u>lunar</u> landing in a series of Apollo missions focused on exploring Earth's closest neighbor. The three-man crew onboard included James A. Lovell, Jr., commander; John L. Swigert, Jr., command module pilot; and Fred W. Haise, Jr., lunar module pilot. The spacecraft they flew had two main*
10 *components: the Command/Service module,* Odyssey, *and the two-part Lunar Module,* Aquarius.

> ### Use the Clues A: Vocabulary Strategies
> - Read lines 1–11.
> - Reread line 5 and the underlined word **lunar**.
> - Use substitution clues to find
>   a) a word that renames **lunar**: _____
>   b) a phrase that renames **lunar**: _____

Their launch into space didn't attract much attention in the news. Previous missions around the moon and moon landings had gone well and yielded moon rocks and
15 *spectacular space photos of the moon and Earth. Fifty-six hours into the flight, the* Apollo 13 *mission became <u>anything but routine</u> when an electrical short circuit in the fans in cryogenic oxygen tank 2 caused an explosion that seriously damaged the lines that supplied the fuel cells. In addition,*
20 *one oxygen tank was gone, and one was leaking.*

(continued)

Use the Clues B: Vocabulary Strategies

- Read lines 12–20.

- Reread lines 16–17 and the underlined phrase **anything but routine**.

- Find a phrase in the text that means the opposite of the phrase **anything but routine**. _____

- Underline examples in the text that made the Apollo 13 mission **anything but routine**.

Comprehend It

- What two things was the *Odyssey* running out of?

  _____

- How was the *Odyssey* going to get more power?

  _____

- What device were the astronauts going to build that would clean the air of carbon dioxide?

  _____

Take Note

Circle the names of four people who were based at the Mission Control Center in Houston.

All the caution and warning lights on Odyssey *lit up, and command module pilot Swigert radioed Mission Control the following message: "Okay Houston, we've had a problem here." They were rapidly running out of power and oxygen. Mission*
25 *Control, headed by flight director Gene Kranz, immediately started analyzing what had happened and how to save* Odyssey *and her crew. They first figured out a way to power up* Aquarius *as a lifeboat just as the power was dying in* Odyssey.

In this excerpt from Lost Moon: The Perilous Journey of
30 Apollo 13, *Jim Lovell and Jeffrey Kluger tell of how urgently the astronauts need an air scrubber to keep carbon dioxide from rising to toxic levels. Ed Smylie, chief of the Crew Systems division, and his assistant, Jim Correale, have just spent a frantic twenty-four hours designing and testing a*
35 *scrubber made out of only the components that can be found aboard the space craft. The astronauts are about to build the component, and everyone is holding their breath to see if it will actually work.*

This was just one of a series of complex problems faced by
40 *the people responsible for rescuing the* Apollo 13 *crew.*

The combined knowledge and courage of many people made it possible for the crippled spacecraft to return to Earth safely three days later.

Fred Haise rather enjoyed being alone in his LEM.[a] He
45 liked the unaccustomed [1] quiet, he liked the unaccustomed

---

[a] **LEM**—Lunar excursion module

[1] **unaccustomed:** uncommon or unusual

(continued)

elbow room, and he liked, more than either, the brief chance to be in charge of his own ship. Unlike the commander of the three-man lunar crew, who enjoyed near-absolute authority over the vehicles and the men placed in his charge,
50 and unlike the command module pilot, who would assume total command of the mother ship during the two days his crewmates were off flying their LEM, the lunar module pilot would never take the helm of either ship he was aboard. For men who, before joining NASA,[b] made their living test-flying
55 planes, this could rankle a bit. At three o'clock Wednesday morning, however, as Jim Lovell and Jack Swigert were entering the second hour of their sleep shift in *Odyssey*,[c] Fred Haise—third in command of a crew of three—found himself drifting around his well-loved *Aquarius*[d] alone.

60   "Houston[e], Aquarius," Haise radioed quietly to Jack Lousma[f] as he floated toward Lovell's vacant [2] station.

"Go, Fred," said Lousma.

"I'm looking back at the left-hand corner of the moon," Haise said, "and I can just barely make out the foothills of
65 the Fra Mauro[g] formation. We never did get to see it when we were in there close."

"O.K.," Lousma said. "It looks like you're not in so close anymore. I'm reading on my monitor here, Fred, that you're 16,214 miles away from the moon and moving at over
70 4,500 feet per second."

"When this flight is over," Haise said, nodding to himself, "we'll really be able to figure out what a LEM can do. If it had a heat shield, I'd say bring it home."

---

[b] **NASA**—National Aeronautics and Space Administration

[c] **Odyssey**—The command module for *Apollo 13*

[d] **Aquarius**—The lunar excursion module for *Apollo 13*

[e] **Houston**—Location of NASA's Manned Spacecraft Center and Mission Control

[f] **Jack Lousma**—A Capcom (capsule communicator) for *Apollo 13* at Mission Control

[g] **Fra Mauro**—A high, hilly area of the moon's surface

[2] **vacant:** empty; unoccupied

(continued)

Text Connection 8 (continued)

"Well, at least you gave the folks at home a good look
75 at the inside of the ship during that last broadcast Monday
night," Lousma said. "That was a good show you guys put on."

"It would have been an even better one about ten
minutes later."

"Yes," Lousma said, "things sure turned to worms in a
80 hurry there after that."

Haise pushed away from the window and drifted
backward toward Swigert's station atop the ascent engine
cover. Reaching into a storage bag, he poked through a few of
the food packets Swigert had carried over from *Odyssey* early
85 yesterday.

"And just for your information, Jack," Haise radioed, "I'm
going to pass the time by tearing into some beef and gravy
and other assorted goodies."

"I presume you're doing this with the full permission of
90 the commander," Lousma said.

"And at this very moment," Haise said with a smile, "just
who do you think the commander is."

"All the same, if I was him, I'd make you sign out
everything you ate, so he could keep track of it."

95 "Understood."

1 "And Fred," Lousma added, "sometime when you're not
too busy chewing on that beef, how about telling us <u>what that
CO_2 reads</u>."

Lousma's nonchalance [3] belied the sense of urgency
100 behind this request. Ed Smylie's[h] visit to Mission Control
had been a happy one for both the engineer and the flight
controllers. The makeshift air scrubber had intrigued
Slayton, Kranz, Kraft,[i] and the knot of LEM environmental
officers who crowded around the Capcom's[j] desk, and
105 the report of the successful test in the vacuum chamber

---

[h] **Ed Smylie**—Chief of the Crew Systems Division at the Manned
Spacecraft Center

[i] **Slayton, Kranz, Kraft**—NASA officials at the Manned
Spacecraft Center; former astronauts and flight directors for the
U.S. space program

[j] **Capcom**—Capsule communicator located at Mission Control

[3] **nonchalance:** an unconcerned manner and attitude

(continued)

Comprehend It

• What sat on top of
Lousma's desk?

_____

_____

• Why were people so
interested in it?

_____

_____

_____

_____

_____

Comprehend It

• At what point would the carbon dioxide begin poisoning the crew?

_____

• What was the carbon dioxide reading when Haise checked it?

_____

in Building 7 had convinced them that the inelegant contraption could indeed work. [2] Now, after Smylie had come and gone, his prototype remained atop Lousma's console, attracting controllers <u>who would amble by and poke at it</u>.

110   The fact that Smylie's box could be easily assembled in his lab was no guarantee it could be just as easily assembled in space, and the time for getting started on the job was growing short. [3] Carbon dioxide concentrations in the command module and the LEM were tracked with a non-

115 power-consuming instrument resembling a thermometer, <u>which measured the pressure of the toxic gas in the overall atmosphere</u>. In a healthy ship, the needle should climb no higher then 2 or 3 millimeters of mercury. When it rose above 7, the crew was instructed to change their lithium

120 hydroxide canisters. If it was allowed to rise above 15, it meant that the canisters had absorbed about all they could and that before long, the first signs of CO_2 poisoning—lightheadedness, disorientation, nausea—would set in.

[4] As Fred Haise folded up his roast beef packet, left it to

125 float near the back of the cockpit, and drifted over to the carbon dioxide gauge, <u>what he saw</u> brought him up short.

Identify It: Adjective Clauses and Noun Clauses

• Locate the first numbered sentence in the text.

• Determine whether the underlined clause is an **adjectival clause** or a **noun** clause.

• Place an **X** under the correct heading.

• Repeat this procedure with the remaining numbered sentences

	Adjectival Clause	Noun Clause
1.		
2.		
3.		
4.		
5.		

(continued)

"O.K.," Haise said evenly, "I'm reading 13 on the gauge."
He squinted at the needle a second time. "Yeah, 13."

"All right," Lousma said, "that's pretty much what we've
130 got here, so we're going to want to get started putting
together the little canister we've come up with."

"You want me to head up into *Odyssey* and start
collecting materials?"

"Nah," Lousma answered. "We don't want to bother the
135 skipper just yet. We'll give him a few more minutes to sleep."

As Lousma was saying this, Haise heard a rustling noise
in the tunnel. He glanced up and saw Lovell, red-eyed with
fatigue [4], floating head-first into *Aquarius*. The commander
descended toward the ascent engine cover, flipped over,
140 and pulled himself down to a sitting position with a thump.
Bobbing at the level of his eyes was Haise's abandoned beef,
which he regarded with curiosity, plucked out of the air, and
tossed across the cockpit to his LEM pilot. Haise caught the
packet and stowed it quickly in a waste bag.

145 "You're back awful early," Haise said.

Lovell yawned. "It's too cold up there, Freddo."

"You've gotta stay real still."

"I *tried* staying real still. It doesn't help anymore. If it's
much above 34 degrees in there, I'd be surprised."

150 Lovell reached forward, put his headset back on, and
called down to Lousma.

"Hello, Houston, *Aquarius*. This is Lovell here who's got
the duty again."

"Roger, Jim. Is Jack there with you?"

155 "No, he's still sacked out."

"O.K.," Lousma said, "as soon as he gets up, I'd suggest
we go ahead and make a couple of these lithium hydroxide
canisters. It's going to take all three sets of hands, I think."

"All right," Lovell said, clearing his head with a shake and
160 moving back to his left-hand spot. "We'll make that the next
project, then, getting those canisters squared away."

Though there was more than an hour left in the sleep
cycle, and Swigert, unlike Lovell, had managed to fall sound

---

[4] **fatigue:** great tiredness

(continued)

asleep inside the icebox of *Odyssey*, the sudden chatter and
165 bustle coming from the LEM soon roused him. Just minutes
after Lovell dropped down through the tunnel, Swigert
appeared as well. 5 On the ground Joe Kerwin,[k] <u>who was</u>
<u>scheduled to begin his fourth shift as Capcom in as many</u>
<u>days</u>, went on duty too, taking Lousma's place behind the
170 console.

"O.K.," Lovell called down to the new man in Houston,
"Jack's up with me now, and as soon as he gets on his
earphone, we'll be ready to copy."

"Roger that, Jim," Kerwin said, letting his
175 acknowledgement serve as his hello. "Whenever you're ready."

For the next hour, the work aboard *Apollo 13* had little
more orderliness than a scavenger hunt, and little more
technical elegance. With Kerwin reading from the list
of supplies Smylie had provided him, and Kraft, Slayton,
180 Lousma, and other controllers standing behind him and
consulting similar lists, the crew were dispatched around the
spacecraft to gather materials that had never been intended
for the uses to which they were about to be put.

Swigert swam back up into *Odyssey* and collected
185 a pair of scissors, two of the command module's oversized
lithium hydroxide canisters, and a roll of gray duct tape that
was supposed to be used for securing bags of refuse to the
ship's bulkhead in the final days of the mission. Haise dug
out his book of LEM procedures and turned to the heavy
190 cardboard pages that carried instructions for lifting off from
the moon—pages he now had no use for at all—and removed
them from their rings. Lovell opened the storage cabinet
at the back of the LEM and pulled out the plastic-wrapped
thermal undergarments he and Haise would have worn
195 beneath their pressure suits while walking on the moon.
No ordinary long johns, these one-piece suits had dozens of
feet of slender tubing woven into their fabric, through which
water would have circulated to keep the astronauts cool as
they worked in the glare of the lunar day. Lovell cut open the

---

[k] **Joe Kerwin**—A novice Capcom for NASA at the time of
Apollo 13

(continued)

200 plastic packaging, tossed the now useless union suits back into the cabinet, and kept the now priceless plastic with him.

When the materials had been gathered, Kerwin began reading up the assembly instructions Smylie had written. The work was, at best, slow going.

205 "Turn the canister so that you're looking at its vented end," Kewin said.

"The vented end?" Swigert asked.

"The end with the strap. We'll call that the top, and the other end the bottom."

210 "How much tape do we want to use here?" Lovell asked.

Kerwin said, "About three feet."

"Three feet . . ." Lovell contemplated out loud.

"Make it an arm's length."

"You want that tape to go on sticky end down?" Lovell asked.

215 "Yes, I forgot to say that," Kerwin said. "Sticky end down."

"I slip the bag along the canister so that it's oriented along the sides of the vent arch?" Swigert asked.

"Depends what you mean by 'sides,'" Kerwin responded.

"Good point," Swigert said. "The open ends."

220 "Roger," Kerwin responded.

This back-and-forth went on for an hour, until finally the first canister was done. The crewmen, whose hoped-for technical accomplishment this week involved nothing less ambitious than a soft touchdown in the Fra Mauro foothills

225 of the moon, stood back, folded their arms, and looked happily at the preposterous tape-and-paper object hanging from the pressure-suit hose.

"O.K.," Swigert announced to the ground, more proudly than he intended, "our do-it-yourself lithium hydroxide

230 canister is complete."

"Roger," Kerwin answered. "See if air is flowing through it."

With Lovell and Haise standing over him, Swigert pressed his ear against the open end of the canister. Softly, but unmistakably, he could hear air being drawn through

235 the vent slats and, presumably, across the pristine [5] lithium hydroxide crystals. In Houston, controllers crowded around

---

[5] **pristine:** remaining in a pure state; unspoiled

Comprehend It

How do you think the process of building the "do-it-yourself lithium hydroxide canister" is different from the other procedures that the astronauts performed on the mission?

_____

_____

_____

_____

_____

_____

_____

(continued)

Comprehend It

Identify the form of writing. What is the author's purpose?

_____

_____

_____

_____

_____

_____

_____

the screen at the TELMU's[1] console, staring at the carbon dioxide readout. In the spacecraft, Swigert, Lovell, and Haise turned to their instrument panel and did the same. Slowly,
240 all but imperceptibly [6] at first, the needle on the CO_2 scale began to fall, first to 12, then to 11.5, then to 11 and below. The men on the ground in Mission Control turned to one another and smiled. The men in the cockpit of *Aquarius* did the same.

"I think," Haise said to Lovell, "I might just finish that
245 roast beef now."

"I think," the commander responded, "I might just join you."

Excepted with permission from Houghton Mifflin Company

---

[1] **TELMU**—Telemetry, electrical, EVA (Extravehicular activity) mobility unit officer for NASA space missions

[6] **imperceptibly:** slightly; unnoticeably

The Raven: A Romantic Imagination

As we have learned, Edgar Allan Poe wrote fiction and literary criticism, but he was first and foremost a poet. As a young man, he was influenced by the English Romantic poets John Keats, Percy Bysshe Shelley, and Samuel Taylor
5 *Coleridge. These poets wrote about humankind's relationship to nature. They reflected on the limitations of society and often had a fascination with an idealized past. Poe was also influenced by Gothic literature, popular at the time, which included stories filled with a sense of terror, the supernatural,*
10 *and exotic locations such as castles or crumbling mansions.*

When Poe's poem "The Raven" was published in 1845, it was instantly popular for the haunting story it told and the music of its verse. In the preface to one of his volumes of poetry, Poe defined poetry as follows: "A poem, in my opinion,
15 *is opposed to a work of science by having, for its immediate object, pleasure, not truth.... Music, when combined with a pleasurable idea, is poetry."*

Readers are often puzzled by "The Raven." Is the raven real or just a product of the speaker's imagination? Why is
20 *it perched upon the bust of Pallas Athena, Greek goddess of wisdom? Who is Lenore? What happened to her? Poe's wife was ill with tuberculosis at the time "The Raven" was published, and she later died in 1847. Is Poe anticipating this sad event in his life, or does Lenore represent something*
25 *else? What does the refrain "Nevermore" mean? The dark, mysterious quality of the poem and its entrancing music give the reader's imagination free rein to consider the intriguing possibilities.*

Preview the Text

Read the highlighted words. Write words you cannot pronounce in the margin or on a self-stick note. Circle words that you can't define.

Comprehend It

Reread lines 18–28. Think of the six elements of poetry you have studied. Which element does the writer of this introduction address as she describes the poem as being "dark" and "mysterious"?

(continued)

Take Note

1. Underline the **metaphor** in lines 38–39.

2. Circle the words that **rhyme** at the end of lines 37–53.

3. Underline the letters that illustrate **alliteration** in line 43.

4. Underline the letters that illustrate **consonance** in line 46. (**Hint**: Look for words with the / s / sound.)

5. Underline the letters that illustrate **assonance** in line 55. (**Hint**: Look for words with **r**-controlled **o**.)

The Raven
by Edgar Allan Poe

Once upon a midnight dreary[1], while I pondered
30   weak and weary,
Over many a quaint[2] and curious volume of forgotten lore,
While I nodded, nearly napping, suddenly there came
       a tapping,
As of someone gently rapping, rapping at my chamber door.
35 ' 'Tis some visitor,' I muttered, 'tapping at my chamber door—
Only this, and nothing more.'

Ah, distinctly I remember it was in the bleak December,
And each separate dying ember wrought its ghost upon
       the floor.
40 Eagerly I wished the morrow;—vainly I had sought to borrow
From my books surcease of sorrow—sorrow for the lost
       Lenore—
For the rare and radiant maiden whom the angels named
       Lenore—
45 Nameless here for evermore.

And the silken sad uncertain rustling of each purple curtain
Thrilled me—filled me with fantastic terrors never
       felt before;
So that now, to still the beating of my heart, I stood
50   repeating
' 'Tis some visitor entreating entrance at my chamber door—
Some late visitor entreating entrance at my chamber door;—
This it is, and nothing more.'

[1] **dreary:** cheerless; gloomy

[2] **quaint:** charmingly unusual

(continued)

Presently my soul grew stronger; hesitating then no longer,
55 'Sir,' said I, 'or madam, truly your forgiveness I implore[3];
But the fact is I was napping, and so gently you came
    rapping,
And so faintly you came tapping, tapping at my chamber door,
That I scarce was sure I heard you'— Here I opened wide
60   the door;—
Darkness there, and nothing more.

Deep into that darkness peering, long I stood there
    wondering, fearing,
Doubting, dreaming dreams no mortal ever
65   dared to dream before
But the silence was unbroken, and the darkness gave no token,
And the only word there spoken was the whispered word,
    'Lenore!'
This I whispered, and an echo murmured back the word,
70   'Lenore!'
Merely this and nothing more.

Back into the chamber turning, all my soul within me
    burning,
Soon again I heard a tapping something louder than before.
75 'Surely,' said I, 'surely that is something at my window lattice;
Let me see then, what thereat is, and this mystery explore—
Let my heart be still a moment and this mystery explore;—
'Tis the wind and nothing more.'

---

[3] **implore:** beg; plead

(continued)

Comprehend It

Reread lines 29–87.

• What is the setting of the poem?

_____

_____

_____

• What is the speaker doing as the poem begins?

_____

_____

_____

• What happens when the speaker opens the window shutter?

_____

_____

_____

_____

_____

Reread lines 88–96.

• Paraphrase what the speaker asks the raven.

_____

_____

_____

_____

• How does the raven reply?

_____

Open here I flung the shutter, when, with many a flirt and
80   flutter,
In there stepped a stately raven of the saintly days of yore.
Not the least obeisance made he; not a minute stopped
    or stayed he;
But, with mienᵃ of lord or lady, perched above my
85   chamber door—
Perched upon a bust of Pallasᵇ just above my chamber door—
Perched, and sat, and nothing more.

Then this ebony bird beguiling⁴ my sad fancy into smiling,
By the grave and stern decorum of the countenance it wore,
90 'Though thy crest be shorn and shaven, thou,' I said, 'art
    sure no craven.
Ghastly grim and ancient raven wandering from the
    nightly shore—
Tell me what thy lordly name is on the Night's Plutonianᶜ
95   shore!'
Quoth the raven, 'Nevermore.'

Much I marvelled this ungainly⁵ fowl to hear discourse
    so plainly,
Though its answer little meaning—little relevancy bore;
100 For we cannot help agreeing that no living human being
Ever yet was blessed with seeing bird above his
    chamber door—
Bird or beast above the sculptured bust above his
    chamber door—
105 With such name as 'Nevermore.'

---

⁴ **beguiling:** enchanting by deception

⁵ **ungainly:** awkward; clumsy

ᵃ **mien**—appearance or manner

ᵇ **Pallas Athena**—the Greek goddess of wisdom

ᶜ **Plutonian shore**—the underworld realm of the Roman god Pluto

(continued)

But the raven, sitting lonely on the placid bust, spoke only,
That one word, as if his soul in that one word he did outpour.
Nothing further then he uttered—not a feather then he
    fluttered—
110 Till I scarcely more than muttered 'Other friends have
    flown before—
On the morrow will he leave me, as my hopes have flown before.'
Then the bird said, 'Nevermore.'

Startled at the stillness broken by reply so aptly spoken,
115 'Doubtless,' said I, 'what it utters is its only stock and store,
Caught from some unhappy master whom unmerciful
    disaster
Followed fast and followed faster till his songs one burden
    bore—
120 Till the dirges[d] of his hope that melancholy burden bore
Of 'Never—nevermore.' '

But the raven still beguiling all my sad soul into smiling,
Straight I wheeled a cushioned seat in front of bird and bust
    and door;
125 Then, upon the velvet sinking, I betook myself to linking
Fancy unto fancy, thinking what this ominous bird of yore—
What this grim, ungainly, gaunt, and ominous[6] bird
    of yore
Meant in croaking 'Nevermore.'

130 This I sat engaged in guessing, but no syllable expressing
To the fowl whose fiery eyes now burned into my
    bosom's core;
This and more I sat divining, with my head at ease reclining
On the cushion's velvet violet lining that the lamp-light
135   gloated o'er,
But whose velvet violet lining with the lamp-light
    gloating o'er,
She shall press, ah, nevermore!

---

[6] **ominous:** menacing; threatening

[d] **dirges**—funeral hymns or laments

(continued)

Comprehend It

Reread lines 130–138. As the speaker's head rests against a cushion, he thinks of a woman whose head will never press the cushion again. Who do you think he is thinking of?

_____

_____

_____

_____

_____

Text Connection 9 (continued)

Comprehend It

Reread lines 139–157. The speaker appears to get more and more angry at the raven. Why do you think this might be?

_____

_____

_____

_____

_____

Then, methought, the air grew denser, perfumed from an
140   unseen censer[e]
Swung by Seraphim[f] whose foot-falls tinkled on the
    tufted floor.
'Wretch,' I cried, 'thy God hath lent thee—by these angels he
    has sent thee
145 Respite—respite and nepenthe[g] from thy
    memories of Lenore!
Quaff, oh quaff this kind nepenthe, and forget this lost Lenore!'
Quoth the raven, 'Nevermore.'

'Prophet!' said I, 'thing of evil!—prophet still, if bird or devil!—
150 Whether tempter sent, or whether tempest tossed thee
    here ashore,
Desolate yet all undaunted, on this desert land
    enchanted—
On this home by horror haunted—tell me truly, I implore—
155 Is there—is there balm in Gilead?[h]—tell me—tell me I
    implore!'
Quoth the raven, 'Nevermore.'

'Prophet!' said I, 'thing of evil—prophet still, if bird or devil!
By that Heaven that bends above us—by that God we
160   both adore—
Tell this soul with sorrow laden if, within the distant
    Aidenn[i],
It shall clasp a sainted maiden whom the angels named
    Lenore—
165 Clasp a rare and radiant maiden, whom the angels named
    Lenore?'
Quoth the raven, 'Nevermore.'

---

[e] **censer**—a container for burning incense

[f] **seraphim**—angels

[g] **nepenthe**—a drink that makes one forget sorrow

[h] **Is there balm in Gilead?**—a quote from the Bible, Jeremiah 8:22. Balm of Gilead was known for its healing powers.

[i] **Aidenn**—the Garden of Eden

(continued)

Text Connection 9 (continued)

'Be that word our sign of parting, bird or fiend!' I shrieked, upstarting—

170   'Get thee back into the tempest and the Night's Plutonian shore!
Leave no black plume as a token of that lie thy soul hath spoken!
Leave my loneliness unbroken!—quit the bust above my door!
Take thy beak from out my heart, and take thy form from off my door.'

175   Quoth the raven, 'Nevermore.'

And the raven, never flitting, still is sitting, still is sitting
On the pallid bust of Pallas just above my chamber door;
And his eyes have all the seeming of a demon's that is dreaming

180   And the lamp-light o'er him streaming throws his shadow on the floor;
And my soul from out that shadow that lies floating on the floor
Shall be lifted—nevermore!

Comprehend It

What does the raven do to cause the speaker to cry, "Take thy beak from out my heart"?

_____

_____

_____

_____

_____

Identify the form of writing. What is the author's purpose?

_____

_____

_____

_____

_____

_____

_____

_____

_____

Preview the Text

Read the highlighted words. Write the words you cannot pronounce in the margin or on a self-stick note. Circle words that you can't define.

Take Note

Reread lines 25–32. Circle the names of the team members, and underline the contribution that each member made to the team.

La Vida Robot: Imagination Rules!

Imagine a team of high school students designing a fantastic underwater robot. Would the students have the expertise and the commitment to do it? Could it be done in a short time on a limited budget? Would it be competitive

5 *in a national contest against college teams? Allan Cameron, computer science teacher, and fellow science teacher Fredi "Ledge" Lajvardi imagined that a team of students from Carl Hayden High School could do it all.*

In spring of 2004 in Phoenix, Arizona, they put up flyers

10 *around their high school inviting students to join a team to compete in the third annual Marine Advanced Technology Education Center's Remotely Operated Vehicle Competition. The robot competition (sponsored in part by the Office of Naval Research and NASA) required students to build a bot*

15 *that could survey a sunken mock-up[a] of a submarine. The teachers decided to enter the Hayden team in the expert-level Explorer class instead of the beginner Ranger class, which meant they would be competing against college students. It seemed ambitious to assemble such a team from Carl Hayden*

20 *High School, where many of the students came from poor families and struggled academically. The teachers set such a high goal because they wanted to show these kids what they could achieve. The students who signed up included Lorenzo Santillan, Cristian Arcega, Luis Aranda, and Oscar Vazquez.*

25 *Little did the teachers know what an exceptional set of talent they had put together when they set to work. Lorenzo Santillan was the mechanical specialist. Cristian Arcega had one of the highest GPAs in the school district and wanted to be an engineer. Luis Aranda was strong and would be the*

30 *100-pound bot's tether[b] man, and Oscar Vazquez was the leader who persuaded local businesses to donate $800 to the team to pay for the materials they needed. The team had limited resources but lots of creative imagination. In four months they assembled an impressive bot built out*

[a] **mock-up**—a model

[b] **tether**—a rope used to pull something

(continued)

Text Connection 10 (continued)

35   *of PVC[c] pipe and equipped with cameras, lights, a laser,*
depth detectors, pumps, an underwater microphone, and
an articulated pincer[d]. At the top was a black, waterproof
briefcase containing a nest of hacked processors[e], minuscule
fans, and LEDs[f]. It was a cheap but astoundingly functional
40   *underwater robot capable of recording sonar[g] pings and*
retrieving objects 50 feet below the surface. But would Stinky,
the name they gave their bot, be able to match up to the
college competition and especially to the rival bot from MIT[h]?

    The team arrived at the Olympic-size UC Santa Barbara[i]
45   pool on a sunny Thursday afternoon. The pool was concealed
under a black tarp—the contest organizers didn't want the
students to get a peek at the layout of the mission. Students
from cities across the country—Miami; New Haven,
Connecticut; Galveston, Texas; Long Beach, California; and
50   half a dozen others—milled around the water's edge. The
Carl Hayden teammates tried to hide their nervousness, but
they were intimidated[1]. Lorenzo had never seen so many
white people in one place. He was also new to the ocean.
He had seen it for the first time several months earlier on
55   a school trip to San Diego. It still unnerved him to see so
much water. He said it was "incredifying"—incredible and
terrifying at the same time.

    Even though Lorenzo had never heard of MIT, the team
from Cambridge scared him, too. There were 12 of them—six
60   ocean-engineering students, four mechanical engineers, and
two computer science majors. Their robot was small, densely

---

[1] **intimidated:** filled with fear

[c] **PVC pipe**—plastic tubing

[d] **articulated pincer**—a tool with prongs for picking things up

[e] **hacked processors**—processors put together using parts from
several computers

[f] **LEDs (Light-Emitting Diodes)**—tiny electronic devices that
emit light like a light bulb

[g] **sonar**—a system for navigating that sends out sound waves or
pings

[h] **MIT**—Massachusetts Institute of Technology, one of the most
prestigious engineering schools in the world

[i] **UC Santa Barbara**—University of California at Santa Barbara

(continued)

Comprehend It

Summarize what made Lorenzo feel so nervous.

_____

_____

_____

_____

_____

_____

_____

Take Note

Circle the two problems that the Phoenix team discovered after they lowered their robot into the water, tested it, and brought it back up.

Underline the two actions that Oscar told the team they would have to undertake in order to solve their problems. (**Note**: To **solder** means to melt metal in order to join it to other metal. The team had to **resolder**, or solder wires again, to make sure they were properly connected in the robot.)

packed, and had a large ExxonMobil sticker emblazoned on the side. The largest corporation in the US had kicked in $5,000. Other donations brought the MIT team's total budget 65 to $11,000.

As Luis hoisted Stinky to the edge of the practice side of the pool, Cristian heard repressed snickering. It didn't give him a good feeling. He was proud of his robot, but he could see that it looked like a Geo Metro compared with the 70 Lexuses and BMWs around the pool. He had thought that Lorenzo's paint job was nice. Now it just looked clownish.

Things got worse when Luis lowered Stinky into the water. They noticed that the controls worked only intermittently[2]. When they brought Stinky back onto the 75 pool deck, there were a few drops of water in the waterproof briefcase that housed the control system. The case must have warped on the trip from Arizona in the back of Ledge's truck. If the water had touched any of the controls, the system would have shorted out and simply stopped working. Cristian 80 knew that they were faced with two serious problems: bad wiring and a leak.

Oscar sketched out the situation. They'd have to resolder every wire going into the main controller in the next 12 hours. And they would either have to fix the leak or find something 85 absorbent to keep moisture away from the onboard circuitry.

Someone had to be well rested for the contest, so Cristian and Luis slept that night. Oscar and Lorenzo stayed up resoldering the entire control system. It was nerve-racking work. The wires were slightly thicker than a human hair, and 90 there were 50 of them. If the soldering iron got too close to a wire, it would melt and there'd be no time to rip the PVC and cable housing apart to fix it. One broken wire would destroy the whole system, forcing them to withdraw from the contest.

95 By 2 in the morning, Oscar's eyesight was blurring, but he kept at it. Lorenzo held the wires in place while Oscar lowered the soldering gun. He dropped one last dab of alloy

---

[2] **intermittently:** periodically; unpredictably

(continued)

on the connection and sat back. Lorenzo flipped the power switch. Everything appeared to work again.

100   On the day of the contest, the organizers purposely made it difficult to see what was happening under the water. A set of high-powered fans blew across the surface of the pool, obscuring the view below and forcing teams to navigate by instrumentation alone. The side effect was that no one had a

105 good sense of how the other teams were doing.

     The task was to withdraw 500 milliliters of fluid from the container 12 feet below the surface. Its only opening was a small, half-inch pipe fitted with a one-way valve. Though the Carl Hayden team didn't know it, MIT had designed an

110 innovative system of bladders and pumps to carry out this task. MIT's robot was supposed to land on the container, create a seal, and pump out the fluid. On three test runs in Boston, the system worked fast and flawlessly.

     MIT's ROV motored smoothly down and quickly located

115 the 5-gallon drum inside the plastic submarine mock-up at the bottom of the pool. But as the robot approached the container, its protruding mechanical arm hit a piece of the submarine frame, blocking it from going farther. The MIT team tried a different angle but their robot still couldn't

120 reach the drum. The bot wasn't small enough to slip past the gap in the frame, making their pump system useless. There was nothing they could do—they had to move on to the next assignment.

     When Stinky entered the water, it careened wildly as

125 it dived toward the bottom. Luis stood at the pool's edge, paying out the tether cable. From the control tent, Cristian, Oscar, and Lorenzo monitored Stinky's descent on their videoscreens.

     "*Vámonos*, Cristian, this is it!" Oscar said, pushing

130 his control too far forward. They were nervous and overcompensated for each other's joystick movements, causing Stinky to veer off course. They settled down and knocked off the first two tasks. When they reached the submarine, they saw the drum and tried to steady the robot. Stinky had a

135 bent copper proboscis, a bilge pump, and a dime-store balloon. They had to fit their long, quarter-inch-wide sampling

(continued)

Comprehend It

How did the size of the MIT robot end up being a disadvantage?

_____

_____

_____

_____

_____

_____

_____

Comprehend It

What feature of the Carl Hayden robot enabled it to succeed in getting the fluid sample where the MIT robot had failed?

_____

_____

_____

_____

Comprehend It

Based on the fact that this article describes the fluid sampling task in great detail, what can you infer about the difficulty of that task?

_____

_____

_____

_____

_____

Comprehend It

• How many total underwater tasks did each team have to perform?

_____

• How much did the report and the interview count in the overall score?

_____

_____

_____

tube into a half-inch pipe and then fill the balloon for exactly 20 seconds to get 500 milliliters. They had practiced dozens of times at the scuba pool in Phoenix, and it had taken them,
140 on average, 10 minutes to stab the proboscis into the narrow tube. Now they had 30 minutes total to complete all seven tasks on the checklist.

It was up to Oscar and Cristian. They re-adjusted their grip on the joysticks and leaned into the monitors.
145 Stinky hovered in front of the submarine framing that had frustrated the MIT team. Because Stinky's copper pipe was 18 inches long, it was able to reach the drum. The control tent was silent. Now that they were focused on the mission, both pilots relaxed and made almost imperceptibly small
150 movements with their joysticks. Oscar tapped the control forward while Cristian gave a short backward blast on the vertical propellers. As Stinky floated forward a half inch, its rear raised up and the sampling pipe sank perfectly into the drum.
155 Oscar looked at Lorenzo, who had already activated the pump and was counting out 20 seconds in a decidedly unscientific way.

"_Uno, dos, tres, quatro,_" Lorenzo whispered.

Oscar backed Stinky out of the sub. They spun the robot
160 around, piloted it back to Luis at the edge of the pool, and looked at the judges, who stood in the control tent behind them.

"Can we make a little noise?" Cristian asked Pat Barrow, a NASA lab operations manager supervising the contest.
165 "Go on ahead," he replied.

Cristian started yelling, and all three ran out to hug Luis, who held the now-filled blue balloon. Luis stood there with a silly grin on his face while his friends danced around him.

It was a short celebration. They still had four more tasks.
170 Luis quickly lowered the ROV back into the water.

Tom Swean was the gruff 58-year-old head of the Navy's Ocean Engineering and Marine Systems program. He developed million-dollar autonomous[3] underwater robots

---

[3] **autonomous:** independent; capable of operating without outside control

(continued)

for the SEALs at the Office of Naval Research. He was not
175 used to dealing with Mexican-American teenagers sporting
gold chains, fake diamond rings, and patchy, adolescent
mustaches.

The Carl Hayden team stood nervously in front of him.
He stared sullenly [4] at them. This was the engineering
180 review—professionals in underwater engineering evaluated
all the ROVs, scored each team's technical documentation,
and grilled students about their designs. The results counted
for more than half of the total possible points in the contest.

"How'd you make the laser range finder work?" Swean
185 growled. MIT had admitted earlier that a laser would have
been the most accurate way to measure distance underwater,
but they'd concluded that it would have been difficult to
implement.

"We used a helium neon laser, captured its phase shift
190 with a photo sensor, and manually corrected by 30 percent
to account for the index of refraction," Cristian answered
rapidly, keyed up on adrenaline. Cameron had peppered them
with questions on the drive to Santa Barbara, and Cristian
was ready.

195 Swean raised a bushy, graying eyebrow. He asked about
motor speed, and Lorenzo sketched out their combination
of controllers and spike relays. Oscar answered the question
about signal interference in the tether by describing how
they'd experimented with a 15-meter cable before jumping
200 up to one that was 33 meters.

"You're very comfortable with the metric system," Swean
observed.

"I grew up in Mexico, sir," Oscar said.

Swean nodded. He eyed their rudimentary [5] flip chart.

205 "Why don't you have a PowerPoint display?" he asked.

"PowerPoint is a distraction," Cristian replied. "People use
it when they don't know what to say."

"And you know what to say?"

"Yes, sir."

---

[4] **sullenly:** gloomily; resentfully

[5] **rudimentary:** simple; basic

(continued)

Take Note

- Circle Tom Swean's first question.

- Underline Cristian's response to Swean's question.

- Draw a box around the detail in line 195 that suggests that Swean was surprised and impressed by Cristian's response.

Comprehend It

How did the Carl Hayden team do compared to the other teams in the seven underwater tasks?

_____

_____

_____

_____

Comprehend It

Why was the Carl Hayden team disappointed to win the special prize?

_____

_____

_____

_____

_____

210   In the lobby outside the review room, Cameron and Ledge waited anxiously for the kids. They expected them to come out shaken, but all four were smiling—convinced that they had answered Swean's questions perfectly. Cameron glanced nervously at Ledge. The kids were too confident.
215 They couldn't have done that well.

    Still, both teachers were in a good mood. They had learned that the team placed third out of 11 in the seven underwater exercises. Only MIT and Cape Fear Community College from North Carolina had done better. The overall
220 winner would be determined by combining those results with the engineering interview and a review of each group's technical manual. Even if they did poorly on the interview, they were now positive that they hadn't placed last.

    The awards ceremony took place over dinner, and the
225 Carl Hayden team was glad for that. They hadn't eaten well over the past two days, and even flavorless iceberg lettuce looked good to them. Their nerves had calmed. After the engineering interview, they decided that they had probably placed somewhere in the middle of the pack, maybe fourth or
230 fifth overall. Privately, each of them was hoping for third.

    The first award was a surprise: a judge's special prize that wasn't listed in the program. Bryce Merrill, the bearded, middle-aged recruiting manager for Oceaneering International, an industrial ROV design firm, was the
235 announcer. He explained that the judges created this spontaneously to honor special achievement. He stood behind a podium on the temporary stage and glanced down at his notes. The contestants sat crowded around a dozen tables. Carl Hayden High School, he said, was that special
240 team.

    The guys trotted up to the stage, forcing smiles. It seemed obvious that this was a condescending pat on the back, as if to say, "A for effort!" They didn't want to be "special"—they wanted third. It signaled to them that they'd missed it.
245   They returned to their seats, and Cameron and Ledge shook their hands.

    "Good job, guys," Ledge said, trying to sound pleased. "You did well."

(continued)

After a few small prizes were handed out (Terrific Tether
250 Management, Perfect Pickup Tool), Merrill moved on to
the final awards: Design Elegance, Technical Report, and
Overall Winner. The MIT students shifted in their seats and
stretched their legs. While they had been forced to skip the
fluid sampling, they had completed more underwater tasks
255 overall than Carl Hayden or Cape Fear. The Cape Fear team
sat across the room, fidgeted with their napkins, and tried
not to look nervous. The students from Monterey Peninsula
College looked straight ahead. They placed fourth behind
Carl Hayden in the underwater trials. They were the most
260 likely third-place finishers. The guys from Phoenix glanced
back at the buffet table and wondered if they could get more
cake before the ceremony ended.

Then Merrill leaned into the microphone and said that
the ROV named Stinky had captured the design award.

265   "What did he just say?" Lorenzo asked.

"Oh my..." Ledge shouted. "Stand up!"

Before they could sit down again, Merrill told them that
they had won the technical writing award.

"Us illiterate people from the desert?" Lorenzo thought.
270 He looked at Cristian, who had been responsible for a large
part of the writing. Cristian was beaming. To his analytical[6]
mind, there was no possibility that his team—a bunch of ESL
students—could produce a better written report than kids
from one of the country's top engineering schools.

275   They had just won two of the most important awards. All
that was left was the grand prize. Cristian quickly calculated
the probability of winning but couldn't believe what he was
coming up with.

"And the overall winner for the Marine Technology ROV
280 championship," Merrill continued, looking up at the crowd,
"goes to Carl Hayden High School of Phoenix, Arizona!"

Reprinted with permission from the author.

---

[6] **analytical:** tending to examine things very carefully

Take Note

• Circle the names of the three teams that the Carl Hayden team felt were most likely to be the top three finishers.

• Underline the description of each of these teams.

Comprehend It

List two reasons why Lorenzo was so surprised that they had won the technical writing award.

_____

_____

_____

_____

_____

_____

Identify the form of writing. What is the author's purpose?

_____

_____

_____

_____

_____

_____

_____

Text Connection 11

Preview the Text

Read the highlighted words. Write the words you cannot pronounce in the margin or on a self-stick note. Circle words that you can't define.

Comprehend It

What is a **syllabary**?

_____

_____

_____

_____

_____

• Use the invented syllabary to encode the word **transform**.

_____

• Then use it to decode this word: ❗ ❤

_____

Sequoyah: Brilliant Code-Maker

"When I have heard anything, I write it down, and lay by it and take it up again at some future day. And there find all that I have heard exactly as I heard it."
—Sequoyah

5   If you can read this sentence, you have mastered the code of written English. Without stopping to think about it, you automatically, rapidly, and fluently [1] associate the symbols (letters) you see with the phonemes (sounds) those letters represent. You're a code-breaker.

10   But try to imagine listening to a spoken language and *inventing* a code, a system that could be used to transform [2] spoken words into writing. Sequoyah (c. 1776–1843), famed Cherokee chief, did just that. He invented an orthographic system—a system for writing—for his native language. But

15   Sequoyah didn't base his code on an alphabet; instead, he created a syllabary. What's the difference? Like an alphabet, a syllabary uses symbols. But each symbol in a syllabary represents an entire syllable—not just a sound.

To understand how a syllabary works, study this invented

20   English syllabary, and use it to write some English words.

Try to encode the word *consider*, using the syllabary above. (answer = ✖★❭)

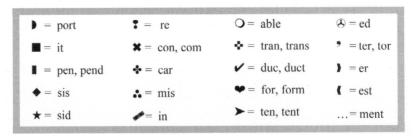

❭ = port	❗ = re	◯ = able	⊛ = ed
■ = it	✖ = con, com	✤ = tran, trans	⁹ = ter, tor
▮ = pen, pend	✤ = car	✔ = duc, duct	❭ = er
◆ = sis	⋰ = mis	❤ = for, form	❨ = est
★ = sid	✦ = in	➤ = ten, tent	… = ment

---

[1] **fluently:** with ease and accuracy

[2] **transform:** to change in shape or appearance

(continued)

Now try to code these English words:

reconsider	*former*	*consistent*	*misinform*
25 *carpenter*	*contentment*	*forage*	*conform*
sister	*transit*	*carport*	*reporter*
portage	*transistor*	*mister*	*conducted*
misconduct			

30 Finally, using your math skills, attempt to calculate the difficulty of using a syllabary, rather than an alphabet, to learn written English. Here are some factors to consider:

Most linguists agree that well over a million words can be formed in English.

English has seven syllable types.

35 Most English words have more than one syllable.

In your calculations, consider these questions:

How many syllable symbols would be needed to create an English syllabary?

How might the various English syllable types complicate 40 the system?

How long would it take to learn an English syllabary?

Would it be more difficult to learn written English in an alphabet or a syllabary?

In general, which orthographic system would be most 45 efficient for learning any language—alphabetic, syllabic, or hieroglyphic? As you consider this question, think about your own language skills. If you're able to *think about and discuss this question*, you're not just a code-breaker; you've become a linguist! Congratulations.

(continued)

Text Connection 11 (continued)

Take Note

Reread lines 64–72.

• Which best sums up the main idea of that paragraph? (check one)

_____ Sequoyah's experience in the Creek War convinced him that written language was needed.

_____ Cherokee soldiers could not write letters home.

• Draw checkmarks (√) next to three details that support the main idea you chose.

Why Did He Do It?

50   "Talking leaves" interested Sequoyah. Some native people used this term to mean book pages that contained written words. For Sequoyah, written language was a new concept. His people's language had been spoken for millennia, but like most languages that have ever been spoken, there was

55 no written form. It hadn't yet been invented. Sequoyah realized that written language allowed people to collect and communicate great amounts of knowledge. He understood that a people who had a written language could record their history and share their legends; they could create literature

60 for their descendants. He understood that writing was the secret of power. Sometime around 1809, Sequoyah began developing an orthographic system—a written representation of his people's spoken language.

    In 1813, Sequoyah's work was interrupted. He joined the

65 United States Army's Cherokee Regiment and fought in the Creek War[a]. This experience deepened his belief about the importance of written language. His fellow Cherokee soldiers couldn't read military orders. They couldn't record events as they happened. They couldn't write letters home to their

70 loved ones. **1** During the war, Sequoyah became ever more convinced that literacy was critical[3] to the survival of his people.

    2 After the war, Sequoyah concentrated on the development of a written code for Cherokee. An old shed

75 became his literacy workshop. **3** Day after day he worked, making marks on wood chips and scraps of paper. Friends and family believed he was crazy. Someone burned his workshop to the ground. Sequoyah kept on working.

    4 In 1821, his masterpiece of a lifetime was completed.

80 Written forms of other languages had developed over

---

[3] **critical:** very important; essential

[a] The Creek War (1813–1814) was fought between the Creek Indians (then living in what in what is now Georgia and Alabama) and the U.S. Army. The Creeks were defeated and made to give up their land.

(continued)

centuries. They had developed with the input of many people. But Sequoyah completed his work within a single lifetime. 5 In just a few years, he had created a written code of the Cherokee language.

Identify It: Transitional Words and Phrases

- Locate the first numbered sentence in the text.
- Identify the transitional word or phrase, underline it, and write it on the line.
- Identify and underline the transitional word or phrase in each of the remaining numbered sentences.
- Determine the relationship created in each sentence and list it below. Refer to the **Transitional Words and Phrases** chart as needed.

Transitional Word or Phrase   **Relationship**

1. _____

2. _____

3. _____

4. _____

5. _____

85   According to legend, Sequoyah and his daughter went to the tent where tribal leaders were waiting. Sequoyah told them that he had created a way to write the Cherokee language. The elders were doubtful and demanded that Sequoyah prove his claim. Sequoyah's daughter exited

90 the tent. After she left, one of the tribal leaders dictated a whispered message. Sequoyah wrote the message. His daughter re-entered the tent, looked at her father, and then looked at what he had written. As the astonished elders looked on, she read her father's message aloud. A written

95 language had been born. A civilization's record would be saved for all of history. An entire people had been given a key to communicating their knowledge of the world.

Comprehend It

Why might some of Sequoyah's people not have supported his work?

_____

_____

_____

_____

_____

_____

_____

_____

_____

(continued)

Unit 36

Take Note

Reread lines 105–110.

• Draw a box around the first sentence.

• Draw checkmarks (√) next to three details that explain or support this main idea.

Comprehend It

What symbols did Sequoyah use for his syllabary?

_____

_____

_____

_____

_____

Identify this form of writing. What is the author's purpose?

_____

_____

_____

_____

_____

_____

_____

How Did He Do It?

At first, Sequoyah set out to devise a set of pictographs. Pictographs are symbols that stand for words. Sequoyah soon
100 realized that thousands of pictographs would be needed to represent every word in the Cherokee language. Imagine how long it would take to memorize thousands of symbols! It would be like trying to learn a symbol for every word in the English language.

105 After the pictographs, Sequoyah tried a new direction. Instead of using pictures to represent words, he decided to use symbols to represent the sounds in words. Sequoyah began to divide every word in the Cherokee language into syllables. He figured out that the Cherokee language was
110 made up of about 85 vowel and consonant combinations.

Next, Sequoyah faced the challenge of assigning a symbol to every sound. Eventually he came up with a symbol to represent every syllable he had identified. Some symbols resembled [4] letters of the Roman alphabet. Others drew from
115 the Greek and Hebrew alphabets. Sequoyah invented many of the symbols himself. These symbols became known as the Cherokee alphabet.

Once Sequoyah convinced the tribal leaders that his syllabary was successful, he set out to teach it to his people.
120 Some records say that within six months, thousands of Cherokee were literate .[5] The Cherokee became the first Native American tribe to publish a newspaper. The *Cherokee Phoenix* was first published in 1828. It is still being published today.

125 Creating a written code for an entire language is a complicated matter, as Sequoyah discovered. However, written language is a priceless commodity .[6] Because of Sequoyah's syllabary, his language has not only survived—it has thrived. Today the Cherokee language is spoken by
130 approximately 15,000 people.

---

[4] **resembled:** appeared alike or similar to

[5] **literate:** able to read and write

[6] **commodity:** something useful or valued

The Miracle Worker: Dawning of Brilliance

By William Gibson

1   *Audiences all over the world have been moved and inspired by the poignant tragedy, painful conflict, and ultimate triumph portrayed in the drama titled* The Miracle Worker *by William Gibson. Originally written for television,*
5   *the play opened on Broadway in 1959. In three memorable acts, Gibson reveals the true-life childhood story of Helen Keller, who was afflicted by an illness that left her blind and deaf at the age of 19 months.*

Locked inside a sightless and soundless world, Helen in
10   *her frustration throws tantrums and physically lashes out at her family and her surroundings. Her father, Captain Keller, is at a loss as to how to help his daughter and tends either to ignore or indulge her. Helen's mother, Kate Keller, grows desperate as remedies suggested by doctors fail, and*
15   *she convinces her husband to hire a governess for Helen. Twenty-year-old Anne Sullivan, the new hire, arrives at the Keller home from the Perkins Institute for the Blind, where she has been treated for blindness and has had partial vision restored. Her life has also been filled with tragedy; she is*
20   *haunted by memories of her brother, who died after they were separated at an orphanage.*

Captain and Kate Keller are skeptical that this young girl can help their daughter. Captain Keller's son, James, is sullen and sarcastic as a result of ineffective ways that his father
25   *and Kate have dealt with Helen's disruption of the family. Undaunted by their lack of confidence in her, Anne takes on the task of teaching Helen proper behavior. She insists that the family stop indulging Helen's tantrums. She physically forces Helen to eat from her own plate with a spoon and fold her*
30   *napkin. She also starts spelling words in Helen's hand. She*

Preview the Text

Read the highlighted words. Write the words you cannot pronounce in the margin or on self-stick notes. Circle words that you can't define.

Comprehend It

• What would be challenging about teaching a person who could neither see nor hear to read?

_____

_____

_____

_____

_____

• Why does Annie spell words on Helen's hand?

_____

_____

_____

_____

_____

_____

(continued)

Take Note

• Draw a box around the setting of the play.

• Look at the **Cast of Characters**. Circle the names of four members of Helen's family. (Note that James is Captain Keller's son and Kate's stepson.)

knows that the most important thing she can teach Helen is the meaning of language.

35 *As the third act opens, Helen has been living with Anne in the Keller's garden house for almost two weeks. Anne has asked the Kellers to give her two weeks alone with Helen so that Helen will be forced to focus on Anne as her teacher. Time is running out for Anne to achieve the miracle that she is looking for with Helen; she wants the child to show an understanding of the words she spells in her hand.*

40 Time: The 1880s
Place: The Keller homestead in Tuscumbia, Alabama

Cast of Characters
Helen Keller—Blind and deaf child

Captain Arthur Keller—Helen's father; fought in the Civil War

Kate Keller—Helen's mother

45 James Keller—Captain Keller's son and Helen's half-brother

Aunt Ev—Helen's Aunt

Annie Sullivan—Helen's governess and teacher

Michael Anagnos—Annie's counselor and director of the Perkins Institute for the Blind

50 Viney—Servant

Martha and Percy—Viney's children

(continued)

Act Three

Scene 1

The stage is totally dark, until we see ANNIE *and* HELEN *silhouetted on the bed in the garden house.* ANNIE'S *voice is* audible ,[1] *very patient, and worn; it has been saying this for a*
55 *long time.*

Annie. Water, Helen. This is water. W, a, t, e, r. It has a *name.* (*A silence. Then:*) Egg, e, g, g. It has a *name*, the name stands for the thing. Oh, it's so simple, simple as birth, to explain. (*The lights have commenced to rise, not on the garden house*
60 *but on the homestead. Then:*) Helen, Helen, the chick *has* to come out of its shell, sometime. You come out, too. (*In the bedroom upstairs, we see* VINEY *unhurriedly washing the window, dusting, turning the mattress, readying the room for use again; then in the family room a diminished group at one*
65 *end of the table—*KATE, KELLER, JAMES—*finishing up a quiet breakfast; then outside, down right, the other servant on his knees, assisted by* MARTHA, *working with a trowel around a new trellis and wheelbarrow. The scene is one of everyday calm, and all are oblivious to* ANNIE'S *voice.*) There's only one
70 way out, for you, and it's language. To learn that your fingers can talk. And say anything, anything you can name. This is mug. Mug, m, u, g. Helen, it has a *name.* It—has—a—*name.*

[KATE *rises from the table.*]

Keller (*gently*). You haven't eaten, Katie.

75 **Kate** (*smiles, shakes her head*). I haven't the appetite. I'm too—restless, I can't sit to it.

Keller. You should eat, my dear. It will be a long day, waiting.

James (*lightly*). But it's been a short two weeks. I never thought life could be so—noiseless, went much too quickly for me.

---

[1] **audible:** capable of being heard

(continued)

Read the stage directions at the beginning of Scene 1. Underline the place where Annie and Helen are as the scene begins.

Underline where Helen's family is and what they are doing while she and Annie are in the garden house.

Unit 36

Comprehend It

Read lines 80–105. Is Annie speaking to James and Captain Keller? If not, why do you think the dialog is written this way?

_____

_____

_____

_____

_____

_____

80 [KATE *and* KELLER *gaze at him, in silence.* JAMES *becomes uncomfortable.*]

Annie. C, a, r, d. Card. C, a—

James. Well, the house has been practically normal, hasn't it?

Keller *(harshly).* Jimmie.

85 **James.** Is it wrong to enjoy a quiet breakfast, after five years? And you two even seem to enjoy each other—

Keller. It could be even more noiseless, Jimmie, without your tongue running every minute. Haven't you enough feeling to imagine what Katie has been undergoing, ever since—

90 [KATE *stops him, with her hand on his arm.*]

Kate. Captain. *(To* JAMES*)* It's true. The two weeks have been normal, quiet, all you say. But not short. Interminable. *(She rises, and wanders out; she pauses on the porch steps, gazing toward the garden house.)*

95 **Annie** *(fading).* W, a, t, e, r. But it means *this*. W, a, t, e, r. *This*. W, a, t—

James. I only meant that Miss Sullivan is a boon. Of contention, though, it seems.

Keller *(heavily).* If and when you're a parent, Jimmie, you
100 will understand what separation means. A mother loses a—protector.

James *(baffled).* Hm?

Keller. You'll learn, we don't just keep our children safe. They keep us safe. *(He rises, with his empty coffee cup and saucer.)*
105 There are of course all kinds of separation. Katie has lived

(continued)

with one kind for five years. And another is disappointment. In a child.

[*He goes with the cup out the rear door.* JAMES *sits for a long moment of stillness. In the garden house the lights commence*
110 *to come up;* ANNIE, *haggard* [2] *at the table, is writing a letter, her face again almost in contact with the stationery;* HELEN, *apart on the stool, and for the first time as clean and neat as a button, is quietly crocheting an endless chain of wool, which snakes all around the room.*]

115 **Annie.** "I, feel, every, day, more, and, more, in—" (*She pauses, and turns the pages of a dictionary open before her; her finger descends the words to a full stop. She elevates her eyebrows, then copies the word.*) "—adequate."

[*In the main house* JAMES *pushes up, and goes to the front*
120 *doorway, after* KATE.]

James. Kate? (KATE *turns her glance.* JAMES *is rather wary.*) I'm sorry. Open my mouth, like that fairy tale, frogs jump out.

Kate. No. It has been better. For everyone. (*She starts away,*
125 *up center.*)

Annie (*writing*). "If, only, there, were, someone, to, help, me, I, need, a, teacher, as, much, as, Helen—"

James. Kate. (KATE *halts, waits.*) What does he want from me?

130 **Kate.** That's not the question. Stand up to the world, Jimmie, that comes first.

James (*a pause, wryly*). But the world is him.

---

[2] **haggard:** appearing worn and exhausted

Comprehend It

Infer what Captain Keller means when he says that his wife has lived with one kind of separation for five years.

(Hint: How old was Helen when she lost her sight and hearing?)

_____

_____

_____

_____

_____

_____

_____

Read line 115. Why do you think the author of the play put commas between every word?

_____

_____

_____

_____

(continued)

Comprehend It

• Why are Annie's eyes bothering her?

_____

_____

_____

_____

_____

• Why do you think Annie is still learning how to spell?

_____

_____

_____

_____

_____

• What does Annie mean when she says, "It's like a surprise party, the most unexpected characters turn up." (lines 157–158)?

_____

_____

_____

_____

_____

_____

• What "unexpected character" turns up in the word **discipline**?

_____

_____

_____

_____

_____

Kate. Yes. And no one can do it for you.

James. Kate. *(His voice is humble.)* At least we—Could you—
135 be my friend?

Kate. I am.

[KATE *turns to wander, up back of the garden house.* ANNIE'S *murmur comes at once; the lights begin to die on the main house.*]

140 **Annie.** "—my, mind, is, undisciplined, full, of, skips, and, jumps, and—" *(She halts, rereads, frowns.)* Hm. (ANNIE *puts her nose again in the dictionary, flips back to an earlier page, and fingers down the words;* KATE *presently comes down toward the bay window with a trayful of food.)* Disinter—
145 disinterested—disjoin—dis— *(She backtracks, indignant.)* Disinterested, disjoin—Where's discipline? *(She goes a page or two back, searching with her finger, muttering.)* What a dictionary, have to know how to spell it before you can look up how to spell it, disciple, *discipline!* Diskipline. *(She*
150 *corrects the word in her letter.)* Undisciplined.

[*But her eyes are bothering her, she closes them in exhaustion and gently fingers the eyelids.* KATE *watches her through the window.*]

Kate. What are you doing to your eyes?

155 [ANNIE *glances around; she puts her smoked glasses on, and gets up to come over, assuming a cheerful energy.*]

Annie. It's worse on my vanity! I'm learning to spell. It's like a surprise party, the most unexpected characters turn up.

Kate. You're not to overwork your eyes, Miss Annie.

(continued)

160 **Annie.** Well. *(She takes the tray, sets it on her chair, and carries chair and tray to* HELEN.*)* Whatever I spell to Helen I'd better spell right.

Kate *(almost wistful).* How—serene she is.

Annie. She learned this stitch yesterday. Now I can't get her
165 to stop! *(She disentangles one foot from the wool chain, and sets the chair before* HELEN. HELEN *at its contact with her knee feels the plate, promptly sets her crocheting down, and tucks the napkin in at her neck, but* ANNIE *withholds the spoon; when* HELEN *finds it missing, she folds her hands in*
170 *her lap, and quietly waits.* ANNIE *twinkles at* KATE *with mock devoutness.)* Such a little lady, she'd sooner starve than eat with her fingers.

[*She gives* HELEN *the spoon, and* HELEN *begins to eat, neatly.*]

Kate. You've taught her so much, these two weeks. I would
175 never have—

Annie. Not enough. *(She is suddenly gloomy, shakes her head.)* Obedience isn't enough. Well, she learned two nouns this morning, key and water, brings her up to eighteen nouns and three verbs.

180 **Kate** *(hesitant).* But—not—

Annie. No. Not that they mean things. It's still a finger-game, no meaning. *(She turns to* KATE, *abruptly.)* Mrs. Keller— *(But she defers it; she comes back, to sit in the bay, and lifts her hand.)* Shall we play our finger-game?

185 **Kate.** How will she learn it?

Annie. It will come.

[*She spells a word;* KATE *does not respond.*]

(continued)

Kate. How?

Annie *(a pause).* How does a bird learn to fly? *(She spells*
190 *again.)* We're born to use words, like wings, it has to come.

Kate. How?

Annie *(another pause, wearily).* All right. I don't know
how. *(She pushes up her glasses to rub her eyes.)* I've done
everything I could think of. Whatever she's learned here—
195 keeping herself clean, knitting, stringing beads, meals,
setting up exercises each morning, we climb trees, hunt eggs,
yesterday a chick was born in her hands—all of it I spell,
everything we do, we never stop spelling. I go to bed with—
writer's cramp from talking so much!

200 **Kate.** I worry about you, Miss Annie. You must rest.

Annie. Now? She spells back in her *sleep*, her fingers make
letters when she doesn't know! In her bones those five fingers
know, that hand aches to—speak out, and something in her
mind is asleep, how do I—nudge that awake? That's the one
205 question.

Kate. With no answer.

Annie *(long pause).* Except keep at it. Like this.

[*She again begins spelling—I, need—and* KATE's *brows gather,
following the words.*]

210 **Kate.** More—time? *(She glances at* ANNIE, *who looks her in
the eyes, silent.)* Here?

Annie. Spell it.

[KATE *spells a word—no—shaking her head;* ANNIE *spells two
words—why, not—back, with an impatient question in her
215 eyes; and* KATE *moves her head in pain to answer it.*]

(continued)

Text Connection 12 (continued)

Kate. Because I can't—

Annie. Spell it! If she ever learns, you'll have a lot to tell each other, start now.

[KATE *painstakingly spells in air. In the midst of this the rear*
220 *door opens, and* KELLER *enters with the setter* BELLE *in tow.*]

Keller. Miss Sullivan? On my way to the office, I brought Helen a playmate—

Annie. Outside please, Captain Keller.

Keller. My dear child, the two weeks are up today, surely you
225 don't object to—

Annie *(rising).* They're not up till six o'clock.

Keller *(indulgent).* Oh, now. What difference can a fraction of one day—

Annie. An agreement is an agreement. Now you've been very
230 good, I'm sure you can keep it up for a few more hours.

[*She escorts* KELLER *by the arm over the threshold; he obeys, leaving* BELLE.]

Keller. Miss Sullivan, you are a tyrant.³

Annie. Likewise, I'm sure. You can stand there, and close the
235 door if she comes.

Kate. I don't think you know how eager we are to have her back in our arms—

---

³ **tyrant:** a harsh, controlling person

Comprehend It

Read lines 219–230. When Captain Keller walks in bringing their dog Belle, how does Annie react?

_____

_____

_____

_____

_____

A **tyrant** is a ruler who exercises power in a harsh, cruel manner. Why does Keller call Annie a tyrant?

_____

_____

_____

_____

_____

_____

_____

(continued)

Annie. I do know, it's my main worry.

Keller. It's like expecting a new child in the house. Well,
240 she *is*, so— composed ,[4] so— *(Gently)* attractive. You've done
wonders for her, Miss Sullivan.

Rewrite It: Quotation Marks

- Rewrite each line of script below as a direct quotation.

- Place quotation marks and other punctuation as needed.

- Add a word or phrase to indicate how the person spoke
  these words. Do not use the word **said**.

  1. Miss Sullivan, you are a tyrant Captain Keller _____

  2. Likewise, I'm sure Annie _____

  3. Kate _____ I don't think you
     know how eager we are to have her back in our arms

  4. I do know. It's my main worry Annie _____

  _____

  5. It's like expecting a new child in the house the captain

  _____

Annie *(not a question)*. Have I.

Keller. If there's anything you want from us in repayment tell
us, it will be a privilege to—

245 **Annie.** I just told Mrs. Keller. I want more time.

Kate. Miss Annie—

Annie. Another week.

[HELEN *lifts her head, and begins to sniff.*]

---

[4] **composed:** calm

(continued)

Keller. We miss the child. *I* miss her, I'm glad to say, that's a
250 different debt I owe you—

Annie. Pay it to Helen. Give *her* another week.

Kate *(gently)*. Doesn't she miss us?

Keller. Of course she does. What a wrench this
unexplainable— exile⁵ must be to her, can you say it's not?

255 **Annie.** No. But I—

[HELEN *is off the stool, to grope about the room; when she
encounters* BELLE, *she throws her arms around the dog's neck
in delight.*]

Kate. Doesn't she need affection too, Miss Annie?

260 **Annie** *(wavering)*. She—never shows me she needs it, she
won't have any—caressing or—

Kate. But you're not her mother.

Keller. And what would another week accomplish? We are
more than satisfied, you've done more than we ever thought
265 possible, taught her constructive—

Annie. I can't promise anything. All I can—

Keller *(no break)*. —things to do, to behave like—even look
like—a human child, so manageable, contented, cleaner, more—

Annie *(withering)*. Cleaner.

270 **Keller.** Well. We say cleanliness is next to godliness, Miss—

---

⁵ **exile:** a forced absence from one's home

(continued)

Take Note

Read lines 260–270 and take note of the stage directions. Underline two words that show how Annie reacts to what is being said. If you don't know the meanings of these words, look them up in a dictionary.

Comprehend It

Read lines 267–277. Paraphrase these lines.

_____

_____

_____

_____

_____

_____

_____

_____

_____

Annie. Cleanliness is next to nothing, she has to learn that everything has its name! That words can be her *eyes*, to everything in the world outside her, and inside too, what is she without words? With them she can think, have ideas, be
275 reached, there's not a thought or fact in the world that can't be hers. You publish a newspaper, Captain Keller, do I have to tell you what words are? And she has them already—

Keller. Miss Sullivan.

Annie. —eighteen nouns and three verbs, they're in her
280 fingers now, I need only time to push *one* of them into her mind! One, and everything under the sun will follow. Don't you see what she's learned here is only clearing the way for that? I can't risk her unlearning it, give me more time alone with her, another week to—

285 **Keller.** Look. *(He points, and* ANNIE *turns.* HELEN *is playing with* BELLE's *claws; she makes letters with her fingers, shows them to* BELLE, *waits with her palm, then manipulates the dog's claws.)* What is she spelling?

[*A silence.*]

290 **Kate.** Water?

[ANNIE *nods.*]

Keller. Teaching a dog to spell. *(A pause.)* The dog doesn't know what she means, any more than she knows what you mean, Miss Sullivan. I think you ask too much, of her and
295 yourself. God may not have meant Helen to have the—eyes you speak of.

Annie *(toneless).* I mean her to.

(continued)

Keller *(curiously).* What is it to you? (ANNIE's *head comes slowly up.)* You make us see how we indulge[6] her for our
300 sake. Is the opposite true, for you?

Annie *(then).* Half a week?

Keller. An agreement *is* an agreement.

Annie. Mrs. Keller?

Kate *(simply).* I want her back.

305 [*A wait;* ANNIE *then lets her hands drop in surrender, and nods.*]

Keller. I'll send Viney over to help you pack.

Annie. Not until six o'clock. I have her till six o'clock.

Keller *(consenting).* Six o'clock. Come, Katie.

310 [KATE *leaving the window joins him around back, while* KELLER *closes the door; they are shut out. Only the garden house is daylit now, and the light on it is narrowing down.* ANNIE *stands watching* HELEN *work* BELLE's *claws. Then she settles beside them on her knees, and stops* HELEN's *hand.*]

315 **Annie** *(gently).* No. *(She shakes her head, with* HELEN's *hand to her face, then spells.)* Dog. D, o, g, Dog. *(She touches* HELEN's *hand to* BELLE. HELEN *dutifully pats the dog's head, and resumes spelling to its paw.)* Not water. (ANNIE *rolls to her feet, brings a tumbler of water back from the tray, and*
320 *kneels with it, to seize* HELEN's *hand and spell.)* Here. Water. Water. *(She thrusts* HELEN's *hand into the tumbler.* HELEN *lifts her hand out dripping, wipes it daintily on* BELLE's *hide, and taking the tumbler from* ANNIE, *endeavors to thrust*

---

[6] **indulge:** to yield to; be lenient with

(continued)

Text Connection 12 (continued)

Comprehend It

What is Annie trying to do at the end of Scene 1?

_____

_____

_____

_____

_____

BELLE'S *paw into it.* ANNIE *sits watching, wearily.)* I don't
know how to tell you. Not a soul in the world knows how
to tell you. Helen, Helen. *(She bends in compassion to touch
her lips to* HELEN'S *temple, and instantly* HELEN *pauses, her
hands off the dog, her head slightly averted. The lights are still
narrowing, and* BELLE *slinks off. After a moment* ANNIE *sits
back.)* Yes, what's it to me? They're satisfied. Give them back
their child and dog, both housebroken, everyone's satisfied.
But me, and you. *(*HELEN'S *hand comes out into the light,
groping.)* Reach. *Reach!* *(*ANNIE *extending her own hand grips*
HELEN'S; *the two hands are clasped, tense in the light, the rest
of the room changing in shadow.)* I wanted to teach you—oh,
everything the earth is full of, Helen, everything on it that's
ours for a wink and it's gone, and what we are on it, the—
light we bring to it and leave behind in—words, why you can
see five thousand years back in a light of words, everything
we feel, think, know—and share, in words, so not a soul is
in darkness, or done with, even in the grave. And I know, I
know, one word and I can—put the world in your hand—and
whatever it is to me, I won't take less! How, how, how do I tell
you that *this—* *(She spells:)* —means a *word*, and the word
means this *thing*, wool? *(She thrusts the wool at* HELEN'S
hand; HELEN *sits, puzzled.* ANNIE *puts the crocheting aside.)*
Or this—s, t, o, o, l—means this *thing*, stool? *(She claps*
HELEN'S *palm to the stool.* HELEN *waits, uncomprehending.*
ANNIE *snatches up her napkin, spells:)* Napkin! *(She forces it
on* HELEN'S *hand, waits, discards it, lifts a fold of the child's
dress, spells:)* Dress! *(She lets it drop, spells:)* F, a, c, e, face!
(She draws HELEN'S *hand to her cheek, and pressing it there,
staring into the child's responseless eyes, hears the distant
belfry begin to toll, slowly: one, two, three, four, five, six.)*

How To Guides

Technical Manual:
How to Make a Slide Show

Using a computer, your job is to create a slide show to share with the rest of the class. To do this, you will research your topic, plan your presentation, and use a software application to create a slide show. Software applications are programs that direct the operation of a computer. There are a number of software applications that can make slide shows. Many of them are similar, so these directions should apply to almost any software application you use.

Follow these seven steps to creating your slide show.

1. Open the Application

First, open up the software application. This can be done by double clicking on the icon for the application on your computer screen. An icon is a small graphic symbol. Or, if there is no such icon, open up the Applications menu and select the software you want to use. Once the application is open, look at the toolbar at the top of your screen. This toolbar will have many of the commands you need to create your slide show. Some that you will probably see include:

File	Edit	View	Format	Insert	Tools	Slide Show

Each command in the tool bar has a drop down menu with more specific actions. To see a drop down menu, put your cursor on a word on the tool bar and click. Begin by putting your cursor on the word FILE and clicking. The drop down menu is the list of commands that appears below the word FILE. Now, move your cursor so that "New" is highlighted, then click it.

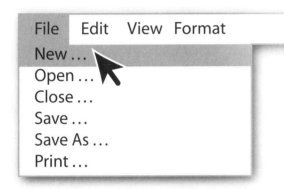

2. Create the Title Slide

Choose the size and style of font you want by selecting "font" from the FORMAT menu. Where it says "click to add title," type the title of your slide show. Then, where it says "click to add subtitle," type the subtitle.

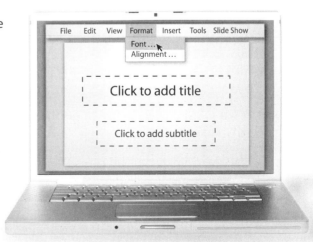

3. Save Your Work

Now make sure to save this slide with a unique file name, remembering to save it someplace you can retrieve it. If this is your own computer you can save the file to its hard drive. The hard drive is the storage disk inside the computer. That way you store your work in the computer's memory.

If you are not working at your own computer, you can save your work to a CD or a flash drive so that you can remove it and take your work with you.

To save the slide show go back to the toolbar and once again click on the FILE command, but this time select "Save As." A screen appears that prompts you to type in a file name. Type the file name, then check to see that the slide show is being saved where you want it to go (to the hard drive or a removable storage device). Once you have named the file and everything is OK, click "Save."

computer's hard drive   **CD**   **flash drive**

Tip!
Save your work every
10 minutes!

4. Create Additional Slides

Now you are ready to add information to your presentation. With your cursor, click on the INSERT command. When the drop down menu appears, click on "New Slide." A new blank slide should appear on the screen. Type text in the space where it says "Add slide title." Then click on the space where it says "Click to add text." Informational text on the slides should appear as a list of talking points. Each point is preceded by a bullet.

Press ENTER on your keyboard each time you want to start a new line. Each line of text should be short and need not be written as a complete sentence.

In most cases a slide should only contain about five to seven lines of basic points. If you have more to say, add another slide and continue your list of points. Click on the TOOLS command and select "Spelling" from the drop down menu to spell check your work.

5. Add Pictures

You may want to add pictures or graphics to your slide show. To make room for a picture, you may have to change the type of slide you are working with. To change the format of a slide, click on the FORMAT command and select "Slide Format" from the drop down menu. Look for a slide format that has two columns: one for text and one for a picture.

Put your cursor in the column where you want a picture to go. Click on the INSERT command on the toolbar, and then click on "Picture." Now you have another choice to make. If you already have a picture on your computer that you want to insert, find that picture and select it. The picture should be imported into your slide show. You may have to adjust the size by dragging one corner of the picture.

You can also look for an appropriate picture on the Internet. In that case, you search on the Internet for "Clip Art" and search for an image that is relevant to your topic and also adds visual interest to your slide show.

After you have added the pictures you want, it is a good idea to save your work again.

6. Add Sound, Music, or Video

You may want to add sound or a movie to your slide show. You can add sound or music to any slide or have background music playing throughout the slide show.

To do this, you can search the Internet for a sound clip and download it to your desktop. Then, to add sound to your presentation, go back to the title slide. Click on the INSERT command on the toolbar, and then select "Movies or Sound" from the drop down menu. Then, click on "Sound from File." A screen will appear, prompting you to select the sound file. Select the file you want and click "Insert."

You can decide whether you want this sound to play automatically. When you insert the file, a small icon of a loudspeaker will appear on your slide, telling you that sound is included. You can move this icon anywhere on the slide. The sound will not play until you actually view the slide show.

7. Present Your Slide Show

To share your presentation with the class, open the slide show in your software application. Select the SLIDE SHOW command and "View Show" from the drop down menu. To move to the next slide, press the spacebar, click the left mouse button, or press N on the keyboard.

  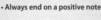

Summary

Here are the steps for making a slide show:

1. Open the software application.
2. Make a title slide.
3. Save your work.
4. Create additional slides.
5. Add pictures.
6. Add sound, music, and video.
7. Present your slide show.

Technical Manual: How to Make a Slide Show

Mini-Lesson: How to Create a Slide Show on a Computer

▶ Read the **Technical Manual**, pages G2–G6, with your teacher. Refer to the manual to answer the questions below.

▶ Read the sentences and the choices in the **Word Bank**. Select the correct answer from the **Word Bank** and write it in the blank.

Word Bank

spell check	flash drive	software
toolbar	hard drive	drop down menu
CD	save	print

1. _____ applications are programs that direct the operation of a computer.

2. Commands such as FILE, EDIT, VIEW, FORMAT, INSERT, TOOLS, and SLIDE SHOW appear at the top of the computer screen in a _____.

3. The _____ is the list of commands that appears below a command, such as FILE, in the toolbar.

4. The storage disk inside a computer is called the _____.

5. It is important to _____ your work about every ten minutes so that your work isn't accidentally lost.

▶ The **Technical Manual** outlines seven steps for making a slide show on a computer. Use your technical manual to identify the seven steps, and write below.

1. _____

2. _____

3. _____

4. _____

5. _____

6. _____

7. _____

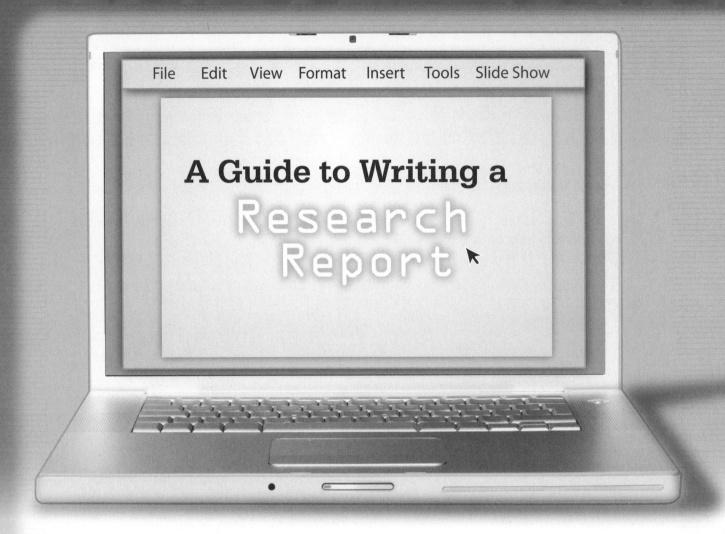

File Edit View Format Insert Tools Slide Show

A Guide to Writing a
Research Report

Table of Contents

Introduction to Writing a Research Report

Writing a research report involves a number of steps. Knowing the steps can assist you in planning and completing your report. Use the Ten Steps for Writing a Research Report checklist to keep track of the sequence and completion of the steps.

Ten Steps for Writing a Research Report

1. Select and shape your topic. ☐

2. Create questions to guide your research. ☐

3. Research the topic and keep track of resources. ☐

4. Take notes from your reference sources. ☐

5. Organize your notes to create an outline.
   (Do more research if there are "holes" in your outline.) ☐

6. Write a first draft and do more research if necessary. (Include footnotes.) ☐

7. Create a bibliography. ☐

8. Revise your first draft. ☐

9. Proofread your final draft. ☐

10. Assemble and publish your research report. ☐

1. Selecting and Shaping the Topic

Selecting and shaping your topic is an important first step.

Select your topic

- Choose a topic that interests you. If a specific topic is assigned, choose an aspect of the assigned topic that interests you.

> **Assignment**: *Select one of the amendments to the United States Constitution. Write a research report describing why the amendment was added and whether you think it is an important right.*

- Do some preliminary research on your topic. Find information about your topic in a valid source so that you understand what the subtopics might be.

Shape your topic

- Focus on an aspect or aspects of the topic that you can manage given the following:
  - what you already know about the topic
  - how much information is available
  - how long your research paper is supposed to be
- Write down the preliminary topic of the paper in one sentence:

> *The First Amendment to the United States Constitution is important to American democracy.*

2. Creating Questions to Guide Research

Brainstorming basic questions that you want answered before you begin your research focuses your research efforts.

- Write down the questions and have them available when you begin your research. Answers to these questions can become subtopics of your report.

What?	What is the United States Constitution? What is the First Amendment?
When?	When were these documents created?
Who?	Who created these documents?
Why?	Why were these documents created? Why does it matter to us today?

3. Researching the Topic: Selecting Information Sources and Keeping Track of Sources

Selecting sources with the most accurate and current information provides valid information on which to base your report.

- Track selected sources using the **Keeping Track of Resources** template.

Selecting Information Sources

Online

- Access web sites of libraries, museums, government agencies, and businesses.
- Locate magazine, journal, and newspaper articles.
- Locate and contact people knowledgeable about the subject, such as university professors and government officials.

At the library

- Use the online card catalog to locate books on the topic. Libraries group materials according to the Dewey Decimal System. This numbering system organizes material into 10 broad areas. For example, 000 General Knowledge, 300 Social Studies, 500 Science, and 900 History and Geography.

- Use different resources and references, such as newspapers, magazines, dictionaries, encyclopedias, atlases, and almanacs.

- Explore online resources, especially those unique to the library.

- Use organizational features of print and online text (e.g., citations and bibliographical references) to locate other relevant information.

Keeping Track of Sources

- Keep track of sources for footnote references and bibliography content. Set up a system and keep using it during the research process.

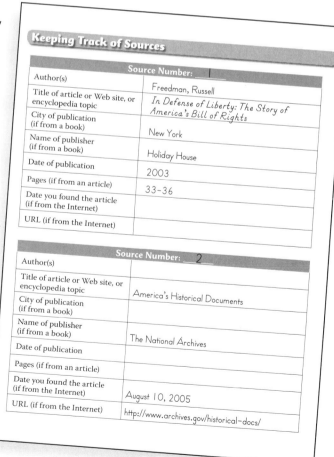

Keeping Track of Sources

	Source Number: 1
Author(s)	Freedman, Russell
Title of article or Web site, or encyclopedia topic	*In Defense of Liberty: The Story of America's Bill of Rights*
City of publication (if from a book)	New York
Name of publisher (if from a book)	Holiday House
Date of publication	2003
Pages (if from an article)	33–36
Date you found the article (if from the Internet)	
URL (if from the Internet)	

	Source Number: 2
Author(s)	
Title of article or Web site, or encyclopedia topic	America's Historical Documents
City of publication (if from a book)	
Name of publisher (if from a book)	The National Archives
Date of publication	
Pages (if from an article)	
Date you found the article (if from the Internet)	August 10, 2005
URL (if from the Internet)	http://www.archives.gov/historical-docs/

4. Taking Notes from Reference Sources

Taking effective notes will make drafting an outline much easier to do.

- Use different colored index cards and assign a color to each subtopic in your report.
- At the top of each index card, write the number of the source you recorded on your **Keeping Track of Sources** template. Also write the page number of the material from which you have taken notes in case you need to find it again.
- Write only on one side of each card and include only one main point per card.
- Write notes in your own words. To **paraphrase** a source:
  - Skim the material first to understand the main ideas.
  - Read the selection carefully.
  - Copy down important dates and spell names correctly. If you are writing down a direct quotation, record the name of the person you are quoting.
  - Look away from the source to recall the main ideas and supporting details and then write them down in a bulleted list in your own words. Do not write down text directly from the source.
- Copy down exact quotations only under the following circumstances:

> You need to state information from an historical document, such as the U.S. Constitution or the Bill of Rights.
>
> *"We hold these truths to be self-evident, that all men are created equal...."*
> *The Declaration of Independence*

> You need to show exactly how a writer wrote or said something.
>
> *Doing so was called "seditious libel."* *Lucy Bledsoe*

> An author or speaker expresses something in a unique way, often with the use of images, similes, or metaphors.
>
> *"Nature's first green is gold."* *Robert Frost*

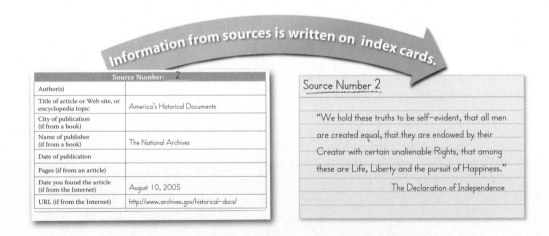

Information from sources is written on index cards.

Source Number: 2	
Author(s)	
Title of article or Web site, or encyclopedia topic	America's Historical Documents
City of publication (if from a book)	
Name of publisher (if from a book)	The National Archives
Date of publication	
Pages (if from an article)	
Date you found the article (if from the Internet)	August 10, 2005
URL (if from the Internet)	http://www.archives.gov/historical-docs/

Source Number 2

"We hold these truths to be self-evident, that all men are created equal, that they are endowed by their Creator with certain unalienable Rights, that among these are Life, Liberty and the pursuit of Happiness."

The Declaration of Independence

5. Organizing Notes into an Outline

Creating a preliminary outline lets you see what information you have and what information you still need. The final outline forms the backbone of your report.

- Sort your index cards into subtopics. Each subtopic should be on a different colored card.
- Put the subtopics in a logical order and then put the cards within each subtopic in a logical order.
- Given what you have learned about your topic, restate it again in one sentence.

> *The five basic freedoms guaranteed by the First Amendment of the U.S. Constitution are the heart of American democracy.*

- Draft a preliminary outline of your report based on the refined topic and the information on the index cards.

Source Number 1

Question: What is the history of the first amendment?
– colonist from Europe
– Countries ruled by kings and queens
– dangerous to express ideas or practice religion different from ruler (could be fined, killed, or put in prison)

e.g., Queen Mary 1,(ruled 1553–1558): had many non-Catholics burned at stake

Topic **The First Amendment**

Main Idea I. **Definition of the First Amendment**
  A. separation between church and state
  B. freedom of speech and press
  C. right to assemble
  D. right to petition government

Main Idea II. **Historical Purpose of the First Amendment**
  A. colonists from Europe couldn't express ideas different from rulers
  B. press could not criticize government
  C. original U.S. Constitution omitted Bill of Rights
  D. T. Jefferson drafted amendments

Main Idea III. **Relevance in Today's World**
  A. First Amendment cornerstone of American democracy
  B. Supreme Court upholds U.S. Constitution
  C. Other parts of world, these rights not guaranteed
  D.

Conclusion First Amendment guarantees the precious rights to citizens.

- Look for any missing or incomplete information in your outline and do more research if necessary.
- Finalize your outline.

6. Writing a First Draft

At last, you can put your ideas on paper. Be clear, logical, complete, and specific.

- Use your sentence that states the topic to write your introductory paragraph.
- Refer to your outline and your index cards to write each paragraph in the body of your paper.
- Focus on writing one section of your report at a time.
- Include examples, evidence, and/or explanations to develop each paragraph.
- Create transitions from one point to the next.
- Write a conclusion that restates the topic, summarizes the ideas in the body of the paper, and gives the reader something to think about.

Using Direct Quotations

- If you use a direct quotation from a source, do the following:
  - Introduce the quotation with a verb of attribution, such as:
    said (that)   stated (that)   declared (that)   wrote (that)
  - Place quoted material in quotation marks.

> For a complete sentence, capitalize the first word of a quotation.
>
> **Patrick Henry declared, "Give me liberty or give me death!"**

> For part of a sentence, do not capitalize the first word if it wasn't capitalized in the original.
>
> **Thomas Jefferson wrote, "all men are created equal."**

> Add a comma before a verb of attribution, unless you also use the word **that** or you are quoting a phrase rather than a whole sentence.
>
> **Thomas Jefferson wrote that "all men are created equal."**
>
> **Gouverneur Morris said Zenger's trial was "the germ of American freedom."**

> Include end punctuation inside the quotation marks unless the end punctuation was not in the original.
>
> **Patrick Henry declared, "Give me liberty or give me death!"**
> **Why did Patrick Henry declare, "Give me liberty or give me death"?**

Including Footnotes

- Footnotes are necessary if you include direct quotations or if you paraphrase another person's words or ideas very closely.
- Keep track of footnotes as you draft your report by doing the following:
  - Number your footnotes with a small superscript number (starting with [1]) at the end of the sentence where you need to reference a source.
  - At the bottom of the page, begin your footnote by writing the number to match the reference you made in your text.
  - Number your footnotes consecutively throughout your report, that is, [1, 2, 3, 4,] and so on.
- Follow these formats based on whether or not the work has an author.

> **Footnote of source with author**
> [3] Dueland, "A Voice from Paris," 36.
>   (last name)   (title)   (page number)

> **Footnote of source with no author**
> [1] Constitution of the United States of America, Amendment I, 1.
>   (title)   (page number)

7. Creating a Bibliography

A good bibliography will show the quality and the variety of sources you used to write your research report.

To create a bibliography, do the following:

- Arrange your sources in alphabetical order by author's last name, or, if there is no author listed, by the title of the work. The first line is flush left and the next lines are indented. This is called a hanging indent.
- Follow these formats based on the type of resource you used. Remember that titles of long works, such as books and magazines, are in italics. Titles of short works, such as book chapters or poems, are in quotation marks.

Books with one author
Farish, Leah. *The First Amendment: Freedom of Speech, Religion, and the Press.* Berkeley Heights, NJ: Enslow Publishers, Inc. 1998.

Books with more than one author
Lovell, Jim and Jeffrey Kluger. *Lost Moon: The Perilous Voyage of Apollo 13.* New York: Houghton Mifflin, 1994.

Magazines and newspapers
Calkins, Virginia. "Mr. Madison Keeps His Promise." *Cobblestone* Sept. 1991:24.

Online source with author
Jefferson, Thomas. Letter to the Danbury Baptists. Jan. 1 1802. LC *Information Bulletin*, Library of Congress, June 1998.
http: www.loc.gov/lcib/9806/ danpre.html
(accessed August 5, 2005).

Online source with no author
"About the First Amendment." First Amendment Center. August 10, 2005.
http://www.firstamendmentcenter.org/aboutaspxitem=about_firstamd
(accessed August 10, 2005).

8. Revising the First Draft

Revision is a time to make certain that your report is both informative and interesting.

- Read through your paper carefully again and use the **Research Report Checklist** on page G19 of this guide to check for the following:

Ideas and Content

- Have you clearly stated the thesis of your report?
- Does each paragraph focus on a topic?
- Do you include details, examples, and quotations from several recent, relevant, and reliable sources?
- Do you include your own examples and explanations?
- Have you accurately paraphrased your sources?
- Do you have footnotes to indicate text that is quoted or paraphrased?
- Have you included a title and a bibliography?

Organization

- Have you written an introductory paragraph that captures the reader's interest, expresses a clear viewpoint, and provides a "map" for the rest of the report?
- Have you divided your report into sections, each of which focuses on one subtopic?
- Is the sequence of your paragraphs logical and do you use transition words to make clear the relationship among ideas?
- Do you have a conclusion that restates your thesis and summarizes your ideas?

Voice and Audience Awareness

- Does the tone of your paper suit your audience and purpose?
- Have you written in a clear and engaging way that makes your audience want to read your work?

9. Proofreading the Final Draft

A good research report has also been carefully proofread for errors.

After you have revised your paper, read through it carefully again, using the **Research Report Checklist** to check for the following:

Word Choice

- Have you explained any technical terms or unfamiliar expressions?
- Have you used words that are lively, accurate, and specific to the content?
- Have you varied the words so that your writing doesn't sound repetitive?

Sentence Fluency

- Did you write in complete sentences?
- Did you expand some sentences by painting the subject and the predicate?
- Did you write in complex sentences?
- Did you avoid sentence fragments and run-on sentences?

Conventions

- Did you edit your work for:
  - capitalization
  - punctuation
  - grammar and usage
  - spelling

Refer to the Handbook section of the *Student Text* for specific rules regarding any of these items.

10. Publishing the Report

Research reports should be published to look clean and professional.

- Type your paper, double spaced, in black ink on white paper, in a readable size and style of font.
- Make certain your paper has the following parts:
  - Cover sheet with the title of your paper, your name, and your classroom information
  - First page with a title and your name repeated. Leave additional space between the heading and the first sentence of your paper.
  - Body of your paper, with the first line of each paragraph indented.
  - Footnotes appearing on the same page that the reference in the text appears. Leave adequate room for footnotes at the bottom of the page.
  - Bibliography
- Spell check your paper on the computer and verify unknown spellings with a dictionary.
- Print an additional copy of your paper and keep it.
- Unless your teacher asks for a different type of binding, affix one staple to the upper left-hand corner of your paper.

Congratulations. You're done!

Research Report Checklist

Ideas and Development

- ☐ My report is well focused on the topic of my chosen amendment.
- ☐ My report is interesting and informative.
- ☐ My report contains details, examples, and quotations from several outside sources. It also contains my own examples and explanations.
- ☐ The sources I have included are recent, relevant, and reliable.
- ☐ I have accurately paraphrased or quoted my sources, and I have corrected cited source information in footnotes.

Organization

- ☐ My report is clearly divided into sections, each of which focuses on one subtopic under the main topic.
- ☐ Each of my body paragraphs has a clear purpose, and each contains a topic sentence.
- ☐ My paragraphs are in a logical order
- ☐ The sentences within each paragraph are in a logical order.
- ☐ My report includes a title and a bibliography.

Voice and Audience Awareness

- ☐ The tone of my writing suits my audience and my purpose for writing.
- ☐ My report is written in such a way as to interest my audience.
- ☐ My report includes enough descriptions, explanations, and background information that my audience can understand my points.

Word Choice

- ☐ I have explained any technical terms or unfamiliar expressions.
- ☐ The words in my report are vivid, specific, and convey just the right meaning.
- ☐ The words in my report are varied so that my writing does not sound repetitive.

Sentence Fluency

- ☐ My sentences are clear and flow easily from one to the other.
- ☐ My sentences vary in length.
- ☐ My sentences vary in structure.
- ☐ I have effectively used connecting words to make the relationship between ideas clear.

Written Language Conventions

- ☐ The grammar in my report is correct.
- ☐ There are no spelling errors in my report.
- ☐ Sentences in my report are correctly punctuated.
- ☐ Words in my report are correctly capitalized.

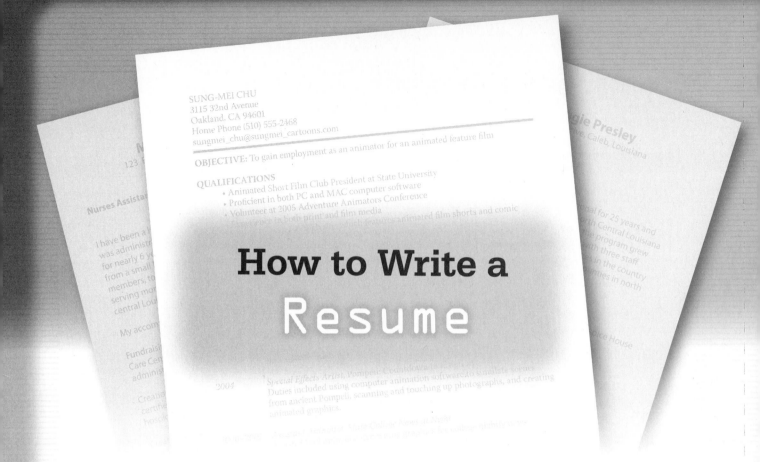

How to Write a Resume

Provide the following information on a resume:

- Your **name** and **address.**

- An **objective:** State the position you are interested in. Begin your objective with an infinitive such as **to gain employment**, or with a noun phrase such as **position as an animator**.

- A summary of **qualifications:** Summarize your major achievements and the special skills you bring to a job.

- **Education:** Summarize the education you have received. Be sure to list any classes that are related to the job you are seeking.

- **Employment:** List the jobs you have had and briefly describe your responsibilities there. List your jobs in reverse chronological order. Begin your job descriptions with action verbs such as **created** or **assisted**, or with noun phrases such as **Duties included**. Include volunteer positions as well as paid jobs.

SUNG-MEI CHU
3115 32nd Avenue
Oakland, CA 94601
Home Phone (510) 555-2468
sungmei_chu@sungmei_cartoons.com

OBJECTIVE: To gain employment as an animator for an animated feature film

QUALIFICATIONS
- Animated Short Film Club President at State University
- Proficient in both PC and MAC computer software
- Volunteer at 2005 Adventure Animators Conference
- Experience in both print and film media
- Maintain personal Web site, which features animated film shorts and comic strips (http://www.sungmei_cartoons.com)

EDUCATION

2000–2004   Bachelor of Fine Arts in Graphic Design, State University. Coursework included computer animation, graphic design, and film.

1996–2000   Graduate of Central High School. Classes included art, journalism, and computer programming.

EMPLOYMENT

2005   *Lead animator, Baby Betty Doll commercial*
Duties included organizing and leading a team of designers to create an animated 30-second commercial for Baby Betty Dolls.

2004   *Special Effects Artist*, Pompeii: Countdown to Eruption
Duties included using computer animation software to simulate scenes from ancient Pompeii, scanning and touching up photographs, and creating animated graphics.

2000–2002   *Assistant Animator, State College News at Night*
Assisted lead animator in creating graphics for college nightly news program.

1998–2000   *Cartoonist, The Central High Bugle*
Created a comic strip, *High School Hijinks*, for the Central High School newspaper. Responsibilities included conceptualizing the strip, organizing its layout, and animating the strip on a weekly basis.

How to Read and Complete an Application

Reading an Application

To fill out an application correctly, you must first learn to read it carefully. Here are some tips that will help you read and understand an application:

- **Survey the application**. Read headings, identify the different sections, and think about what kind of information is being asked for in each section.

- **Read the directions**. There are usually instructions for completing the application at the very beginning of the application or at the top of each section.

- **Note any sections to be filled in by others**. Some forms will ask for a signature, or request information to be provided by another person, such as a parent or guardian. Sometimes there are spaces you should leave blank. They will often be labeled Do Not Write Below This Line or For Office Use Only.

- **Read the entire application**.

- **Look for abbreviations**. Because there is not a lot of space on an application form, abbreviations such as these are often found on applications: St. (Street), Apt. (Apartment), Zip (Zip Code), and SSN (Social Security Number).

▸ Read and complete the following application for a library card.

Oakville Public Library
Library Card Application

Photo identification and proof of address are required for all registrants. If you are 12 years of age or under, your parent/guardian must sign the application form.

PLEASE PRINT

_____

Last Name   First Name   Middle

_____

Mailing Address   Apt. #

_____

City   County   State   ZIP

_____/_____/_____

Date of Birth: Month   Day   Year   Age (circle one)   0–12 years   13–17   18–64   65 and over

_____

E-mail   Telephone 1   Telephone 2

Driver's License/Student ID

I agree to abide by library rules and to pay for any loss of, or damage to, library materials and to pay for overdue fines accumulated on this card. I understand I am responsible for notifying the library in case of loss or theft of this card. Failure to do so will result in my being held liable for materials on this card and for fines incurred on the card. I also agree to inform the library of any street address or e-mail changes or change in the status of parent/guardian.

_____

Your Signature

_____

Signature of Parent/Guardian (if applicant is 12 years of age or younger)

PLEASE DO NOT WRITE BELOW THIS LINE

Type: JV YA AD SR ST BU RC VC   Agency _____

PID# 21223 _____   Initials _____

NEW
Energy Drink
Beats the Rest by a Mile!
Are you looking for a drink that will power you through your next 10K or just get you through the day?
Try Energy,
the drink that's got it all.
• Less than 10 calories of sugar
• Contains protein for long-lasting energy
• B6 and B12 vitamins
• Natural herbs to focus your mind
• 6 thirst-quenching fruit flavors
• smooth taste
Joe Runner powered to victory with Energy Drink
142
Proven in a test of elite runners to improve endurance by 20%
Over a million people have already tried it.
Are you ready to catch up?
Energy Drink
Go for it!

Why I Want to Be Class President

By I.M. Student

I want to thank you for coming to this assembly today to hear why I think you should vote for me as class president. There are many good candidates running for office, but I feel that I am the kind of leader this class needs.

First of all, I have been at this school longer than the other candidates. I have done a lot of things at this school. I have been on the football team, and I have acted in the school play. I was the person that the principal chose as "Student of the Month" in September for getting a speed bump put in the front of our school so that people wouldn't drive so fast. The principal knows that I would be an excellent leader. So, I would say that a vote for me is a vote for this school, and any other vote is a vote against making this school a better place.

Second, I have more friends at this school than the other candidates. The football team is going to vote for me and so is the drama club. The last class president told me yesterday that she was going to vote for me and you know how popular she is. All of these people are making the right choice. Don't you want to be one of them?

Third, I think that all of you remember last year when I lost the election by only five votes. Why? I couldn't make this speech at the assembly last year because I had just broken my ankle and I was in the hospital recovering. So, knowing what I have been through, I think you will agree that I am the most deserving candidate.

Let me just add that a vote for anyone else will start a series of events that can't benefit anyone of us at this school. If we elect a class president who isn't popular then no one will listen to him or her, and then nothing will be accomplished this year.

Vote for me and I promise that I will be the best class president this school has ever had.

Resources

Resources

ē
1. me
2. these
3. see
4. eat
5. chief
6. happy
7. key
8. either

ĭ
1. sit
2. gym
3. build

ā
1. baby
2. make
3. rain
4. play
5. ___
6. vein
7. they
8. great
9. ___

ĕ
1. pet
2. head

ă
1. cat

ī
1. item
2. time
3. pie
4. my
5. ___
6. guide

ə
1. about
2. lesson
3. elect
4. definition
5. circus

ŏ
1. fox
2. swap
3. quad
4. ___
5. ___

ŭ
1. cup
2. tough
3. ___
4. ___
5. ___

aw
1. saw
2. pause
3. call
4. dog
5. wall
6. talk

ō
1. go
2. vote
3. boat
4. show
5. toe
6. soul

ŏŏ
1. took
2. put
3. could
4. neuron

ōō
1. moo
2. ruby
3. tube
4. chew
5. blue
6. suit
7. soup
8. sleuth

êr → er
1. her
2. fur
3. sir

âr → ar
1. cart

ôr → or
1. sport

oi	oy
ou	ow

oi — oil
oy — boy
ou — out
ow — cow

Consonant Chart

Mouth Position

Type of Consonant Sound	Lips	Lips/Teeth	Tongue Between Teeth	Tongue Behind Teeth	Roof of Mouth	Back of Mouth	Throat
Stops	/ b / / p /			/ t / / d /		/ k / / g /	
Fricatives		/ f / / v /	/ th / / <u>th</u> /	/ s / / z /	/ sh /		/ h /
Affricatives					/ j / / ch /		
Nasals	/ m /			/ n /		/ ng /	
Lateral				/ l /			
Semivowels	/ w / / hw /			/ r /	/ y /		

Steps for Syllable Division	Example: disconnected
First, check the word for prefixes and suffixes. Circle them. Next, look at the rest of the word:	(dis)connect(ed)
1. Underline the **first** vowel. Write a **v** under it.	(dis)connect(ed) v
2. Underline the **next** vowel. Write a **v** under it.	(dis)connect(ed) v v
3. Look at the letters **between** the vowels. Mark them with a **c** for consonant.	(dis)connect(ed) v cc v
4. Look at the pattern and divide according to the pattern.	(dis)con/nect(ed) v cc v
5. Place a diacritical mark over the vowels. Cross out the **e** at the end of final silent **e** syllables. Listen for schwa in the unaccented syllable, cross out the vowel, and place a ə symbol above it.	(dis)cŏn/nĕct(ed) v̄ cc v̄
Finally, blend each syllable and read the word.	disconnected

Diacritical Marks and Symbols

Diacritical marks and **symbols** are used to indicate the correct sound for the vowel graphemes.

breve / brĕv /	ă	short vowel phonemes
macron	ā	long vowel phonemes
circumflex	âr	**r**-controlled phonemes
schwa	ə	schwa phoneme

Pattern	How to Divide	Examples
VCCV	vc / cv • Divide between the consonants. • The first syllable is closed. • The vowel sound is short.	năp/kĭn VCCV
VCV	v/cv • **Usually**, divide after the first vowel. • The first syllable is open. • The vowel sound is long. **Note:** If the first vowel is followed by an **r**, the syllable is **r**-controlled. or vc/v • If the first division does not result in a recognizable word, divide after the consonant. • The first syllable is closed. • The vowel sound is short.	sī/lᵊnt VCV mâr/kĕt V CV nĕv/êr VCV
VCCCV	• vc/ccv or vcc/cv • Divide before or after the blend or digraph. • Do not split the blend or digraph.	ăth/lēte VCCCV
VV	• v/v • Divide between the vowels if they are not a vowel team or diphthong. • The first syllable is open. • The vowel sound is long.	nē/ŏn V V
c + le	• /cle • Count back three and divide.	crā/dle 321

Six Elements of Poetry

Element of Poetry	Definition	Example	Unit
form	The element that defines the poem's actual structure.	quatrain, sonnet, blank verse, limerick, ballad, and free (open) verse	25, 29
thought	The element that contains the poem's message.	One component of thought is the theme, which is often stated as a statement of universal truth.	25, 29
imagery	The poem's creation of mental pictures, or images, for the reader.	Metaphor, simile, and personification are examples of techniques that poets use to create imagery.	28, 29
mood			
melody			
meter			

Use the Clues Strategies

▶ **Use Meaning Signals:** Use meaning signals to find definitions in the context. Signal words provide cues to the definition of a word in context. These signal words include **is/are**, **it means**, **which stands for**, and **can be defined as**.

▶ **Use Context Cues:** Use contextual analysis to identify cues to the meaning of an unfamiliar word.

▶ **Use Substitutions:** Use words or phrases that rename nouns to increase understanding of the text. These substitutions are often synonyms or distinctive features of the noun.

▶ **Use Examples Given in Text:** Use examples provided in surrounding text to inform the meaning of an unknown word. Signal words such as **for example** and **such as** indicate examples.

▶ **Use Words That Show Comparison:** Use signal words to identify comparisons to help determine the meaning of unfamiliar words. Words and phrases such as **like**, **as**, or **similar to** signal comparison.

▶ **Use Visual Information:** Use pictures, charts, and other visual information that accompany the text to understand the meaning of new vocabulary words.

Other Vocabulary Strategies

▶ **Use Morpheme Parts:** Use the meaning of prefixes, roots, and suffixes to inform the meaning of words.

▶ **Use a Dictionary:** Use the dictionary to locate word meanings and select meanings to fit the context.

Six Traits of Effective Writing Rubric

	Ideas and Development	Organization	Voice and Audience Awareness	Word Choice	Sentence Fluency	Conventions
5	The paper is very clear and well focused. Supporting details make the paper interesting and very easy to understand.	Ideas are very clearly organized. All parts of the essay (introduction, body, and conclusion) work together to support the thesis.	The writer's voice is distinctive and shows an interest in the topic. The writer knows who his or her audience is.	Words are used correctly and are very well chosen. They create pictures in the reader's mind.	Sentences have an easy flow and rhythm. Transitions are very smooth.	There are no grammar errors. There are few or no errors in spelling, capitalization, or punctuation.
4	The paper is clear and well focused. Supporting details make the paper easy to understand.	Ideas are clearly organized. The paper includes all parts of an essay (introduction, body, and conclusion).	The writer's voice is natural and shows an interest in the topic. The writer knows who his or her audience is.	Words are used correctly. Some words may be a bit general.	Sentences are formed correctly and are varied in structure. Transitions are clear.	There are no major grammar errors. There are few errors in spelling, capitalization, or punctuation.
3	The paper has a clear thesis. The ideas are somewhat developed, but there are only a few details.	Ideas are fairly well organized. The paper includes all parts of an essay (introduction, body, and conclusion).	The writer's voice is natural, but the writer is not fully engaged in the topic. At times the writer's viewpoint may be vague.	Most words are used correctly. A few words are too general. Some words are repeated.	Sentences are formed correctly, although they may be similar in structure. Most transitions are clear.	There are a few grammar errors. There are a few errors in spelling, capitalization, or punctuation.
2	The thesis of the paper is unclear. The paper is poorly developed.	Ideas are not clearly organized. The paper may be missing an introduction or a conclusion.	The writer seems somewhat uninterested in the topic and unaware of his or her audience.	Some words are used incorrectly, some are too general, or some words are repeated often.	The sentences do not flow well. They are short and choppy, or long and confusing.	There are many grammar or spelling errors. There are quite a few errors in capitalization and punctuation.
1	The paper is missing a thesis. The paper is very confusing or poorly developed.	The paper has no organization. There is no introduction or conclusion.	The writer is uninterested in the topic and unaware of his or her audience.	Many words are used incorrectly, many words are general, or many words are repeated.	The sentences are not correctly structured and they do not flow well.	There are many spelling and grammar errors. There are many errors in capitalization and punctuation.

Persuasive Essay Writer's Checklist

Trait	Did I...?	Unit
Ideas and Content	❏ Clearly state my position on an issue ❏ Focus the content of each paragraph on the topic ❏ Include examples, evidence, and/or explanations that are logically, emotionally, or ethically compelling ❏ When necessary, include recent, relevant, reliable research to validate my position ❏ Create a title	29 7 29 29 20
Organization	❏ Write an introductory paragraph that captures the reader's interest and contains a clear thesis statement that serves as a "map" for my essay ❏ Sequence body paragraphs logically and use transition sentences that make clear the relationship between my ideas ❏ Write a concluding paragraph that restates my position and issues a call to action	29 7 29
Voice and Audience Awareness	❏ Write in a voice that is confident and reasonable * ❏ Write in a tone of voice that suits my audience and my purpose for writing ❏ Demonstrate that I have considered the beliefs and opinions that others might have on the topic * ❏ Acknowledge one or more objections that others may make to my own position *	35 35 29 29
Word Choice	❏ Use words that are lively, accurate, specific to the content, and convey authority ❏ Vary the words so that my writing does not sound repetitive	2 13
Sentence Fluency	❏ Write complete sentences ❏ Expand some of my sentences by painting the subject and predicate ❏ Write complex sentences ❏ Avoid sentence fragments ❏ Avoid run-on sentences	1 3, 6 28 29 25

Conventions	❏ Edit my work for:
	   ❏ Capitalization
	   ❏ Punctuation
	   ❏ Grammar and usage
	   ❏ Spelling
	
	For specific rules governing any of these items, refer to the Handbook section of the *Student Text*.	

*Feature of persuasive writing

Personal Narrative Writer's Checklist

Trait	Did I...?	Unit
Ideas and Content	❑ Tell a single true story	9
	❑ Include enough description and detail to develop the message/lesson learned	9
	❑ Include dialog	28
	❑ Create a title	20
Organization	❑ Write an introductory paragraph that captures the reader's interest and hints at the message/lesson learned	9
	❑ Write middle paragraphs that form the beginning, middle, and end of the story	9
	❑ Use story transitions to connect anecdotes/events	9
	❑ Write a concluding paragraph that explains the message/lesson learned	9
Voice and Audience Awareness	❑ Write in a tone that suits my audience and purpose for writing	6
	❑ Write in a clear and engaging way that makes my audience want to read my work: can my reader "hear" me speaking?	6
	❑ Use the word I to write about myself *	9
Word Choice	❑ Use words that are lively, accurate and specific to the content	2
	❑ Vary the words so that my writing does not sound repetitive	13
Sentence Fluency	❑ Write complete sentences	1
	❑ Expand some of my sentences by painting the subject and predicate	3,6
	❑ Write complex sentences	28
	❑ Avoid sentence fragments	29
	❑ Avoid run-on sentences	25

Conventions	❑ Edit my work for:
	    ❑ Capitalization
	    ❑ Punctuation
	    ❑ Grammar and usage
	    ❑ Spelling
	
	For specific rules governing any of these items, refer to the Handbook section of the *Student Text*.	

*Feature of personal narratives

Problem-Solution Essay Writer's Checklist

Trait	Did I...?	Unit
Ideas and Content	❑ Clearly identify a problem ❑ Propose workable solutions and their probable results ❑ Include recent, relevant, reliable research to validate the problem and the possible solutions ❑ Focus each paragraph on the topic ❑ Describe the impact of the solution on the problem ❑ Create a title	27 27 27 7 27 20
Organization	❑ Write an introductory paragraph that captures the reader's interest, identifies the problem, and validates its scale ❑ Write a second paragraph that explains the problem in detail ❑ Write body paragraphs that offer research-backed possible solutions to the problem ❑ Use transition sentences that make clear the relationship between my ideas ❑ Write a concluding paragraph that draws a conclusion about how my proposed solution will impact the problem	27 27 27 7 27
Voice and Audience Awareness	❑ Write in a voice that is confident and reasonable * ❑ Write in a tone of voice that suits my audience and my purpose for writing	35 35
Word Choice	❑ Use words that are lively, accurate, specific to the content, and convey authority * ❑ Vary the words so that my writing does not sound repetitive	2, 27 13
Sentence Fluency	❑ Write complete sentences ❑ Expand some of my sentences by painting the subject and predicate ❑ Write complex sentences ❑ Avoid sentence fragments ❑ Avoid run-on sentences	1 3, 6 28 29 25

Conventions	❑ Edit my work for:
	  ❑ Capitalization
	  ❑ Punctuation
	  ❑ Grammar and usage
	  ❑ Spelling
	
	For specific rules governing any of these items, refer to the Handbook section of the *Student Text*.	

*Feature of problem-solution essays

Literary Analysis Writer's Checklist

Trait	Did I...?	Unit
Ideas and Content	❏ Clearly state the thesis of my essay ❏ Analyze and evaluate one element in a work of literature ❏ Focus each paragraph on the topic ❏ Include effective support for my thesis by giving details, examples, explanations, and quotations from the work ❏ Create a title	7 20 7 20 20
Organization	❏ Write an introductory paragraph that captures the reader's interest and cites the title of the work and the name of the author ❏ Include in my introductory paragraph a clear viewpoint on the topic and a "map" for the essay that follows ❏ Sequence body paragraphs logically and use transition sentences that make clear the relationship between my ideas ❏ Write a conclusion that ties the analysis together and offers my evaluation of the element about which I am writing	20 20 7 20
Voice and Audience Awareness	❏ Write in a tone that suits my audience and purpose for writing ❏ Write in a clear and engaging way that makes my audience want to read my work: can my reader "hear" me speaking?	6 6
Word Choice	❏ Use words that are lively, accurate, and specific to the content ❏ Vary the words so that my writing does not sound repetitive	2 13
Sentence Fluency	❏ Write complete sentences ❏ Expand some of my sentences by painting the subject and predicate ❏ Write complex sentences ❏ Avoid sentence fragments ❏ Avoid run-on sentences	1 3,6 28 29 25

Conventions	❏ Edit my work for:
	   ❏ Capitalization
	   ❏ Punctuation
	   ❏ Grammar and usage
	   ❏ Spelling
	
	For specific rules governing any of these items, refer to the Handbook section of the *Student Text*.	

Fictional Narrative Writer's Checklist

Trait	Did I...?	Unit
Ideas and Content	❏ Include characters, setting, plot ❏ Create an opening that grabs the reader's attention ❏ Include enough description so that the reader can picture the characters and setting ❏ Include dialog between characters ❏ Create a title for my story	22 22 23 23 20
Organization	❏ Create an initiating event, conflict (or rising action), and climax ❏ Include a resolution, as well as a conclusion that ties everything up ❏ Create a clear sequence of events	22 22 22
Voice and Audience Awareness	❏ Write in a tone that suits my audience and purpose ❏ Write in a clear and engaging way that makes my audience want to read my work: can my reader "hear" me speaking? ❏ Select a point of view (1st or 3rd person) for a fictional narrative and maintain it consistently *	6 6 28
Word Choice	❏ Use words that are lively, accurate, and specific to the content ❏ Vary the words so that my writing does not sound repetitive	2 13
Sentence Fluency	❏ Write complete sentences ❏ Expand some of my sentences by painting the subject and predicate ❏ Write complex sentences ❏ Avoid sentence fragments ❏ Avoid run-on sentences	1 3, 6 28 29 25

Conventions	❏ Edit my work for:
	  ❏ Capitalization
	  ❏ Punctuation
	  ❏ Grammar and usage
	  ❏ Spelling
	
	For specific rules governing any of these items, refer to the Handbook section of the *Student Text*.	

*Feature of fictional narratives

Research Report Writer's Checklist

Trait	Did I...?	Unit
Ideas and Content	❑ Clearly state the thesis of my report ❑ Focus each paragraph on the topic ❑ Include details, examples, and quotations from several recent, relevant, and reliable outside sources ❑ Include my own examples and explanations ❑ Accurately paraphrase my sources ❑ Correctly cite source information in footnotes ❑ Include a title and a bibliography	33 7 33 33 33 33 33
Organization	❑ Write an introductory paragraph that captures the reader's interest, expresses a clear viewpoint on the topic, and provides a "map" for the rest of the report ❑ Divide my report into sections, each of which focuses on one subtopic under the main topic ❑ Sequence body paragraphs logically and use transition sentences that make clear the relationship between my ideas ❑ Write a conclusion that restates the introduction or summarizes my ideas.	33 33 7 7
Voice and Audience Awareness	❑ Write in a tone that suits my audience and purpose for writing ❑ Write in a clear and engaging way that makes my audience want to read by work: can my reader "hear" me speaking?	6 6
Word Choice	❑ Explain any technical terms or unfamiliar expressions * ❑ Use words that are lively, accurate, and specific to the content ❑ Vary the words so that my writing does not sound repetitive	33 2 13
Sentence Fluency	❑ Write complete sentences ❑ Expand some of my sentences by painting the subject and predicate ❑ Write complex sentences ❑ Avoid sentence fragments ❑ Avoid run-on sentences	1 8 28 29 25
Conventions	❑ Edit my work for: ❑ Capitalization ❑ Punctuation ❑ Grammar and usage ❑ Spelling For specific rules governing any of these items, refer to the Handbook section of the *Student Text*.	

*Feature of research report

Personal Essay Writer's Checklist

Trait	Did I...?	Unit
Ideas and Content	❑ Clearly state the thesis of my essay ❑ Focus each paragraph on the topic ❑ Include examples, evidence, and/or explanations and make clear how they support my thesis ❑ Create a title	7 7 7 20
Organization	❑ Write an introductory paragraph that captures the reader's interest and provides a clear statement of the topic and a "map" for the essay that follows ❑ Sequence the body paragraphs logically and use transition topic sentences to make clear the relationship between my ideas ❑ Write a concluding paragraph that explains the message/lesson learned.	36 7 9
Voice and Audience Awareness	❑ Write in a tone that suits my audience and purpose for writing ❑ Write in a clear and engaging way that makes my audience want to read my work: can my reader "hear" me speaking? ❑ Use the first person to write my essay *	6 6 9
Word Choice	❑ Use words that are lively and specific to the content ❑ Vary the words so that my writing does not sound repetitive	2 13
Sentence Fluency	❑ Write complete sentences ❑ Expand some of my sentences by painting the subject and predicate ❑ Write complex sentences ❑ Avoid sentence fragments ❑ Avoid run-on sentences	1 8 28 29 25

Conventions	❑ Edit my work for:
	  ❑ Capitalization
	  ❑ Punctuation
	  ❑ Grammar and usage
	  ❑ Spelling
	
	For specific rules governing any of these items, refer to the Handbook section of the *Student Text*.	

*Feature of personal essays

Peer Writing Review

IDEAS AND DEVELOPMENT

- Is the draft focused on the assigned topic?
- Does the draft include an introduction, body paragraphs, and a conclusion?
- Are the main ideas or main events easy to understand?
- Are there enough details to make the ideas clear and well supported?

Things That Work Well:

_____

_____

_____

Things You Might Improve:

_____

_____

ORGANIZATION AND FLOW

- Does the beginning catch your interest? How can it be improved?
- Do the ideas flow in an order that makes sense?
- Has the writer used transition words to help make the flow of ideas clear? Give examples.
- Does the writing have a strong ending? How could the ending be stronger?

Things That Work Well:

_____

_____

_____

Things You Might Improve:

_____

_____

STRONG SENTENCES

- Has the writer used a variety of sentence types? Give examples.
- If any sentences seem unclear, how can they be improved?
- Has the writer used specific verbs and nouns? What are some examples of these?
- Has the writer used colorful adjectives to create pictures in readers' minds? Can any be added or changed?

Things That Work Well:

_____

_____

_____

Things You Might Improve:

_____

_____

mark

Use this to insert text. Use it to add a letter, word, sentence, or passage to your draft.

Use this mark to delete text ~~from your draft~~. Use it to take a letter, word, sentence, or passage out of your draft.

correct

Use this mark to ~~replace~~ text. Use it to replace a letter, word, sentence, or passage with new text.

Unit 31 Fluency

Word Fluency 1

	Correct	Errors
1st Try		
2nd Try		

bury	buy	cough	penguin	soldier	toward	cough	bury	penguin	toward	10
cough	bury	soldier	buy	toward	penguin	buy	cough	toward	bury	20
buy	toward	penguin	bury	soldier	cough	soldier	cough	bury	toward	30
penguin	soldier	cough	toward	buy	buy	penguin	bury	toward	buy	40
toward	cough	penguin	soldier	buy	bury	buy	toward	penguin	cough	50
cough	toward	bury	buy	penguin	soldier	cough	penguin	bury	buy	60
bury	buy	soldier	cough	toward	penguin	cough	toward	soldier	bury	70
toward	soldier	penguin	buy	cough	penguin	buy	toward	cough	toward	80
penguin	toward	cough	soldier	soldier	buy	toward	bury	penguin	cough	90
cough	soldier	bury	buy	penguin	soldier	penguin	toward	bury	buy	100

Word Fluency 2

		Correct	Errors
1st Try			
2nd Try			

chair	care	very	merry	serious	various	here	issue	sure	10
very	here	chair	heard	care	issue	merry	sure	various	20
here	merry	care	very	chair	serious	heard	various	issue	sure	30
care	serious	here	merry	very	sure	chair	issue	various	heard	40
heard	issue	various	serious	here	care	very	merry	chair	sure	50
merry	various	issue	serious	here	sure	heard	care	very	chair	60
serious	heard	merry	issue	here	very	chair	sure	care	70
various	here	merry	chair	sure	chair	care	merry	issue	heard	80
here	chair	serious	heard	serious	issue	various	very	sure	merry	90
issue	serious	here	chair	various	merry	sure	heard	care	very	100

Word Fluency 3

	Correct	Errors
1st Try		
2nd Try		

primary · library · measure · treasure · repair · prepare · paragraph · paraphrase · compare · comparison	10
measure · paragraph · primary · paraphrase · library · compare · treasure · comparison · repair · prepare	20
paragraph · treasure · measure · library · primary · repair · paraphrase · prepare · compare · comparison	30
library · repair · paragraph · treasure · measure · comparison · primary · compare · prepare · paraphrase	40
compare · paraphrase · repair · prepare · paragraph · library · measure · comparison · primary · treasure	50
treasure · prepare · paraphrase · paragraph · repair · comparison · compare · library · measure · primary	60
repair · compare · treasure · prepare · paraphrase · measure · paragraph · primary · comparison · library	70
prepare · paragraph · repair · measure · comparison · primary · library · treasure · compare · paraphrase	80
paragraph · primary · library · compare · repair · paraphrase · prepare · measure · comparison · treasure	90
paraphrase · repair · paragraph · primary · prepare · treasure · comparison · compare · library · measure	100

Word Fluency 4

	Correct	Errors
1st Try		
2nd Try		

triceps biceps hexagon heptagon decathlon pentathlon hexameter decimeter megawatts kilowatts	10
hexagon hexameter triceps decimeter megawatts heptagon biceps kilowatts decathlon pentathlon	20
kilowatts heptagon hexagon biceps triceps decimeter decathlon pentathlon megawatts hexameter	30
biceps decathlon hexameter heptagon kilowatts triceps hexagon megawatts pentathlon decimeter	40
decimeter megawatts decathlon pentathlon hexameter biceps hexagon heptagon triceps kilowatts	50
heptagon pentathlon megawatts kilowatts decathlon hexameter decimeter hexagon biceps triceps	60
decathlon decimeter heptagon pentathlon megawatts hexagon triceps kilowatts hexameter biceps	70
pentathlon hexameter decathlon hexagon kilowatts triceps biceps heptagon megawatts decimeter	80
hexameter triceps biceps decimeter decathlon megawatts pentathlon hexagon kilowatts heptagon	90
megawatts decathlon hexameter triceps pentathlon heptagon kilowatts decimeter biceps hexagon	100

Passage Fluency

	Correct	Errors
1st Try		
2nd Try		

Adapted from "The Heart of Our Land"

The upper Midwestern part of the United States is | 9
often called the Heartland. This region sits in the | 18
middle, or heart, of the country. The region's name, | 27
the Heartland, reflects more than its position in the | 36
country. The name also reflects important American | 43
values and traditions that thrive there. | 49

Geographical Characteristics and Location | 53

In parts of the Heartland, flat plains stretch across | 62
the landscape. Some areas have hills and trees. Others | 71
have beautiful forests and rivers. The Heartland | 78
centers on the Ohio, Missouri, and Mississippi rivers. | 86
The Heartland lies between the Appalachian and | 93
Rocky Mountains. | 95

Which states make up the Heartland region? | 102
Most geographers include Ohio, Indiana, Illinois, | 108
Minnesota, Wisconsin, Iowa, Missouri, Kansas, | 113
Nebraska, North Dakota, and South Dakota on this | 121
list. Also, most geographers consider Michigan, which | 128
borders four of the five Great Lakes, as being part of | 139
the Heartland region. | 142

History | 143

The early United States was a country of farms and | 153
farmers. Keeping a farm was hard work. It took | 162
independence, and it took appreciation for the land. | 170
A healthy dose of neighborly spirit was also needed. | 179
Americans see these traits as valuable in all parts of | 189
life, and these traits themselves provide yet another | 197
reason for the region's name. | 202

The Heartland Today | 205

Today, there are fewer farms, but the farms are much | 215
bigger. Fewer farms are run by families. Instead, | 223
most are run by large companies, and this new way of | 234
farming is called agribusiness. | 238

Some of the Heartland's people still farm, and | 246
Heartland values remain the same. The people still | 254
take pride in their work, and they share their love of | 267
the land. | 269

Word Fluency 1

	Correct	Errors
1st Try		
2nd Try		

floor	flood	both	door	floor	pint	flood	door	blood	both	10
both	door	floor	blood	flood	floor	blood	pint	both	door	20
floor	both	door	pint	door	pint	both	flood	floor	blood	30
blood	floor	both	flood	both	blood	floor	door	pint	flood	40
door	flood	floor	both	blood	both	pint	flood	door	floor	50
blood	both	door	flood	pint	flood	blood	both	floor	door	60
both	pint	floor	door	flood	floor	door	pint	pint	both	70
floor	door	blood	flood	door	blood	flood	both	both	floor	80
door	flood	both	blood	blood	both	pint	door	floor	flood	90
blood	both	floor	flood	pint	flood	blood	both	pint	door	100

Word Fluency 2

	Correct	Errors
1st Try		
2nd Try		

10	wild	child	remind	behind	foremost	almost	scroll	stroll	scold	cold
20	foremost	almost	wild	scroll	child	scold	remind	cold	behind	stroll
30	wild	child	foremost	remind	almost	cold	scold	stroll	scroll	behind
40	remind	foremost	child	cold	wild	stroll	scroll	behind	almost	scold
50	scroll	cold	wild	stroll	scold	behind	foremost	behind	remind	child
60	cold	scroll	stroll	child	wild	almost	behind	almost	foremost	scroll
70	scold	stroll	scold	behind	stroll	remind	foremost	scroll	child	almost
80	remind	child	scroll	scold	cold	wild	stroll	almost	behind	foremost
90	scroll	scroll	stroll	foremost	remind	almost	child	scold	cold	behind
100	stroll	scold	child	wild	scroll	foremost	cold	behind	almost	remind

Word Fluency 3

	Correct	Errors
1st Try		
2nd Try		

bold	behold	scaffold	threshold	enroll	payroll	control	patrol	unkind	unwind	10
scaffold	control	bold	patrol	behold	unkind	threshold	unwind	enroll	payroll	20
unwind	threshold	scaffold	behold	bold	enroll	patrol	payroll	unkind	control	30
behold	enroll	control	threshold	scaffold	unwind	bold	unkind	payroll	patrol	40
patrol	unkind	enroll	payroll	control	behold	behold	threshold	unwind	unwind	50
threshold	payroll	unkind	enroll	unwind	control	patrol	behold	scaffold	bold	60
enroll	patrol	unwind	enroll	unkind	scaffold	unwind	bold	control	behold	70
payroll	control	scaffold	threshold	payroll	bold	behold	threshold	unkind	patrol	80
control	bold	behold	patrol	enroll	unkind	payroll	scaffold	unwind	threshold	90
unkind	enroll	control	bold	payroll	threshold	unwind	patrol	behold	scaffold	100

Word Fluency 4

	Correct	Errors
1st Try		
2nd Try		

autograph	biography	phonogram	phonograph	telegraph	paragraph	microscope	micrograph	skeptic	skeptical	10
phonogram	microscope	autograph	micrograph	biography	skeptic	phonograph	skeptical	telegraph	paragraph	20
skeptical	phonograph	phonogram	biography	autograph	telegraph	micrograph	paragraph	skeptic	microscope	30
biography	phonogram	microscope	phonogram	phonogram	skeptical	autograph	skeptic	paragraph	micrograph	40
micrograph	skeptic	telegraph	paragraph	microscope	biography	phonogram	phonograph	autograph	skeptical	50
phonograph	paragraph	skeptic	skeptical	telegraph	microscope	microscope	biography	phonogram	autograph	60
telegraph	micrograph	phonograph	paragraph	skeptic	phonogram	skeptical	autograph	microscope	biography	70
paragraph	microscope	telegraph	phonogram	skeptical	autograph	biography	phonograph	skeptic	micrograph	80
microscope	autograph	biography	micrograph	telegraph	skeptic	skeptic	phonogram	skeptical	phonograph	90
skeptic	telegraph	autograph	microscope	paragraph	phonograph	paragraph	micrograph	biography	phonogram	100

	Correct	Errors
1st Try		
2nd Try		

Adapted from "Good as Gold"

Through the ages, gold has been valued more	8
than most materials. Because of its brilliant color	16
and durability, gold was one of the first metals to	26
attract human interest. Throughout the world, gold	33
became a symbol of wealth, and leaders of ancient	42
civilizations hoarded gold. Wars were fought over	49
gold. Thousands of people left their homes in search	58
of gold. And gold was used as money. Gold is an	69
excellent conductor of electricity, and because of	76
that, today many computers have gold in them. Even	85
cell phones contain gold. Gold has many special	93
properties. When we want to praise the quality of	102
something, we say it is as "good as gold."	111
The United States set up its first national system of	121
money in 1792. A bimetallic standard was established.	129
This meant that two metals, gold and silver, would	138
be the basis for the value of all the money. In 1900,	150
the United States changed to the gold standard. The	159
United States guaranteed that it would trade any U.S.	168
coin or bill for the same value in gold. The gold that	180
stood behind all the U.S. money has been stored at	190
Fort Knox in Kentucky since 1937. Other countries	198
used gold as a standard for their money as well, and	209
this made trade among countries easier. In 1971,	217
poor economic conditions forced the United States to	225
abandon the gold standard. Nevertheless, gold is still	233
a valued national resource—the United States holds	241
147.3 million ounces of gold at Fort Knox.	249

Word Fluency 1

	Correct	Errors
1st Try		
2nd Try		

10	tongue	ocean	daughter	mortgage	tongue	auxiliary	ocean	mortgage	dinosaur	daughter
20	daughter	mortgage	tongue	dinosaur	ocean	tongue	daughter	auxiliary	daughter	mortgage
30	tongue	daughter	mortgage	auxiliary	mortgage	auxiliary	ocean	daughter	tongue	dinosaur
40	dinosaur	tongue	ocean	daughter	tongue	dinosaur	daughter	mortgage	ocean	tongue
50	mortgage	ocean	daughter	dinosaur	tongue	daughter	dinosaur	auxiliary	ocean	auxiliary
60	dinosaur	daughter	mortgage	tongue	ocean	mortgage	ocean	daughter	mortgage	daughter
70	daughter	auxiliary	mortgage	tongue	ocean	tongue	mortgage	auxiliary	mortgage	dinosaur
80	tongue	mortgage	dinosaur	ocean	mortgage	dinosaur	ocean	dinosaur	auxiliary	daughter
90	mortgage	ocean	daughter	tongue	daughter	auxiliary	dinosaur	mortgage	tongue	auxiliary
100	dinosaur	daughter	tongue	auxiliary	ocean	dinosaur	tongue	daughter	auxiliary	daughter

Word Fluency 2

10	tight	slight	sight	right	night	might	light	fright	bright	fight
20	night	might	tight	light	slight	bright	fight	right	fright
30	tight	slight	night	sight	might	bright	fight	light	right
40	sight	night	slight	fight	tight	light	fright	might	bright
50	light	fight	tight	fright	bright	right	might	night	slight
60	fight	fright	bright	slight	tight	might	sight	right	night
70	bright	tight	fight	right	fright	sight	fight	light	might
80	sight	slight	light	bright	tight	fight	night	slight	right
90	light	tight	fright	night	sight	might	slight	bright	fight
100	fright	bright	slight	tight	light	night	tight	right	might

Word Fluency 3

	Correct	Errors
1st Try		
2nd Try		

uptight	upright	delight	tonight	sigh	high	thorough	although	weight	eight	10
sigh	high	uptight	thorough	upright	weight	delight	eight	tonight	although	20
tonight	upright	sigh	delight	high	eight	weight	although	thorough	uptight	30
delight	sigh	uptight	eight	uptight	although	thorough	sigh	high	weight	40
uptight	eight	thorough	although	weight	tonight	sigh	high	uptight	delight	50
eight	although	weight	delight	tonight	high	uptight	although	sigh	thorough	60
weight	tonight	eight	uptight	although	upright	although	high	eight	high	70
delight	upright	thorough	weight	eight	uptight	high	delight	high	sigh	80
thorough	uptight	although	sigh	uptight	weight	delight	thorough	weight	tonight	90
although	weight	delight	uptight	thorough	sigh	eight	high	tonight	upright	100

Word Fluency 4

	Correct	Errors
1st Try		
2nd Try		

geography	photography	chronology	geology	perimeter	thermometer	geometry	geologist	polygon	octagon	10
chronology	geometry	geography	geologist	photography	polygon	geology	octagon	perimeter	thermometer	20
octagon	geology	chronology	photography	geography	perimeter	geologist	thermometer	polygon	geometry	30
photography	perimeter	geometry	geology	chronology	octagon	thermometer	polygon	geography	geologist	40
geologist	polygon	perimeter	thermometer	geometry	photography	chronology	geology	geography	octagon	50
geology	thermometer	polygon	octagon	perimeter	thermometer	geometry	geologist	photography	geography	60
perimeter	geologist	geology	thermometer	polygon	chronology	octagon	geography	chronology	photography	70
thermometer	geometry	perimeter	chronology	octagon	polygon	photography	geology	polygon	geologist	80
geometry	geography	photography	geologist	perimeter	thermometer	geography	chronology	octagon	geology	90
polygon	perimeter	geometry	geography	thermometer	geology	octagon	geologist	photography	chronology	100

Passage Fluency

	Correct	Errors
1st Try		
2nd Try		

**Adapted from "Playing with the Logic of
Space: The Art of M.C. Escher"**

As a boy, the Dutch graphic artist M.C. Escher   9
(1898–1972) often created a puzzle when   16
making a cheese sandwich.   20

He would divide the cheese into small bits, and   29
then he would piece the bits together on the   38
bread so they just fit. Satisfied, he would eat the   48
sandwich. This childhood interest with the way   55
shapes fit together continued throughout his life.   62

Escher was not good at math in school, but he   72
was fascinated by many of its principles. He   80
once said that mathematicians had "opened   86
the gate" to a wide and wonderful world. But,   95
he added, "By their very nature they are more   104
interested in the way in which the gate is   113
opened than in the garden lying behind it."   121

For Escher, this garden was filled with   128
opportunities to play with the logic of space. He   137
found that by turning, stacking, and rotating   144
basic shapes, he could make surprising images.   151
He took joy in drawing shapes that tricked   159
the human eye. In Escher's drawings, a flat   167
square with four right angles can change into   175
a 3-D star, and a grid of squares can reshape   185
itself until a flock of geese seems to fly out of a   197
checkerboard. Water can flow uphill.   202

To create these illusions, Escher drew from the   210
world of geometry. Escher used both Necker   217
cubes and the Penrose triangle in many of his   226
most famous works. Escher was famous in his   234
lifetime, and his works still intrigue us with   242
their puzzling perspectives.   245

Word Fluency 1

	Correct	Errors
1st Try		
2nd Try		

bargain	clothes	island	ninth	often	sword	island	bargain	ninth	sword	10
island	bargain	often	clothes	sword	ninth	clothes	sword	island	bargain	20
clothes	sword	ninth	bargain	often	island	often	island	bargain	sword	30
ninth	often	island	sword	clothes	bargain	ninth	bargain	sword	clothes	40
sword	island	ninth	often	bargain	clothes	bargain	sword	ninth	island	50
island	sword	bargain	clothes	ninth	often	ninth	island	bargain	clothes	60
bargain	clothes	often	island	sword	ninth	island	sword	often	bargain	70
sword	often	bargain	ninth	clothes	island	ninth	clothes	island	sword	80
ninth	sword	island	often	bargain	clothes	sword	bargain	ninth	island	90
island	often	bargain	clothes	ninth	often	ninth	sword	bargain	clothes	100

Word Fluency 2

	Correct	Errors
1st Try		
2nd Try		

	Words									
10	tobacco	rhythm	sight	calm	column	comb	sign	knowledge	knew	write
20	column	comb	tobacco	sign	rhythm	knew	sight	write	calm	knowledge
30	tobacco	rhythm	column	sight	comb	write	knew	knowledge	sign	calm
40	sight	column	rhythm	write	tobacco	knowledge	sign	calm	comb	knew
50	sign	write	tobacco	knowledge	knew	calm	column	comb	sight	rhythm
60	write	knowledge	knew	rhythm	tobacco	calm	sight	column	comb	sign
70	knew	tobacco	write	calm	knowledge	sight	sign	column	rhythm	comb
80	sight	rhythm	sign	knew	tobacco	calm	comb	write	knowledge	column
90	sign	tobacco	knowledge	column	sight	comb	rhythm	knew	write	calm
100	knowledge	knew	rhythm	tobacco	sign	column	write	calm	comb	sight

	Correct	Errors
1st Try		
2nd Try		

knew	write	wrong	knee	wrist	know	wrote	knife	knock	knot	10
wrong	wrote	knew	knife	write	knock	knee	knot	wrist	know	20
knot	knee	wrong	write	knew	wrist	knife	know	knock	wrote	30
write	wrist	wrote	knee	wrong	knot	knew	knock	know	knife	40
knife	knock	wrist	know	wrote	write	knot	knee	knew	knot	50
knee	know	knock	knot	wrist	wrote	write	knife	wrong	knew	60
wrist	knife	knee	know	knock	wrong	wrote	knot	knew	write	70
know	wrote	wrist	wrong	knew	knock	write	knee	knife	knife	80
wrote	knew	write	knife	knock	know	wrist	knot	knot	knee	90
knock	wrist	wrote	knew	knot	knife	know	knife	write	wrong	100

Unit 34 Fluency

Word Fluency 4

	Correct	Errors
1st Try		
2nd Try		

#	Words								
10	hierarchy	autocratic	democratic	politician	democracy	demography	psychologist	psychology	political
20	autocratic	demography	hierarchy	psychology	anarchy	democratic	political	democracy	politician
30	political	democratic	anarchy	democracy	hierarchy	democracy	psychologist	psychology	demography
40	anarchy	democracy	democracy	political	autocratic	hierarchy	psychology	politician	psychologist
50	psychologist	psychology	politician	anarchy	demography	autocratic	hierarchy	hierarchy	political
60	democratic	psychology	demography	political	political	psychologist	anarchy	autocratic	hierarchy
70	democracy	democratic	politician	hierarchy	autocratic	demography	hierarchy	political	anarchy
80	politician	democracy	autocratic	democracy	anarchy	democracy	democratic	psychology	psychologist
90	political	anarchy	psychologist	autocratic	politician	demography	autocratic	demography	democratic
100	psychology	democracy	political	hierarchy	democratic	demography	psychologist	anarchy	autocratic

Passage Fluency

	Errors	Correct
1st Try		
2nd Try		

Adapted from "The Value of Knowledge"

Knowledge adds value to our lives. With knowledge,	8
we can understand and appreciate our world. Statistics	16
show that knowledge has measurable benefits. Since	23
the 1970s, the United States government has conducted	31
many studies, and these studies show a strong	39
relationship between education and income. One thing	46
is clear: higher levels of education translate into better	55
jobs, and better jobs mean higher wages. When it is all	66
said and done, lifetime earnings increase significantly	73
as a result of having a higher level of education.	83
Studies have examined the relationships among	89
education, employment, and income. Overall, more	95
education translates into better employment and	101
higher wages. Higher annual income adds up to greater	110
lifetime earnings.	112
Education's economic benefits are clear, but there are	120
some intangible benefits, too. The process of acquiring	128
an education gives us skills as well as knowledge.	137
In school, we learn how to learn, and we learn to	148
confidently face a rapidly changing world. We learn	156
to meet challenging new work environments. People	163
used to think that one lifetime = one career. Today, it's	173
possible to have several careers in our lives, and the key	184
to making transitions is education.	189
Acquiring knowledge is the best investment we can	197
make in our future and, as for the added benefits of	208
knowledge, no one can measure those. What's the value	217
of better knowing ourselves and our world? Priceless.	225

Unit 35 Fluency

Word Fluency 1

	Correct	Errors
1st Try		
2nd Try		

arbitrary	ordinary	temporary	voluntary	contemporary	manipulate	predominate	investigate	identical	identify	10
temporary	predominate	arbitrary	investigate	identical	ordinary	voluntary	identify	contemporary	manipulate	20
predominate	voluntary	temporary	ordinary	arbitrary	contemporary	investigate	manipulate	identical	identify	30
ordinary	contemporary	predominate	voluntary	temporary	identify	arbitrary	identical	manipulate	investigate	40
identical	investigate	contemporary	manipulate	predominate	temporary	arbitrary	identify	arbitrary	voluntary	50
voluntary	manipulate	investigate	predominate	contemporary	identify	identical	ordinary	temporary	arbitrary	60
contemporary	identical	voluntary	manipulate	investigate	temporary	ordinary	arbitrary	identify	ordinary	70
manipulate	predominate	contemporary	temporary	identify	arbitrary	voluntary	ordinary	identical	investigate	80
predominate	arbitrary	ordinary	identical	contemporary	investigate	manipulate	temporary	identify	voluntary	90
investigate	contemporary	predominate	arbitrary	manipulate	voluntary	identify	identical	ordinary	temporary	100

Word Fluency 2

	Correct	Errors
1st Try		
2nd Try		

Words										Count
criteria	cursory	malleable	utility	irritable	fidelity	deposition	imagination	interpretation	moderation	10
malleable	deposition	criteria	imagination	cursory	interpretation	utility	moderation	irritable	fidelity	20
deposition	utility	malleable	cursory	criteria	irritable	imagination	fidelity	interpretation	moderation	30
cursory	irritable	deposition	utility	malleable	moderation	criteria	interpretation	fidelity	imagination	40
interpretation	imagination	irritable	fidelity	deposition	cursory	malleable	moderation	criteria	utility	50
utility	fidelity	imagination	deposition	irritable	moderation	deposition	cursory	malleable	criteria	60
irritable	interpretation	utility	fidelity	imagination	malleable	deposition	criteria	moderation	cursory	70
fidelity	deposition	irritable	malleable	moderation	criteria	cursory	utility	interpretation	imagination	80
deposition	criteria	cursory	interpretation	irritable	imagination	fidelity	malleable	moderation	utility	90
imagination	irritable	deposition	criteria	fidelity	utility	moderation	interpretation	cursory	malleable	100

Word Fluency 3

	Correct	Errors
1st Try		
2nd Try		

hemisphere	hydrogen	astrology	hydrology	physics	deposition	physical	physician	physique	10
astrology	hemisphere	physical	hemicycle	physician	hydrogen	physique	hydrology	physics	20
deposition	hemicycle	astrology	hemisphere	hydrology	physical	physics	physician	physique	30
hemicycle	hydrogen	deposition	astrology	physique	hemisphere	physician	physics	physical	40
physician	physics	hydrology	deposition	hemicycle	astrology	physique	hemisphere	hydrogen	50
hydrogen	deposition	physics	hydrology	physician	hemicycle	physique	astrology	hemisphere	60
hydrology	hydrogen	physical	physics	astrology	deposition	hemisphere	physique	hemicycle	70
physics	hydrology	astrology	physique	physical	hemicycle	hydrogen	physician	physical	80
deposition	physician	hemisphere	hydrology	physical	physics	astrology	physique	hydrogen	90
physical	hydrology	deposition	physics	hydrogen	physique	physician	hemicycle	astrology	100

	Correct	Errors
1st Try		
2nd Try		

pyromania	maniac	hydrophobia	claustrophobia	hydrology	atmosphere	biosphere	technical	zoology	zoologist	10
hydrophobia	biosphere	pyromania	technical	maniac	zoology	claustrophobia	zoologist	hydrology	atmosphere	20
biosphere	claustrophobia	hydrophobia	maniac	pyromania	hydrology	technical	atmosphere	zoology	zoologist	30
maniac	hydrology	biosphere	claustrophobia	hydrophobia	zoologist	pyromania	zoology	atmosphere	technical	40
zoology	technical	hydrology	atmosphere	biosphere	maniac	hydrophobia	zoologist	pyromania	claustrophobia	50
claustrophobia	atmosphere	technical	biosphere	hydrophobia	zoologist	zoology	maniac	hydrophobia	pyromania	60
hydrology	zoology	claustrophobia	atmosphere	technical	hydrophobia	biosphere	pyromania	zoologist	maniac	70
atmosphere	biosphere	atmosphere	hydrophobia	zoologist	pyromania	maniac	claustrophobia	zoology	technical	80
biosphere	pyromania	maniac	zoology	hydrology	technical	atmosphere	hydrophobia	zoologist	claustrophobia	90
technical	hydrology	biosphere	pyromania	atmosphere	claustrophobia	zoologist	zoology	maniac	hydrophobia	100

Passage Fluency

	Errors	
Correct		
	1st Try	2nd Try

Adapted from "The Tech of Shrek: Imagination Animated"

Imagine making a movie about a large, green ogre who | 10
really has the heart of a hero inside, and now imagine | 21
that the whole film is made using the latest in computer- | 32
generated (CG) animation. That is what the creators of the | 42
movie *Shrek* did, and they stretched their imaginations | 50
to the limits and earned an Academy Award for Best | 60
Animated Feature. Here's how. | 64

The filmmakers were inspired by a children's book, *Shrek*, | 73
by William Steig. To make a full-length movie, they had | 84
to add a lot to the original story, so the story team met | 97
as a group and elaborated on the story. They parodied | 107
traditional fairy tales and added characters and scenes | 115
that would make both kids and adults laugh. | 123

After the filmmakers wrote the story, they designed the | 132
movie. They made drawings and sketches, and they built | 141
sculptures of the characters. They worked hard to create a | 151
look for Shrek; he couldn't be a typical fairy-tale hero. He | 163
had to look something like a bulldog—ugly but still cute. | 174
They worked on the other characters as well. | 182

Over 275 artists and technicians worked for almost | 190
three years on the art, and their goal was to create a | 202
fully computer-animated film. They faced three major | 210
challenges: they had to make human-like characters that | 219
looked and acted real; they had to create the natural | 229
environment; and they needed to render other special | 237
visual effects, such as fire. | 242

The "tech" of *Shrek* broke new ground in the world of | 253
CG animation. Animation is a rich medium for the | 262
imagination. Ogres may come and go, but nevertheless, | 270
this movie will continue to inspire many more fun and | 280
creative animated films to entertain us. | 286

	Correct	Errors
1st Try		
2nd Try		

company	companion	underlie	government	thereby	compliment	improve	impair	brilliance	resonance	10
underlie	improve	company	impair	companion	brilliance	government	resonance	thereby	compliment	20
improve	government	underlie	companion	company	thereby	impair	compliment	brilliance	resonance	30
companion	thereby	improve	government	underlie	resonance	company	brilliance	compliment	impair	40
brilliance	impair	thereby	compliment	improve	companion	underlie	resonance	company	government	50
government	compliment	impair	improve	thereby	resonance	brilliance	companion	underlie	company	60
thereby	brilliance	government	compliment	impair	underlie	improve	company	resonance	companion	70
compliment	government	underlie	brilliance	resonance	company	companion	government	brilliance	impair	80
improve	company	companion	brilliance	thereby	impair	compliment	underlie	resonance	government	90
impair	thereby	improve	company	compliment	government	resonance	brilliance	companion	underlie	100

Word Fluency 2

	Correct	Errors
1st Try		
2nd Try		

#										
10	prevalent	premature	miser	fervor	divulge	dissent	requisite	respite	imminent	ominous
20	divulge	dissent	prevalent	requisite	premature	imminent	miser	ominous	fervor	respite
30	prevalent	premature	divulge	miser	dissent	ominous	imminent	respite	requisite	fervor
40	miser	divulge	premature	ominous	prevalent	imminent	requisite	fervor	dissent	imminent
50	requisite	ominous	prevalent	respite	imminent	dissent	respite	prevalent	divulge	premature
60	ominous	respite	imminent	premature	respite	fervor	miser	divulge	miser	requisite
70	imminent	prevalent	ominous	imminent	respite	fervor	ominous	fervor	requisite	dissent
80	miser	premature	requisite	premature	dissent	prevalent	respite	dissent	premature	divulge
90	requisite	prevalent	respite	divulge	respite	prevalent	miser	premature	prevalent	fervor
100	respite	imminent	imminent	prevalent	requisite	divulge	ominous	dissent	fervor	miser

Word Fluency 3

	Correct	Errors
1st Try		
2nd Try		

digraph	dialogs	pentagons	hexagons	kiloliter	hectoliter	magabytes	gigabytes	quarts	quartile	10
pentagons	digraph	magabytes	gigabytes	dialogs	quarts	hexagons	quartile	kiloliter	hectoliter	20
magabytes	hexagons	pentagons	dialogs	digraph	kiloliter	gigabytes	hectoliter	quarts	quartile	30
dialogs	kiloliter	magabytes	hexagons	pentagons	quartile	digraph	quarts	hectoliter	gigabytes	40
quarts	gigabytes	kiloliter	hectoliter	magabytes	dialogs	pentagons	quartile	digraph	hexagons	50
hexagons	hectoliter	gigabytes	magabytes	kiloliter	quartile	quarts	dialogs	pentagons	digraph	60
kiloliter	hexagons	quarts	hectoliter	gigabytes	pentagons	magabytes	digraph	quartile	dialogs	70
hectoliter	kiloliter	magabytes	pentagons	quartile	digraph	dialogs	hexagons	quarts	gigabytes	80
magabytes	digraph	dialogs	quarts	kiloliter	gigabytes	hectoliter	pentagons	quartile	hexagons	90
gigabytes	kiloliter	magabytes	digraph	hectoliter	hexagons	quartile	quarts	dialogs	pentagons	100

Word Fluency 4

	1st Try	2nd Try
Correct		
Errors		

telescopic	telegraphic	podiatrist	orthographic	dysgraphia	biometrics	podiatrist	telegraphic	technologies	10
podiatrist	tripod	telescopic	triathlete	telegraphic	unicycles	triathlete	telescopic	biometrics	20
tripod	orthographic	podiatrist	telegraphic	telescopic	dysgraphia	telescopic	orthographic	technologies	30
telegraphic	dysgraphia	tripod	orthographic	podiatrist	technologies	podiatrist	orthographic	triathlete	40
unicycles	triathlete	dysgraphia	biometrics	tripod	telegraphic	telescopic	telegraphic	orthographic	50
orthographic	biometrics	triathlete	tripod	dysgraphia	technologies	unicycles	telegraphic	telescopic	60
dysgraphia	unicycles	orthographic	biometrics	triathlete	tripod	telescopic	technologies	telegraphic	70
biometrics	tripod	dysgraphia	podiatrist	technologies	telescopic	telegraphic	orthographic	triathlete	80
tripod	telescopic	telegraphic	unicycles	dysgraphia	biometrics	podiatrist	technologies	orthographic	90
triathlete	dysgraphia	tripod	telescopic	biometrics	orthographic	technologies	unicycles	podiatrist	100

Correct	Errors	
		1st Try
		2nd Try

Adapted from "Brilliance Through Time and Space"

What exactly is the source of a star's brilliance? 9

A star is a huge ball of hot gases, held together by 21
gravity. The centers of stars are so intensely hot that the 32
hydrogen there changes into helium, and this chemical 40
change releases heat and light. We feel the heat only 50
from the star closest to us, the sun. But we see the light 63
of many, many other stars. 68

Two factors contribute to the brightness of stars as 77
seen from Earth: (1) the distance from Earth, and 86
(2) how much energy the star emits. If a bright star 97
is very far away from Earth, it appears less brilliant 107
than a less bright star that is much closer to Earth. 118
Think of comparing the brightness of a candle flame 127
and a bonfire. If these two sources of light are at equal 139
distances from your eyes, the bonfire will appear much 148
brighter. However, if the candle flame is on a table next 159
to you, and the bonfire is a mile down the beach, then 171
the candle flame will look brighter. 177

In space, distance is measured in light-years. A light- 187
year is the distance light travels in one year. The speed 198
of light is about 186,000 miles (300,000 kilometers) per 207
second, so a light-year is about 5.9 trillion miles (9.5 218
trillion kilometers). 220

The sun is like the candle flame in the previous example. 231
It is a medium-sized star and releases only a medium 242
amount of light, but because it is only about eight light- 253
minutes away—meaning light emitted from the sun 261
reaches Earth in eight minutes—it appears much, much 270
brighter to us than any other star. 277

Fluency Charts

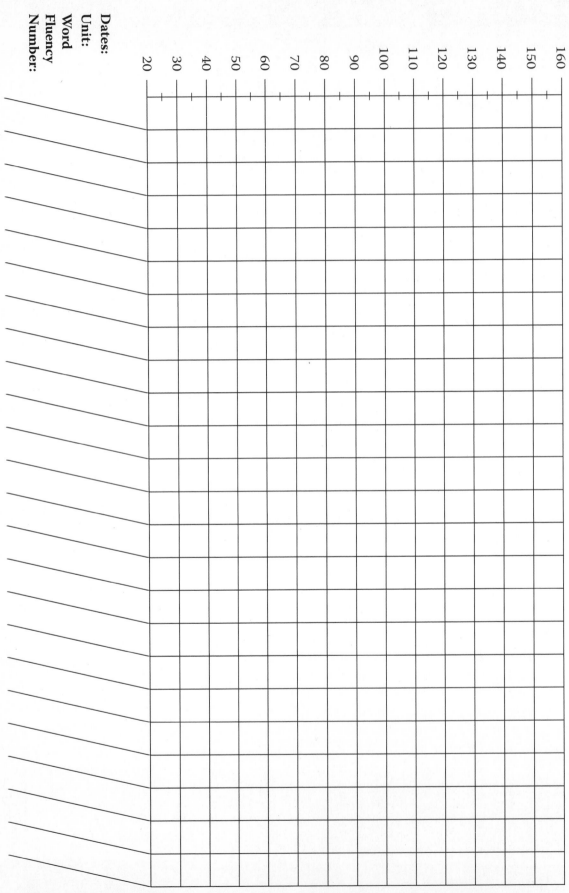

Dates:
Unit:
Word
Fluency
Number:

160
150
140
130
120
110
100
90
80
70
60
50
40
30
20

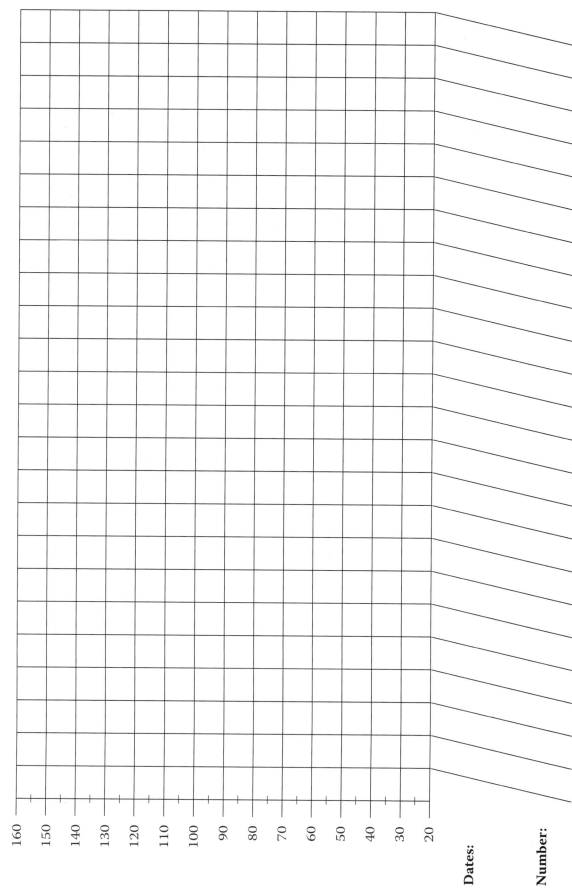

Passage Fluency Chart

Correct Phrases Per _____

160
150
140
130
120
110
100
90
80
70
60
50
40
30
20

Dates:

Number:

Notes

Unit 31	Unit 31	Unit 31
uni-	bi-	ter-
Unit 31	Unit 31	Unit 31
quadr-/ quar-	quint-	sex-
Unit 31	Unit 31	Unit 31
sept-	oct-	nona-/ nove-
Unit 31	Unit 31	Unit 31
dec-	cent-	mille-/ milli-

Unit 31	Unit 31	Unit 31
mono-	di-	tri-
Unit 31	Unit 31	Unit 31
tetra-	penta-/ pent-	hexa-
Unit 31	Unit 31	Unit 31
hepta-	oct-	ennea-
Unit 31	Unit 31	Unit 31
dec-	hect-	kilo-

Unit 31	Unit 31	Unit 31
myria-	mega-	giga-
Unit 31	**Unit 31**	**Unit 31**
tera-	peta-	exa-
Unit 32	**Unit 32**	**Unit 32**
auto	bio	gram
Unit 32	**Unit 32**	**Unit 32**
graphy	macro	micro

Unit 32	Unit 32	Unit 32
phono	**scope**	**skept**
Unit 32	Unit 32	Unit 32
tele	**anthro**	**miso**
Unit 32		
phil		
Unit 33	Unit 33	Unit 33
chrono	**geo**	**gon**

Unit 33	Unit 33	Unit 33
meter	metry	ologist/ logist
Unit 33	Unit 33	Unit 33
ology/ logy	peri	photo
Unit 33	Unit 33	Unit 33
poly	sym	thermo
Unit 33	Unit 33	Unit 33
chrom	morph	biblio

Unit 34 arch	Unit 34 aristo	Unit 34 cracy
Unit 34 crat	Unit 34 demo	Unit 34 derm
Unit 34 pod	Unit 34 polis	Unit 34 polit
Unit 34 psych	Unit 34 theo	Unit 34 path

Unit 34	Unit 34	
pyr	**peudo**	

Unit 35	Unit 35	Unit 35
astro	**hemi**	**hydro**

Unit 35	Unit 35	Unit 35
mania	**phobia**	**phys**

Unit 35	Unit 35	Unit 35
sphere	**tech**	**zoo**

Unit 35	Unit 35	Unit 35
nau	cyclo	neur

Sources

Unit 31

The Heart of Our Land

Answers.com. 2005. "Middle West." Answers Corporation. http://www.answers.com/topic/midwest (accessed June 21, 2005).

Bureau of International Information Programs. 2005. "American Agriculture: Its Changing Significance." U.S. Department of State. http://www.usinfo.state.gov/ (accessed June 15, 2005).

Iowa Department of Agriculture & Land Stewardship. 2004. "Kid's Stuff: Iowa Agriculture Quick Facts." Iowa Department of Agriculture & Land Stewardship. http://www.agriculture.state.ia.us/quickFacts.htm (accessed June 15, 2005).

National Geographic. 1991. "The Heartland." *National Geographic Picture Atlas of Our Fifty States.* Washington, D.C.: National Geographic Society.

Dear Rosita

Candelaria, Nash. 1998. "Dear Rosita," from Uncivil Rights and Other Stories. Copyright © 1998 Bilingual Press/Editorial Bilingüe, Arizona State University, Tempe, AZ. Reprinted with permission.

The Tell-Tale Heart

Poe, Edgar Allan. 1843. "The Tell-Tale Heart." Literature.org, the Online Literature Library. http://www.literature.org/authors/poe-edgar-allan/tell-tale-heart.html (accessed June 21, 2005).

Heroes of the Heart

Azevedo, Mary Ann. 2005. "Dr. Michael DeBakey: A champion of the heart." Houston Business Journal, May 20, 2005. © American City Business Journals. http://houston.bizjournals.com/houston/stories/2005/05/23/story2.html, (accessed May 23, 2005).

Baylor College of Medicine. 1998. "The father of modern cardiovascular surgery: Dr. Michael E. DeBakey." http://www.bcm.edu/pa/debakey_bio.htm (accessed May 23, 2005).

BlackInventor.com. 2005. "Daniel Hale Williams." The Black Inventor Online Museum. http://www.blackinventor.com/pages/danielwilliams.html (accessed May 23, 2005).

Bianco, Carl. 2005. "How Your Heart Works." HowStuffWorks.com © HowStuffWorks, Inc. http://www.howstuffworks.com/heart.htm (accessed May 23, 2005).

Encyclopædia Britannica Online. 2005. "Women in American History." http://www.britannica.com/search?query=Women+in+American+History&go_button.x=17&go_button.y=9&ct= (accessed May 23, 2005).

Foundation for Biomedical Research, The. 2003. "Dr. Michael E. DeBakey." http://www.fbresearch.org/about/debakey.htm (accessed May 23, 2005).

Haber, Louis. 1970. Black Pioneers of Science and Invention. New York, NY: Harcourt, Brace & World, Inc.

Inventions.org. 2005. "Women in Science: Helen Brooke Taussig." Inventors Assistance League. http://www.inventions.org/culture/science/women/taussig.html (accessed May 23, 2005).

MedicalBooks.com. 2005. "History of Surgery." Medical Distributors of America. http://www.medicalbooks.com/skin-surgery.html (accessed June 22, 2005).

Methodist Hospital System, The. 2005. "Heart Health." http://www.methodisthealth.com/ (accessed May 23, 2005).

O'Neill, Lois Decker, ed. 1979. The Women's Book of World Records and Achievements. Garden City, NY: Anchor Press/Doubleday.

PBS Reference Room, Articles A to Z. 2002. "Daniel Hale Williams," from the PBS series, African American World. http://www.pbs.org/wnet/aaworld/reference/articles/daniel_hale_williams.html (accessed May 23, 3005).

Planet-Science.com. 2005. "Fitness Factory: The Heart." Out There. © Nesta. http://www.planet-science.com/outthere/index.html?page=/outthere/

bodybeat/fitness_factory/heart.html (accessed May 23, 2005).

Provident Hospital History. 2005. "History: Dr. Daniel Hale Williams." The Provident Foundation. http://www.providentfoundation.org/history/williams.html (accessed May 23, 2005).

Robinson, Donald. 1976. The Miracle Finders: The Stories Behind the Most Important Breakthroughs of Modern Medicine. New York, NY: David McKay Company, Inc.

Science Friday Kids' Connection. 2004. "Hour One: Heart Health." © KIDSNET.org. http://www.sciencefriday.com/kids/sfkc20041112-1.html (accessed May 23, 2005).

U.S. National Library of Medicine. 2005. "Dr. Helen Brooke Taussig." http://www.nlm.nih.gov/changingthefaceofmedicine/physicians/biography_316.html (accessed May 23, 2005).

Language of the Heart: A Collection of Poems

Bruchac, Joseph. 1971. "Drums," a section of the poem Second Skins A Peyote Song. Copyright © 1971 by Joseph Bruchac. Reprinted in arrangement with Joseph Bruchac and Barbara S. Kouts, Literary Agent.

Dickinson, Emily. 1890. "If I Can Stop One Heart from Breaking." The Poems of Emily Dickinson, Thomas H. Johnson, ed. Cambridge, MA: Harvard University Press.

Rumi, Mowlana Jalaluddin. 1231. "Let Go of Your Worries" from "Poem Seven." Rumi the Path of Love. http://www.rumi.org.uk/love_poems.html (accessed October 17, 2007).

Williams, C.K. 1994. "The World's Greatest Tricycle-Rider," from Selected Poems by C.K. Williams. Copyright © 1994 by C. K. Williams. Reprinted by permission of Farrar, Straus and Giroux, LLC.

Wordsworth, William. 1802. "My Heart Leaps Up." Poetry Out Loud. Chapel Hill, NC: Algonquin Books.

Unit 32

Good as Gold

Arts and Exhibitions International. 2005. "Tutankhamun." http://www.kingtut.org/home (accessed July 11, 2005).

Gold Institute, The. 2002. "Nothing Works Like Gold." http://www.responsiblegold.org/ (accessed July 6, 2005).

National Numismatic Collection. 2005. "Your Money in Transition," National Numismatic Collection of the Smithsonian Institution. http://americanhistory.si.edu/collections/numismatics/moneyintrans/mitindex.htm (accessed July 11, 2005).

United States Mint, The. 2005. "United States Mint at San Francisco." U.S. Department of the Treasury. http://www.usmint.gov/about_the_mint/mint_facilities/index.cfm?flash=yes&action=SF_facilities (accessed July 11, 2005).

Wikipedia. 2005. "Hernán Cortés." http://en.wikipedia.org/wiki/Hern%C3%A1n_Cort%C3%A9s (accessed July 11, 2005).

World Book, The. 2000. "Money." World Book, Volume 13. Chicago, IL: World Book, Inc.

Nothing Gold Can Stay

Frost, Robert. 1923. "Nothing Gold Can Stay," from The Poetry of Robert Frost, edited by Edward Connery Lathem. Copyright 1923, 1969 by Henry Holt and Company. Copyright 1951 by Robert Frost. Reprinted by permission of Henry Holt and Company, LLC.

The Treasure of the Sierra Madre

Naremore, James. 1979. The Treasure of the Sierra Madre. © 1979. Reprinted by permission of The University of Wisconsin Press.

Blue Gold: Earth's Liquid Asset

Vidal, John. 2002. "Blue gold: Earth's liquid asset." Reprinted by permission from The Guardian, 22 August 2002. Copyright Guardian News & Media Limited, 2002.

The Golden Mean: How the Universe Adds Up

Absolute Astronomy. 2005. "Golden Mean," http://www.absoluteastronomy.com/encyclopedia/G/Go/Golden_Mean.htm (accessed June 21, 2005).

Atrise Web Design Software. 2005. "What is Golden Section?," http://www.atrise.com/golden-section/golden-section.html (accessed June 21, 2005).

Britton, Jill. 2005. "Golden Section in Art and Architecture." http://britton.disted.camosun.bc.ca/goldslide/jbgoldslide.htm (accessed June 23, 2005).

Garland, Trudi Hammel. 1987. Fascinating Fibonaccis: Mystery and Magic in Numbers. Palo Alto, CA: Dale Seymour Publications.

"The Golden Section." 2005. Paper from the Classics 189:Greek Science class by Prof. Gregory Crane at Tufts University. http://www.perseus.tufts.edu/GreekScience/Students/Tim/Golden.html (accessed June 21, 2005).

Harris, William. 2005. "The Golden Mean With A New Solution for the Parthenon's GM." http://community.middlebury.edu/~harris/Humanities/TheGoldenMean.html (accessed June 21, 2005).

Huntley, H.E. 1970. The Divine Proportion: A Study in Mathematical Beauty. New York, NY: Dover Publications, Inc.

Jovanovic, Radoslav. 2003. "Golden Section: The Golden Proportion." Rasko Jovanovic's World of Mathematics. http://milan.milanovic.org/math/english/golden/golden.html (accessed June 21, 2005).

Knott, Ron. 2005. "Fibonacci Numbers and the Golden Section." http://www.mcs.surrey.ac.uk/Personal/R.Knott/Fibonacci/fib.html (accessed June 21, 2005).

Livio, Mario. 2002. The Gold Ratio: The Story of Phi, The World's Most Astonishing Number. New York, NY: Broadway Books.

Male, Lydia Sharman. 1990. "In the Mind of the Beholder." *Saudi Aramco World*, May/June 1990. Aramco Services Company. http://www.saudiaramcoworld.com/issue/199003/in.the.mind.of.the.beholder.htm (accessed June 21, 2005).

Unit 33

Playing With the Logic of Space: The Art of M.C. Escher

Math Academy Online. 2004. "The Mathematical Art of M.C. Escher." Platonic Realms MiniText. http://www.mathacademy.com/pr/minitext/escher/index.asp (accessed July 21, 2005).

Project Online. 2005. "Make your own tessellations!" http://www.iproject.com/escher/teaching/maketessel.html (accessed July 21, 2005).

———. 2005. "M. C. Escher: Beyond the Craft." http://www.iproject.com/escher/teaching/maketessel.html (accessed July 21, 2005).

Seckel, Al. 1997. "Art of M.C. Escher." IllusionWorks, LLC. http://www.psychologie.tu-dresden.de/i1/kaw/diverses%20Material/www.illusionworks.com/html/art_of_m._c._escher.html (accessed July 21, 2005).

Wikipedia. 2005. "Necker cube." http://en.wikipedia.org/wiki/Necker_cube (accessed July 21, 2005).

The First Amendment

Blohm, Craig E. 1991. "The Road to Rights," from Cobblestone, vol. 12, no. 9. Carus Publishing, 315 Fifth St., Peru, IL 61354. All rights reserved.

Calkins, Virginia. 1991. "Mr. Madison Keeps His Promise," from Cobblestone, vol. 12, no. 9. Carus Publishing, 315 Fifth St., Peru, IL 61354. All rights reserved.

Dueland, Joy. 1982. "A Voice From Paris," from Cobblestone, vol. 3, no. 9. Carus Publishing, 315 Fifth St., Peru, IL 61354. All rights reserved.

Farish, Leah. 1998. The First Amendment: Freedom of Speech, Religion, and the Press. Berkeley Heights, NJ: Enslow Publishers, Inc.

First Amendment Center Online. 2005. "About the First Amendment." http://www.

Sources

firstamendmentcenter.org/about.aspx?item=about_firstamd (accessed July 10, 2005).

Freedman, Russell. 2003. In Defense of Liberty: The Story of America's Bill of Rights. New York, NY: Holiday House.

Levy, Leonard W. 1999. Origins of the Bill of Rights. New Haven, CT: Yale University Press.

National Archives Experience, The. 2005. "Bill of Rights" from The Charters of Freedom. http://www.archives.gov/national_archives_experience/charters/bill_of_rights.html#more (accessed July 10, 2005).

Schilder, Rosalind. 1982. "Know Your Rights!," from Cobblestone, vol. 3, no. 9. Carus Publishing, 315 Fifth St., Peru, IL 61354. All rights reserved.

Wikipedia. 2005. "Thomas Jefferson." http://en.wikipedia.org/wiki/Thomas_Jefferson (accessed July 10, 2005).

A Printer's Journal in Revolutionary America

Breig, James. 2003. "Early American Newspapering." Colonial Williamsburg Journal. The Colonial Williamsburg Foundation. http://www.colonialwilliamsburg.com/Foundation/journal/spring03/journalism.cfm (accessed July 21, 2005).

E Pluribus Unum Project, The. 2005. "The Problem of Becoming 'One'," from "Would there have been an American Revolution without Newspapers and Mail?" http://www.assumption.edu/ahc/1770s/pcomconvers.html (accessed July 21, 2005).

———. 2005. "The Dangerous Lives of Printers: The Evolution of Freedom of the Press." http://www.assumption.edu/ahc/1770s/ppressfree.html (accessed July 21, 2005).

Library of Congress. 2002. "Declaration of Independence: Right to Institute New Government." http://www.loc.gov/exhibits/jefferson/jeffdec.html (accessed July 21, 2005).

The Right Choice

Frost, Robert. 1915. "The Road Not Taken," from The Poetry of Robert Frost, edited by Edward Connery Lathem. New York, NY: Henry Holt and Company.

"Letter to Alex Haley" from "Dear Author: Students Write About the Books that Changed Their Lives, a collection by Weekly Reader's Reader Magazine." 1995. Special permission granted by Weekly Reader, published and copyrighted by Weekly Reader Corporation. All rights reserved.

'Right Brain' or 'Left Brain'--Myth or Reality

McCrone, John. 1999. "'Right Brain' or 'Left Brain'—Myth Or Reality?" New Scientist, July 3, 1999. http://www.rbiproduction.co.uk. As published in New Scientist © Reed Business Info. Ltd.

Unit 34

The Value of Knowledge

Degrees to Succeed. 2003. "The Value of Higher Education." http://www.degreestosucceed.com/higher_education.html (accessed August 12, 2005).

Maya Angelou: A Love of Knowledge

Angelou, Maya. 1993. "I Love the Look of Words" by Maya Angelou, copyright © 1993 by Maya Angelou, from Soul Looks Back in Wonder by Tom Feelings. Used by permission of Dial Books for Young Readers, A Division of Penguin Young Readers Group, A Member of Penguin Group (USA) Inc., 345 Hudson Street, New York, NY 10014. All rights reserved.

———. 1969. "Mrs. Flowers," from I Know Why the Caged Bird Sings by Maya Angelou, copyright © 1969 and renewed 1997 by Maya Angelou. Used by permission of Random House, Inc. Note: the title "Mrs. Flowers" is not original to Random House, Inc.'s book.

Sources

Apollo 13: Ingenuity Saves the Mission

Lovell, Jim and Jeffrey Kluger. 1994. Excerpt from LOST MOON: The Perilous Voyage of Apollo 13 by Jim Lovell and Jeffrey Kluger. Copyright © 1994 by Jim Lovell and Jeffrey Kluger. Reprinted by permission of Houghton Mifflin Company. All rights reserved.

Alvar Nuñez Cabeza de Vaca: A Man of Knowledge

"Alvar Nuñez Cabeza de Vaca: Pioneer Historian, Ethnologist, Physician. Parts 1 and 2." 2005. http://www.english.swt.edu/CSS/alvar1CDV.HTML and http://www.english.swt.edu/CSS/alvar2CDV.HTML (accessed August 11, 2005).

"Alvar Nuñez Cabeza de Vaca: History and Importance." 2005. http://www.english.swt.edu/CSS/BackgroundCDV.HTML (accessed August 11, 2005).

Columbia Encyclopedia, The. 2001-2005 (Sixth Ed). "Cabeza de Vaca, Alvar Nuñez." http://www.bartleby.com/65/ca/Cabezade.html (accessed August 11, 2005).

PBS Online. 2001. "Alvar Nuñez Cabeza de Vaca." http://www. pbs.org/weta/thewest/people/a_c/cabezadevaca.htm (accessed August 11, 2005).

Sheppard, Donald E. 2005. "Cabeza de Vaca's Trail in Brief." FloridaHistory.com. http://www.floridahistory.com/vaca-brief.html (accessed August 11, 2005).

Marjory Stoneman Douglas: Knowing the River of Life

Breton, Mary Joy. 2000. "Thinking Like A River: Marjory Stoneman Douglas (1890–1998)." Women Pioneers for the Environment. Boston, MA: Northeastern University Press.

Douglas, Marjory Stoneman. 1997. *The Everglades: River of Grass 50th Anniversary Edition*, copyright © 1997 by Marjory Stoneman Douglas. Used by permission of Pineapple Press, Inc.

Friends of the Everglades. 2005. "Marjory Stoneman Douglas." http://www.everglades.org/msd.html (accessed August 24, 2005).

Hiaasen, Carl. 1998. "Author Showed Us the Splendor of Everglades." *The Miami Herald*, May 17, 1998, p. 1B Local. Copyright © 1998 Tribune Media Services, Inc. All rights reserved. Reprinted with permission.

National Park Service. 2005. "Everglades National Park, Florida." U.S. Department of the Interior. http://www.nps.gov/ever/ (accessed August 24, 2005).

U.S. Army Corps of Engineers. 2002. "About CERP: Brief Overview." http://www.evergladesplan.org/about/about_cerp_brief.aspx (accessed August 24, 2005).

Unit 35

The Tech of Shrek: Imagination Animated

About.com. 2005. "The Making of Shrek, Part 1: Principles of Animation." Action Adventure. http://actionadventure.about.com/library/weekly/2001/aa051901a.htm (accessed September 1, 2005).

Blair, Iain. 2004. "The Making of Shrek." http://www.digitalanimators.com/2001/05_may/features/Shrek/TheMakingShrek.htm (accessed September 15, 2005).

Kalin-Casey, Mary. 2005. "Savoring Shrek." Movie Gallery U.S., LLC and Hollywood Entertainment Corporation. http://www.reel.com/reel.asp?node+features/interviews/shrek (accessed September 1, 2005).).

The Raven: A Romantic Imagination

National Park Service. 2005. "The Poet." *Edgar Allan Poe: National Historic Site, Teacher's Handbook.* U.S. Department of the Interior.

Poe, Edgar Allan. 1845. "The Raven." http://www.heise.de/ix/raven/Literature/Lore/TheRaven.html (accessed August 25, 2005).

Sources

The Teaching Company, LLC. 2005. "Lives and Works of the English Romantic Poets." http://www.teach12.com/ttc/Assets/courseDescriptions/2477.asp (accessed August 25, 2005).

La Vida Robot: Imagination Rules!

Davis, Joshua. 2005. "La Vida Robot," originally published in *Wired*, Issue 13.04, April, 2005 at http://www.wired.com/wired/archive/13.04/robot.html (accessed August 24, 2005). Reprinted with permission from the author.

Don Quixote

Cervantes, Miguel de. 2003. Pages 19-24 and 55-60 from Don Quixote by MIGUEL DE CERVANTES. A new translation by Edith Grossman. Introduction by Harold Bloom. Translation copyright © 2003 by Edith Grossman; introduction copyright © 2003 by Harold Bloom. New York, NY: HarperCollins Publishers, pp. 19-24, 55-60. Reprinted by permission of HarperCollins Publishers.

Unit 36

Brilliance Through Time and Space

Badders, William, and J. Lowell Bethel, Victoria Fu, Donald Peck, Carolyn Sumners, Catherine Valentino, and R. Mike Mullane. 2000. "The Life Cycle of a Star." *Discovery Works: Texas Edition.* Boston, MA: Houghton Mifflin Company.

———. 2000. "Measuring Distances in Space." Discovery Works: Texas Edition. Boston, MA: Houghton Mifflin Company.

———. 2000. "How Stars Differ." *Discovery Works: Texas Edition.* Boston, MA: Houghton Mifflin Company.

Freudenrich, Craig C. 2005. "How Stars Work," http://science.howstuffworks.com/star.htm (accessed September 12, 2005).

Guidry, Mike. 2005. "The Speed of Light." http://csep10.phys.utk.edu/guidry/violence/lightspeed.html (accessed September 14, 2005).

High Energy Astrophysics Science Archive Research Center (HEASARC). 2003. "Supernova." NASA's HEASARC: Education & Public Information. http://heasarc.gsfc.nasa.gov/docs/snr.html (accessed October 14, 2005).

NASA. 2005. "Star." World Book at NASA. http://www.nasa.gov/worldbook/star_worldbook.html (accessed September 14, 2005).

Rao, Joe. 2005. "Big Dipper Stars in Summer Sky." SPACE.com © Imaginova Corporation. http://www.space.com/spacewatch/050610_big_dipper.html (accessed October 14, 2005).

"Stars." 2000. http://www.astro.bas.bg/~pi/astro/stars/stars.html (accessed October 14, 2005).

Sequoyah: Brilliant Code-Maker

Bessie Chin Library Online. 2005. "Sequoyah: Inventor of the Cherokee Alphabet." http://www.wccusd.k12.ca.us/elcerrito/library/sequoyah.htm (accessed August 19, 2005).

Brittanica Online. 2005. "Sequoyah." http://www.britannica.com/eb/article-9066812/query=sequoyah&ct=eb (accessed August 22, 2005).

Cherokee Nation, The. 2005. "The Cherokee Language." http://www.cherokk.org/ (accessed August 19, 2005).

Golden Ink. 2003. "Sequoyah's Talking Leaves." About North Georgia. http://ngeorgia.com/history/alphabet.html (accessed August 19, 2005).

———. 2005. "Sequoyah (a.k.a. George Gist)." http://ngeorgia.com/people/sequoyah.html (accessed August 19, 2005).

Houghton Mifflin Company. 2005. "Sequoyah." Houghton Mifflin College Division. http://college.hmco.com/history/readerscomp/naind/html/na_035400_sequoyah.htm (accessed August 22, 2005).

———. 2005. "Cherokee Language," Houghton Mifflin College Division. http://college.hmco.com/history/reaerscomp/naind/html/na_035400_sequoyah.htm (accessed August 19, 2005).

Sources

Native Nashville. 2005. "Reading Tsalagi (Cherokee)—Lesson 1: Small Talk," http://www.nativenashville.com/tutor_syllabary_read1_study.htm (accessed August 23, 2005).

Rose, Lina. 2004. "Sequoyah Invents the Cherokee Written Language." http://si.unm.edu/abq_2003/lina/Documents/Timelineofsequoyah.html (accessed August 22, 2005).

"Sequoyah." 2005. http://www.neosoft.com/powersource/gallery/people/sequoyah.html (accessed August 19, 2005).

Sequoyah Birthplace Museum, The. 2005. "A Brief Biography of Sequoyah." http://www.sequoyahmuseum.org/ (accessed August 26, 2005).

Thomas, N.L. 2005. "Sequoyah's Cherokee Syllabary," http://www.yvwiiusdinvnohii.net/images/syll.htm (accessed August 19, 2005.)

The Miracle Worker: Dawning of Brilliance

American Foundation for the Blind. 2005. "Helen Keller Biography." http://www.afb.org/Section/asp?SectionID=&TopicID=129 (accessed August 30, 2005).

Enotes. 2005. "The Miracle Worker: Introduction." http://www.enotes.com/miracle-worker/ (accessed August 30, 2005).

Gibson, William. 1957. "Act Three," reprinted with the permission of Scribner, an imprint of Simon & Schuster Adult Publishing Group, from The Miracle Worker by William Gibson. Copyright © 1956, 1957 by William Gibson. Copyright © 1959, 1960 by Tamarack Productions, Ltd., George S. Klein, and Leo Garel as trustees under three separate deeds of trust. Copyright renewed 1984, 1985, 1987, 1988 by William Gibson. All rights reserved.

Hall, Frances Benn. 2004. "Dynamic, spirited, and intensely moving...July 28, 2004 performance reviewed by Frances Benn Hall." NewBerkshire.com. http://newberkshire.com/4btf-mw.php (accessed August 29, 2005).

Schuur, Diane, and David Jackson. 2003. "Helen Keller." The Time 100, June 14, 1999. http://www.time.com/time/time100/heroes/profile/keller01.html (accessed August 29, 2005).

Wikipedia. 2005. "Helen Keller." http://wikipedia.org/wiki/Helen_Keller (accessed August 30, 2005).

Islands of Genius

Budris, Bill. 2005. "Brittany Maier: A Gift of Music." ABILITY Magazine. http://www.abilitymagazine.com/Brittany_Maier.html (accessed August 31, 2005).

Carrasco, Joni. 2004. "Blind pianist is autistic . . . and inspiring," New York Daily News. http://www.nydailynews.com/boroughs/v-pfriendly/story/224488p-192844c.html (accessed August 31, 2005).

James, Sara. 2005. "Playing by Ear." MSNBC.com. http://www.msnbc.msn.com/id/8790667/print/l/displaymode/1098/ (accessed August 31, 2005).

Maier, Brittany Mercedes. 2005. "Brittany Maier." http://www.brittanymaier.com/home.html (accessed August 31, 2005).

Mehnert, David. 2004. "Common Myths About Savants." Savant Academy. http://www.savantacademy.org/myths.php (accessed August 31, 2005).

Treffert, Darold A., and Gregory L. Wallace. 2002. Adapted from "Islands of Genius" by Darold A. Treffert and Gregory L. Wallace. Copyright © 2002 by Scientific American, Inc. All rights reserved.

WLTX-TV 19. 2004. "Brittany's Encore: A Voice From Music." News 19. http://www.wltx.com/print/default.asp?storyid=16641 (accessed August 31, 2005).

Faces of Brilliance

Alaska Pacific University. 2005. "Katherine Gottlieb is a Genius." Alaska Pacific University Alumni Magazine. http://alumni.alaskapacific.edu/ (accessed September 22, 2005).

Arellano, Gustavo. 2005. "Genius in Our Midst." Latino Cities, Inc. http://www.latinola.com/story.php?story=2122 (accessed September 20, 2005).

Bay, Joel. 2005. "Genius Awarded: Alaska Native Health Care Leader Wins $500,000 For Creativity." Alaska Pacific University. http://www.alaskapacific.edu/ (accessed September 22, 2005).

Bay, Joel. 2005. "Alaska Native Wins MacArthur Prize." Tribal Connections. http://www.tribalconnections.org/ (accessed September 22, 2005).

Cable News Network. 2005. "Foundation Awards $500,000 'Genius Grants." CNN.com http://www.cnn.com/ (accessed September 22, 2005).

California Teachers Association. 2004. "CTA News Conference Honors Outstanding Bay Area Teacher: Awarded $500,000 Creativity Grant." http://www.cta.org/ (accessed September 21, 2005).

Carter, Majora. 2005. "Balancing Development and the Environment in the South Bronx." Gotham Gazette, March 19, 2001. http://www.gothamgazette.com/commentary/77.carter.shtml accessed September 22, 2005).

Clarke, Kim. 2005. "Changing the Face of Classical Music," *Leaders & Best: Philanthropy at Michigan.* Fall 2004. The University of Michigan Office of Development. http://www.giving.umich.edu/leadersbest/pdf/fall2004.pdf (accessed September 22, 2005).

Commercial Fisheries News. 2005. "New Zone C Lobster Hatchery Well Underway in Stonington, Maine." *Commercial Fisheries News Online Edition.* http://www.fish-news.com/cfn/CFN_pages/editorical_7_05/zone_C_lob (accessed September 22, 2005).

DeFao, Janine. 2004. "The MacArthur Grants: Bay Area Profiles." SFGate.com. http://www.sfgate.com/cgi-bin/article.cgi?f=/c/a/2004/09/28/MNG99 (accessed September 21, 2005).

Detroit Free Press. 2005. "Hometown Genius." http://www.freep.com/voices/editorial/

egenius22e_20050922.htm (accessed September 22, 2005).

Dworkin, Aaron. 2005. "Selections featuring Aaron." Ethnovibe. http://www.ethnovibe.com/Aaronbio.html (accessed September 22, 2005).

Edwards, Sylvia. 2005. "Maya Lin: 1959- Architect, sculptor." http://www.edwardsly.com/linm.htm (accessed September 22, 2005).

Facing History and Ourselves. 2005. "Tommie Lindsey." http://www.facinghistory.org/ (accessed September 20, 2005).

Fish, Jen. 2005. "Lobsterman's Fish Studies Earn Him a 'Genius Grant'" *Portland Press Herald.* http://pressherald.mainetoday.com/ (accessed September 22, 2005).

French-Laetz, Nancy. 2004. "Reuben Martinez Wins MacArthur Fellowship Award." Institute for Social, Behavioral, and Economic Research. University of California Santa Barbara. http://www.isber.ucsb.edu/ (accessed Sept 22, 2005).

Gottlieb, Katherine. 2005. "A Letter From the President." Southcentral Foundation. http://www.southcentralfoundation.com/president.cfm (accessed September 22, 2005).

Gottlieb, Katherine and Doug Eby. 2004. "Putting Healthcare Into Culture, Not Culture Into Healthcare." Diversity Rx. http://www.diversityrx.org/CCCONF/04/C_1.htm (accessed September 22, 2005).

Hewitt, Rich. 2005. "Maine Lobsterman, Researcher Wins $500,000 'Genius' Grant," *Bangor Daily News*, September 20, 2005. http://www.bangornews.com/ (accessed September 22, 2005).

Huetteman, Susan. 2005. "Esmeralda's Dream Essay." Masterpiece Theatre: The American Collection. http://www.ncteamericancollection.org/aaw_dream_essay.htm (accessed September 20, 2005).

Institute for Healthcare Improvement. 2005. "Alaska Native Medical Center: Values-Driven

System Design." http://www.ihi.org/IHI/ (accessed September 22, 2005).

John D. and Katherine T. MacArthur Foundation, The. 2005. "The MacArthur Fellows Program: Tommie Lindsey." http://www.macfound. org/programs/fel/fellows/lindsey_tommie.thm (accessed September 22, 2005).

———. 2005. "The MacArthur Fellows Program: Katherine Gottlieb." http://www.macfound. org/programs/fel/fellows/gottlieb_katherine.htm (accessed September 22, 2005).

———. 2005. "The MacArthur Fellows Program: Ted Ames." http://www.macfound.org/programs/ fel/fellows/ames_ted.htm (accessed September 22, 2005).

———. 2005. "The MacArthur Fellows Program: Maya Lin." http://www.macfound.org/programs/ fel/fellows/lin_maya.htm (accessed September 22, 2005).

———. 2005. "The MacArthur Fellows Program: Reuben Martinez." http://www.macfound. org/programs/fel/fellows/martinez_reuben.thm (accessed September 22, 2005).

———. 2005. "The MacArthur Fellows Program: Majora Carter." http://www.macfound.org/ programs/fel/fellows/carter_majora.htm (accessed September 22, 2005).

———. 2005. "The MacArthur Fellows Program: Aaron Dworkin." http://www.macfound.org/ programs/fel/fellows/dworkin_aaron.htm (accessed September 22, 2005).

Johnson, Lawrence B. 2004. "Aaron P. Dworkin: Minority Musicians Hear Applause Across America, Thanks To His Notable Efforts." *The Detroit News*, May 9, 2004. http://www.detnews. com/2004/project/0405/09/e06-146712.htm (accessed September 2, 2005).

———. 2004. "Competition Builds Classical Harmony." *The Detroit News.* http://www.detnews. com/2004/entertainment/0402/17/d01-6600.htm (accessed September 22. 2005.)

Johnson, Rebecca. 2004. "Innovators All: 23 Fine MacArthur Fellows," USA Today. http://www. usatoday.com/ (accessed September 20, 2005).

Logan, Timothy J.W. 2005. "Majora Carter to Head 'Sustainable South Bronx' Initiative," Green Yes Archives, LCG Communications. http://greenyes. grrn.org/2001/03/msg00045.html (accessed September 22, 2005).

Mac & Ava Productions. 2005. "Tommie Lindsey." Accidental Hero: Room 408. http://www.pbs.org/ accidentalhero/tommie (accessed September 21, 2005).

Malyon, John. 2005. "Maya Lin." Artcyclopedia. http://www.artcyclopedia.com/artists/lin_maya. html (accessed September 22, 2005).

McKeough, Kevin. 2003. "The Sphinx Stands Alone." Strings Magazine, January 2003, no. 107. http://stringsmagazine.com/issues/strings107/ coverstory.html (accessed September 22, 2005).

Mulligan, Michelle Herrera. 2004. "Libreria Martinez's Third Bookstore," LibraryJournal.com, May 1, 2004. http://www.libraryjournal.com/ article/CA420433.html?display=critic (accessed September 22, 2005).

National Association for Urban Debate Leagues. 2005. "Urban Debate Educator Wins Prestigious MacArthur Genius Grant." http://www. urbandebate.org/newsStory?id=64 (accessed September 21, 2005).

Nationalforest.org. 2005. "Speaker Bio: Majora Carter." http://www.natlforest.org/centennial/ speakers/carter/htm (accessed September 22, 2005).

National Oceanic and Atmospheric Administration. 2005. "Ted Ames." NOAA Fisheries National Marine Fisheries Service. http:// www.st.nmfs.noaa.gov/lfkproject/05_Committee. bios.htm (accessed September 22, 2005).

National Women's History Project. 2005. "Maya Lin." The Learning Place. http://www.nwhp.org/ (accessed September 22, 2005).

Sources

Newscenter. 2005. "MacArthur Foundation Award 25 Grants." http://newscenter.mind.net/wed/cz/Ayb81783928.RrhN_FaK.html (accessed September 22, 2005).

Oldenburg, Don. 2005. "Placed at the Feat of Genius: $500,000." *Washington Post.* http://www.washingtonpost.com/ (accessed September 22, 2005).

PBS. 2004. "An Interview With Esmeralda Santiago." Masterpiece Theatre. http://www.pbs.org/wgbh/masterpiece/americancollection/woman/ei_santiago.html (accessed September 20, 2005).

PBS.org. 2002. "Speaking For Success." The Online Newshour. http://www.pbs.org/newshour/bb/education (accessed September 21, 2005).

Penobscot Bay Watch. 2005. "Downeast Groundfish Initiative." http://www.penbay.org/downeast.html (accessed September 22, 2005).

Porter, Aaron. 2004. "Stonington Fisherman's Study Reveals Reality of Cod Stocks." Florida Museum of Natural History. http://www.flmnh.ufl.edu/fish/InNews/stonington2004.htm accessed September 22, 2005).

Puerto Rico Federal Affairs Administration. 2005. "About the Featured Artist: Esmeralda Santiago" http://www.prfaa.com/ (accessed September 20, 2005).

Radio Bilingue. 2005. "Reuben Martinez: A MacArthur Fellow." Linea Abierta. http://www.radiobilingue.org/archive/Lineaprevprogjan2005.htm (accessed September 22, 2005).

Random House, Inc. 2004. "Almost a Woman." Random House Worldwide. http://www.randomhouse.com/acmart/catalog/display.pperl?isbn=978 (accessed September 20, 2005).

———. 2004. "Esmeralda Santiago: A Note to the Reader." Reading Group Center. http://www.randomhouse.com/vintage/read/puerto/santiago.html (accessed September 20, 2005.)

Rasmuson Foundation. 2005. "Southcentral Foundation: Family Wellness Warriors," http://www.rasmuson.org/SiteEditor/index.php?switch=viewpage&pa (accessed September 22, 2005).

Ross, Alex. 2002. "Maya Lin," Stanford Presidential Lectures and Symposia in the Humanities and Arts, Stanford University. http://prelectur.stanford.edu/lecturers/lin/ (accessed September 22, 2005).

Ruiz, Gina. 2005. "Report on LA Times Festival of Books." Xispas web log, April 27, 2005. http://www.xispas.com/blog/2005/04/report-on-la-times-festival-of-books (accessed September 22, 2005).

Santiago, Esmeralda. 2004. "Esmeralda Santiago." http://www.esmeraldasantiago.com/bio/bio.html (accessed September 20, 2005).

Seglin, Jeffrey. 2005. "Reuben Martinez: Libreria Martinez Books and Art Sources Galleries." *26 Most Fascinating Entrepreneurs*, Inc.com. http://www.inc.com/magazine/20050401/26-martinez.html (accessed September 22, 2005).

Sphinx Organization. 2005. "About Us—Staff." http://www.sphinxmusic.org/about/staff.html (accessed September 22, 2005).

Staub, Mary. 2003. "Libreria Martinez Opens Second Store." LibraryJournal.com, December 1, 2003. Reed Business Information. http://www.libraryjournal.com/article/CA337332.html?display=critic.htm (accessed September 22, 2005).

Stryker, Mark. 2005. "Michigan's $500,000 Pioneers." *Detroit Free Press.* http://www.freep.com/entertainment/music/genius20e_20050920.htm (accessed September 22, 2005).

———. 2005. "The Riddle of the Sphinx: Minority Strings Competition Founder Takes Pride in His Player's Success, But Rapid Growth Brings Questions About the Future." *Detroit Free Press.* http://www.freep.com/entertainment/music/sphinx6_20020206.htm (accessed September 22, 2005).

Turner, Khary Kimani. 2005. "Rhapsody in Black." Detroit *Metro Times*, February 9, 2005. Metro Times, Inc. http://www.metrotimes.com/editorial/story.asp?id=7290 (accessed September 22, 2005).

Tysh, George. 2003. "Behind the Sphinx." Detroit *Metro Times*, February 26, 2003. Metro Times, Inc. http://www.metrotimes.com/editorial/story.asp?id=4628 (accessed September 22, 2005).

Wallis, Claudia. 2005. "Majora Carter," Time.com, June 5, 2004. http://www.time.com/time/2004/obesity/speakers/carter/html (accessed September 22, 2005).

WBUR.org. 2005. "Debating for the Future" from The Connection, hosted by Dick Gordon. http://www.theconnection.org/shows/2004/11/20041116_b_main.asp (accessed September 21, 2005).

Zick, William J. 2006. "Aaron Paul Dworkin." Africlassical.com. http://chevalierdesaintgeorges.homestead.com/Dworkin.html (accessed September 22, 2005).

Word History

Alexander, Barb. 2005. "Silent Knight." Suite101.com. http://www.suite101.com/article.cfm/english_grammar_style/53897 (accessed September 26, 2005).

American Heritage Dictionaries. 2004. "Eureka." *Word Histories and Mysteries.* Boston, MA: Houghton Mifflin, pp. 89-90.

British Council, The. 2005. "Grammar. Pronunciation. Silent Letters." Archive. http://www.learnenglish.org.uk/grammar/archive/silentletters01.html (accessed September 26, 2005).

Yourdictionary. 2005. Love to Know Corp. http://www.yourdictionary.com (accessed October 6, 2005).